MAR   8 2005

On the Outside Looking In(dian)

PETER LANG
New York • Washington, D.C./Baltimore • Bern
Frankfurt am Main • Berlin • Brussels • Vienna • Oxford

Phillipa Kafka

On the Outside
Looking In(dian)

Indian Women Writers
at Home and Abroad

PETER LANG
New York • Washington, D.C./Baltimore • Bern
Frankfurt am Main • Berlin • Brussels • Vienna • Oxford

Library of Congress Cataloging-in-Publication Data

Kafka, Phillipa.
On the outside looking in(dian):
Indian women writers at home and abroad / Phillipa Kafka.
p. cm.
Includes bibliographical references and index.
1. Indic literature (English)—Women authors—History and criticism.
2. Indic literature (English)—Foreign countries—History and criticism.
3. Indic literature (English)—20th century—History and criticism. 4. Women, East
Indian—Foreign countries—Intellectual life. 5. Women and literature—India—
History—20th century. 6. India—Intellectual life—20th century. I. Title.
PR9488 .K34   820.9'9287'0954—dc21   2002021416
ISBN 0-8204-5812-0

Bibliographic information published by **Die Deutsche Bibliothek**.
Die Deutsche Bibliothek lists this publication in the "Deutsche
Nationalbibliografie"; detailed bibliographic data is available
on the Internet at http://dnb.ddb.de/.

Cover design by Joni Holst

© 2003 Peter Lang Publishing, Inc., New York
275 Seventh Avenue, 28th Floor, New York, NY 10001
www.peterlangusa.com

Printed in the United States of America

To "The Sisterhood;" to Phyllis Korper, acquisitions editor, Peter Lang Publishing; and to Olavi K. Koskinen, my devoted husband and live-in editor. This book would not be possible without them.

Contents

Preface

Indian society is like a cruel Procrustean bed for women. UMA NEHRU

In writing themselves, women have attempted to render noisy and audible all that had been silenced in phallocentric discourse. TRINH T. MINH-HA

In this text I have discussed works by feminist Indian writers from approximately the middle of the nineteenth century to the present in terms of major societal issues that they focus on: purdah (the confinement of women in certain quarters of the home), veiling, denial of education, property rights, government corruption, exploitation and destruction of the environment, oppression of tribals and women, female infanticide, child marriage, bridal deaths, son preference, widowhood, sati (widow immolation), widow remarriage, expatriation and immigration, domestic violence issues such as rape and physical and verbal abuse, and the suppression and denial of female sexuality.

For the most part, after traveling abroad these writers critique the shortcomings of both India and their host cultures, as well. Gender oppression, especially their gendered sex, makes women outsiders in India solely by virtue of their being women; outsiders when they travel or emigrate; outsiders when they return to India, or even after they have immigrated to other cultures. Gayatri Chakravorty Spivak's "cosmopolitan migrant Indian resident" perspective, that of an outsider looking on at a distance at various culture(s) and institutions—what Inderpal Grewal calls an "oblique connection to the society" (1994, 246)—does not always have a negative connotation. Some Indian/Third World feminists[1] feel that being situated as women on the outside of the structures of power and Old Boy Networks gives them a strategic position from which to launch their challenges to gender oppression (Tripp 2000). Either way, from the middle of the nineteenth century onward, Indian women activists have demanded the transference of women from the outside of the profoundly patriarchal Indian culture to inclusion and full participation in its institutions.

Generally, I have proceeded chronologically. A strict chronological approach to the issues would not work, however, because many have changed very little or remain unchanged. Therefore, I have added/juxtaposed citations from earlier or later authors and critics on these issues in order to provide a historic perspective on them.

In Chapter One: Outsiders Within I, I analyze early feminist responses to the British by focusing on the Christian feminist Krupabai Satthianadhan (1862–1894) who simultaneously critiqued them in some ways (and those influenced by them) while valuing them as a feminist. In this chapter I also cover feminist struggles to expand education for women and to end *purdah* and the enforced wearing of the *burqa* (a voluminous and tent-like covering from head to toe), as illustrated in the work of the great Muslim feminist Rokeya Sakhawat Hossain (1880–1932). Because I see a fundamental relationship between them, I linked the lesbian separatist fantasies of the contemporary writer Suniti Namjoshi (1941–) with Hossain's dream vision, *Sultana's Dream* ([1908] 1988). I also discuss the struggles to permit widows to remarry by other reformer, nationalist, and feminist authors and critics who have written on these issues over time.

In Chapter Two: Outsiders Within II, I discuss the struggles to end caste and gender oppression of tribals and landless women as illustrated in works by Mahasweta Devi (1926–). Devi's commitment to nothing less than the political and social transformation of India through her relentless, intense activism is unrivalled except perhaps by later activists such as Vandana Shiva (1952–) and Arundhati Roy (1961–). It will be evident in this chapter that other Indian women writers share Devi's political and social concerns; that they begin to link societal issues such as the oppression of tribals, corrupt governmental policies, pollution, environmental destruction, the misuse of technology, industrialization, female infanticide, child marriage, bridal death, son preference, widowhood, sati, and widow remarriage with issues of gender (and caste) oppression that result in continued poverty, starvation, marches, and riots, with women and children suffering the most. Coinciding with "the first campaigns of the contemporary Indian feminist movement," protests arose on all sides from feminists against the growing custom of ever more exhorbitant dowry demands on brides' families, dowry-connected "abetment to suicide" (Kumar 1999, 349–351), rape, violence and murders, and the use of ultrasounds and amniocentesis to abort female fetuses—to consciously commit female foeticide for the express purpose of "culling . . . girls" (Harriss-White 1999, 127; Kishwar and Vanita 1984, 10; N. Menon 1999a, 281).

In Chapter Three: Outsiders Abroad, I explore the complex and diverse responses of writers such as Anita Desai (1937–), Bharati Mukherjee (1940–), Susham Bedi (1942?–), Gita Mehta (1943–), Meena Alexander (1951–), Pramila Jayapal (1965–), and others to the host of issues concerning expatriation and immigration, such as the issue of being oppressed and Othered as alien and as inferior women of color, as well as the authors' interesting cross-cultural comparisons between their native countries and the West.

In Chapter Four: Outsiders Silenced, I discuss works by Indian feminist writers on these issues. Despite a wall of powerful external opposition from the patriarchal culture and its religious, social, and political traditions, from their own communities, and from within their familes—not least of all from their own mothers—and despite their own internal struggles, feminists such as Lalika Antherjanam (1909–1987?), Maitreyi Devi (1914–1989), Kamala Das (1934–), Shashi Deshpande (1938–), Bharati Mukherjee (1940–), and Meena Alexander (1951–) focus primarily on the suppression and denial of female sexuality and violence of various kinds, primarily domestic, in the home. Some of them did reach clarity by the 1970s on the issue of women's sexuality and began to identify and name their own needs and desires, and painstakingly attempted to fulfill them. Many of these older feminist writers and critics feel that female sexuality is a crucial issue for the feminist project:

> If sexuality is not incorporated into the main feminist and political agenda, the struggles for freedom will remain on a very superficial level. A problem cannot be solved without going to its roots. . . . I would suggest that if sexuality and women's issues were dealt with from the beginning, wars might be avoided, and revolutionary struggles and movements for liberation would become more effective. Justice cannot be won in the midst of injustice. Each of the levels is connected to the others. (Accad 1991, 244)

The question arises as to whether younger feminists agree, whether their work reflects the constraints, the oppression, and suppression, the incessant struggling with the issue of their sexuality as women, their fears of expressing themselves that Indian women still confront, often in the form of abuse and violence, solely on the basis of their gender. Ever philosophical, Namjoshi calls for the older generation to accept that younger feminists will not necessarily have the same perspectives. They will instead "mutate" in many complex ways: "The feminism that we fought for has mutated into strange shapes. Some we don't like. Some we don't recognize. But that's how it is. That's how it must be. . . . Can we not, may we not, leave a legacy to which others may contribute? True, it will be broken, altered, changed" (1996, xxvii).

What do the latest works in fact reveal? Have younger generations of feminist Indian writers indeed benefited from "the immense project of clearing cultural space for reinscriptions of female subjectivity" (Gopal 1999, 314), especially in regard to gender roles that constrain/deny women's sexuality and subject them to abuse and violence? How different are these younger writers from their foremothers? What fresh perspectives, new insights, new ideas, and new solutions do they bring to the ongoing feminist project?

In Chapter Five: Solutions, I focus on the interesting, unexpected solutions to gender issues proposed by this younger generation of feminist Indian (and some Pakistani) women writers both in India and in the West such as Chitra Banerjee Divakaruni (1956–), Anjana Appachana (1956–), Indira Ganesan (1960–), Sunetra Gupta (1965–), and others. Some of them are the first generation to be born in the West and have begun to describe in literature and the media what this experience is like.[2]

Introduction: Background and Overview of Major Topics

Reform and Nationalism

National boundaries should not define the bounds of feminist imaginations that care about a more equitable and just global and international order. Justice within nations and saner forms of nationalism seem closely connected to our hopes for justice across nations at an international level.   UMA NARAYAN

The sexuality that is seen as the problematic aspect of women's lives forms the opacity that is to be removed if the transparent nation is to be gained and to become a reality.   INDERPAL GREWAL

Women inhabitants of nations were neither imagined as nor invited to imagine themselves as part of the horizontal brotherhood.

MARY LOUISE PRATT, QUOTED IN SANGEETA RAY

In the beginning—the middle of the nineteenth century—men led the movement for women's rights (Kishwar and Vanita 1984, 27; S. Ray 2000, 101). These early male reformers were first inspired to work on Brahmin Hindu women's behalf in order to save them from social injustices, that is, to "patriar-chally [monitor] 'progress' for [their] women" (Natarajan 1994, 82). The crucial issue for most Indian women at that time (as it still is) was not achieving equality, as it was for Western feminists, but simply surviving (M. Basu 2001, 150). These men organized the narrow Hindu-only reform movements that began the larger struggles against social injustices, and Indian women writers and critics reflect (on) these struggles. Consciously feminist Indian women's groups and movements did not emerge until the early to mid-1970s as spinoffs from Leftist organizations (Kumar 1999). This is a similar phenomenon to that of the Second-Wave Western feminist movement spinning off from masculinist Leftist groups, and Chicana and Black feminist movements spinning off from the masculinist La Raza and Black Power movements.[1] Like Western feminists from diverse races, classes, ethnicities, and religions during this exciting time, Indian feminists began to call for economic and employment equality with men (M. Basu 2001, 150–151).

No matter what the issue in terms of gender oppression, both the British and the early Hindu male reformers used women as symbolic abstractions for their own ends (as the nationalists still do). Debates on women, whether in the context of *sati,* widow remarriage, or *zenanas* (separate women's quarters) were not merely about women but were also instances in which the moral challenge of British colonial rule was confronted and negotiated. In this process, women came to represent Indian tradition for all sides: whether viewed as weak, deluded creatures who must be reformed through legislation and education, or the valiant keepers of tradition who must be protected from statutory interventions and be permitted only certain kinds of instruction. For the British, rescuing women became part of the civilizing mission of colonization. For the indigenous male elite, protection of women's status, or its reform, became (and still is) an urgent necessity in maintaining the honor of the collective—religious or national (L. Mani [1989] 1998, 79).

Many feminists credit Mohandas Mahatma Gandhi's attitude toward women as being responsible for inspiring a broad spectrum of women to participate in the nationalist movement (Ramusack 1999, 60). Antoinette Burton informs us that Gandhi had been influenced by the suffragettes in 1906 on a visit to London when he observed their demonstrations and protests at the House of Commons and their willingness to go to prison on behalf of their convictions. She writes that ironically Gandhi saw a parallel between the British feminist struggle to be included as full-fledged citizens of the British Empire through the vote and his own cause—the struggle for Indian independence from the British (1994, 199–200). Nayantara Sahgal (1927–), whose mother was India's first ambassador to the United Nations, whose uncle was Jawaharlal Nehru, and whose cousin was Indira Gandhi, is an excellent novelist in her own right. She objects to Gandhi's suppression of human sexuality. In *Mistaken Identity* (1988a), Sahgal describes what the aimless son of a petty Raja hears about Gandhi while in jail in 1929. "If he hadn't called off the last civil disobedience agitation just because it turned violent, his party would be in better shape today. But with the stab in the back he gave it, it is thoroughly demoralized, and Gandhi's influence is waning. And what else could you expect of a Machiavellian Utopian?" (1988a, 69). This opinion, expressed by a Communist, does not seem to me to reflect Sahgal's own. When she goes on to describe the beliefs of a Gandhian—Bhaiji, and his group—her hero is just as negative toward Gandhi:

> The India of Bhaiji's dreams is a county of vegetarian capitalists and rural handicrafts. A few machines such as sewing machines that won't corrupt the economy or the moral fibre will be welcome. They'll make way for leisure but not too much of it. Some wool and cotton will be spun in cottages. Citizens will abstain from sex and turn the other cheek. Independence will be the dawn of an era washed clean of drink and lust. (Sahgal 1988a, 69)

In contrast, the heroine of Sahgal's *Rich Like Us* ([1986] 1988b) feels that "Gandhi's non-violence had worked like a streak of forked lightning" unlike the other Indian movements which had no ideas of their own, "[that] had cut and paste Western concepts together" as if Europe "were the centre of the universe, and the Bible and Marx were the last word on mankind [*sic*]." Gandhi had sent an empire packing "with an antique idea instead of an atom bomb. . . . And half naked in his middle-class middle-caste skin he'd taken human rights a hundred years ahead in two decades without a glimmer of class war" ([1986]1988b, 98, 101). In this passage, it appears to me that Sahgal is expressing her own opinion.

The initial response of the "lame" heroine Lenny in *Cracking India* (1991) by Bapsi Sidhwa (1938–) is at first both skeptical and sarcastic when she meets "Gandhijee": "[He] certainly is ahead of his times. He already knows the advantages of dieting. He has starved his way into the news and made headlines all over the world" (1991, 94). Then, when she actually comes face to face with him, Lenny suddenly turns adoring and sexual, even though later on in her life she realizes that Gandhi's character also contained elements far different from his carefully cultivated public personality:

> I am puzzled why he's so famous—and suddenly his eyes turn to me. My brain, heart and stomach melt. The pure shaft of humor, compassion,[2] tolerance and understanding he directs at me fuses me to everything that is feminine, funny, gentle, loving. He is a man who loves women. And lame children. . . . He touches my face, and in a burst of shyness I lower my eyes. This is the first time I have lowered my eyes before a man. . . . It wasn't until some years later—when I realized the full scope and dimension of the massacres [following the Partition]—that I comprehended the concealed nature of the ice lurking deep beneath the hypnotic and dynamic femininity of Gandhi's non-violent exterior. (1991, 96)

Bharati Mukherjee is on the other end of the spectrum in her response to Gandhi. One of her male characters, who claims to have been Gandhi's assassin, views

Gandhi as "the enemy of women" because he "had hurt our women. The man who could sleep between virgins and feel no throb of virility had despoiled the women of our country" (1985, 161). Furthermore, Gandhi was too detached from the diurnal problems of the people: "But Gandhi, the spiritual leader, what did he understand about evil and sin? A man with his head in the clouds does not see the shit pile at his feet" (160). In Mukherjee's *Jasmine* (1991), when Muslims sacked Jasmine's father's beloved home in Lahore, he lost his fortune and was forced to flee to the backwater village of Hasnapur after Partition. He never again spoke Hindi because it was "the language of Gandhi" who was responsible for approving the Partition of India and the subsequent "slaughter of millions" (1991, 37).

Like Mukherjee, Meena Alexander also critiques Gandhi from a feminist perspective because he had the hair cut off from the heads of some young women whom he thought guilty of inappropriate sexual conduct and he also severely restrained women's sexuality. Although Gandhi served as an inspiration for millions of female followers, nevertheless he had "a corrosive view of female sexuality" (1996a, 82, 183). The record, however, shows that Gandhi advocated a single standard for men and women, as revealed in the following rhetorical question he asked of Indian men: "And why is there all this morbid anxiety about female purity? We hear nothing of women's anxiety about men's chastity. Why should men arrogate to themselves the right to regulate female purity?" (quoted in Jayawardena 1986, 96). To undertake a response to Gandhi, I would suggest that this "morbid anxiety" began with "the Brahmanical tradition and the ascetic schools that used as their primary means of control "the suppression of women, the purity/impurity polarization":

> Another ... denigration of women was the "problem" of female sexuality. The eschewal of all contact with women—who represented a danger to male vitality (*tejas*), the restrictions of family life, the danger of impurity, and also symbolized carnality—became pivotal for the successful practice of ascetic disciplines. . . . Physical purity-consciousness (*sauca*) and the negative view of embodiment and sexuality that characterized the renouncer tradition, had . . . a negative impact on the lives of women. (Das-Gupta Sherma 2000, 43)

Gandhi perceived women as equal, but only within "the religious sense of the word" and still within patriarchal limitations. Women embodied "sacrifice, silent suffering, humility, faith and knowledge" (Jayawardena 1986, 95) and lived separate lives "complementary" to men's and therefore should have a different education from men. Women were morally superior to men because of their great suffering, although he emphasized that they should neither be passive nor subservient, but free to take part in political life. He needed everyone he could get, including women, in order to build a mass movement with numbers sufficient to oust the British. Still, whatever his motives and despite conservatism in his attitudes toward women, Gandhi's contribution is seen by many feminists as unrivaled to this day

cally, the flux of contemporary Indian society is jeopardized by Hindu nationalist leaders who are fixated on glorifying a mythical Hindu culture much like the immigrant leaders in the West. All deviations from nationalist constructions are subject to insults such as labeling the arguments of those who differ from them "random . . . biased . . . regional . . . narrow-minded." And, for presuming to question the system of gender oppression, feminists are labeled "disruptive" (Bhattacharjee 1998, 180). Although strict adherents of their heritage, the nationalists simultaneously covet expertise in Western technologies in order to achieve upward mobility,[3] while (op)pressing their women into symbolic repositories of the public morality and virtue of the entire Indian immigrant community. Any woman who does not submit to this concept of The Indian Woman is considered a traitor to her family and to the entire community and treated accordingly (Bhattacharjee 1997, 310, 320; Bhattacharjee 1998, 172–173; Shahmaz Khan 1998, 470; B. Mani 1996, 176; R. Mazumdar 1998, 130; S. Mazumdar 1996, 463; M. Roy 1998, 103). It also should be noted here that controlling women metaphorically through the construction of binaries such as goddess/whore, good girl/bad girl is actually a transnational phenomenon and by no means limited to Indian nationalists (Das-Gupta and Das Dasgupta 1998, 116).

At every public celebratory gathering, girls are the objects of much primping and prodding, painstakingly garbed in saris and festooned with paper flowers, while boys are free to wear their baseball caps backward and loose jeans riding low on their hips.[4] For girls, these costumes really reflect Western fashions of fifty to one hundred years ago—a form of Victorian repression in mandated Indian clothing. New generations of Indian children are heavily indoctrinated into the belief that sex is considered bad or vulgar and female bodies embarrassing. These values are then claimed to be totally Indian (Das Dasgupta and DasGupta 1996a, 384, 386; Kishwar 1999, 184). The feminist struggle against nationalist spiritual and cultural regulating of women so that they act in conformity with what the patriarchs of the community decree to be the Ideal Indian Woman continues. Although Ritu Menon and Khamla Bhasin confine their critique of nationalism only to South Asian countries, they view Indian patriarchal nationalist communities as similar in the West on the grounds that this prescribed ideal is common to nationalists and because regulating women's sexuality is vital in order to differentiate their ethnicity and community from other ethnicities and communities. Such self-policing communities are very harsh and repressive toward women (1998, 254, 256). Additionally, by controlling various communities' religious, social, and cultural institutions, as well as the media, the patriarchs control and police differences within the community so that publicly it appears as if it is one monolithic unified community (Das Dasgupta 1998, 5).

Other feminist critics focus on the artificially constructed model of female purity and self-sacrifice imposed on women by having their sexuality tabooed and erased not only in India but in most South Asian cultures in order to unify and symbolize the Indian nation and its lofty spirtual and moral fiber (R. Mazumdar 1998; M. Roy 1998 103, 104; Tharu [1989] 1999, 263). However, it is not only that "*women cannot find home in nation* because nationalism constructs women as subordinates of men and therefore *from a feminist perspective, nationalism—to be precise, the nation—cannot be seen as providing enabling community*" (Ismail 2000, 256, emphasis the author's). But to focus only on the immediate past and current nationalist suppression and denial of women's sexuality denies historic conditions for women. There is a cyclical, faddist quality to this misogynist model based on ruling men's decrees at different times throughout history, but no matter what the decrees, in one way or another they always subordinate and constrain women in every way in relation to themselves. As Madhu Kishwar comments: "It is ironic that whenever men get enamoured with a particular kind of identity assertion, women usually have to carry the burden of implementing it by taking on more restrictive ways of life and cultural markers like dress codes" (1999, 218).

Kishwar and Ruth Vanita do find grounds for agreeing with the nationalists that women were better off in most places before the British occupied India. They enjoyed "personal and property rights" and "were far more secure and more community based" (1984). Similarly, Nandita Gandhi and Nandita Shah, in arguing that patriarchy is responsible for women's "loss of identity . . . freedom and . . . rights" (1999, 339), imply prior possession by the word "loss." Since they define "patriarchy" as the cause of this "loss," they must be envisioning some other system more favorable to women as having prevailed at an anterior period, as the nationalists and others such as Chattopadhyay, Kishwar, and Vanita do. However, they do not elucidate their argument beyond this point. Partha Chatterjee also dismisses claims extolling "Ancient India" on the grounds that they are nationalist strategies. He cites a nationalist historian, Tarinicharan Chattopadhyay (1833–1897), who maintains in his history of India that Hindu women nowadays live like slaves, are imprisoned in their homes, and are illiterate, but that in ancient times women were treated with respect, given educations, lived without constraints, and there were no child marriages (quoted in Chatterjee 1993, 98). Chatterjee fails to note, however, that the ancient Indus valley group was "anarchistic" and did not "originally" have any concept of virginity for brides, nor was it fixed on the idea of legitimating children through paternity (R. Mazumdar 1998, 141).

Clearly, the vast majority of feminist Indian critics insist that "there was no golden age for Hindu women" (Pandita Ramabai [Saraswati] quoted in Chakravarti [1989] 1999, 68). There never has been. They view such glittering times as nothing more than the creations of nineteenth-century nationalists selectively constructing great ancient traditions that were not really old or "authentic" and that had no "sacred" scriptural referents (as Jews view the Old Testament and Christians view the Old and New Testaments) as a source for nationalist claims. Such claims were made to justify their skewing of the distribution of "resources" and "advantages" to their own group of upper-caste men and to themselves (S. Basu 1999, 258; Grewal 1996, 206; N. Menon 1999a, 5). Similarly, Trinh T. Minh-ha sees tradition as:

> the sacred weapon oppressors repeatedly hold up whenever they need to maintain their privileges, hence to impose the form of the old on the content of the new, arises. One can say that fear and insecurity lie behind each attempt at opposing modernism with tradition and, likewise, at setting up ethnicity against womanhood: today, it is more convincing to reject feminism as a whitewashed notion and a betrayal of roots values, or vice versa, to consider the promotion of ethnic identity treacherous to that of female identity or feminism. (1989, 106)

Shamita Das Dasgupta, who identifies herself as first a woman "by nature," then a Muslim American who is a Pakistani by ancestry, extends this point to every culture at present, and apparently to all women globally, when she reminds her readers that we have the responsibility of determining the identity of those whose "machinations" cause women's "disenfranchisement" to become "reified as tradition" and that consign women's freedoms and rights "to obscurity" (1998, 10). In contrast, Kishwar suggests selecting aspects of Indian culture that can be salvaged and then to shape and modify and transform them so that they become productive and uplifting for women rather than oppressive. She does not locate the source for the outbreak, formation, and mobilization of monolithic communal entities that have been responsible for oppressing women in patriarchal nationalist male leadership as Das Dasgupta and other feminists do. Instead, she traces the source of oppression to a "virus of ethnic and secular nationalism" (1999, 255) that has spread from the West.

In 2001, only a year before Muslim fundamentalists slaughtered over one hundred people in Lagos, Nigeria, at the Miss World contest, Rapul Oza did a feminist analysis of an Indian beauty pageant. But, unlike Kishwar, she focused her critique not on a Western virus but on the male, masculinist leaders of both the left and the right within India. As in Nigeria, the pageant caused a battle (although without slaughter) between the right and the progressives, exposing—as in Nigeria—the fundamental conflicts in India in terms of women's sexuality. The right maintained that exposing the female body is obscene and threatening to the nation. They displaced onto "women's sexuality and bodies" their fear of losing their autonomy due to a variety of changes:

> Containment entailed securing the female body and sexuality against transgression. . . . The right wing [claim] that any discourse on sexuality was other, foreign, and not within the parameters of what is considered Indian culture [and] prescribe a certain kind of femininity that controls women's bodies and sexuality, since men's sexuality is naturalized as uncontrollable. Women's bodies, sexuality, and femininity then are intricately woven together so that perceived transgression of any one threatens others and

subsequently threatens Indian culture. . . . Exposure of certain parts of the female body was perceived as a threat to Indian culture and, by extension, to national sovereignty. . . . Such judgments by structures of the state [exposure of women's bodies constitutes obscenity and indecent exposure and therefore must be policed] are crucial because particular ideas of gender and sexuality become . . . embedded within the state's technologies of power. . . . A desexualized Indian womanhood became an effective icon to protect the nation against globalization. . . . [It] does not threaten the nation with sexual transgression. This desexualized narrative was most particularly evidenced in the rhetoric of the political right, which held that women's modernity is acceptable but not Westernization—which was symbolic of uncontrolled sexuality. Conversely, while the progressive coalitions were critical of the conceptions of womanhood adopted by the right, they, too, did not consider women's agency and sexuality, so that the primary arguments about women's sexuality concerned commodification and the threat of sex trade. (Oza 2001, 1078, 1080, 1081, 1085, 1089)

The right's opposition to globalization was therefore constructed through the need to maintain "oppressive gender and sexual codes . . . predicated on erasing women's autonomy over their bodies and sexualities." The leadership on the left chose to ignore gender and sexuality issues and place their priorities on resisting globalizing. To them, gender issues are insignificant, whereas in reality they are inherently and importantly part and parcel "of globalization and of local resistance." To the leaders of the left and right, New India is Hindu and "gendered in terms of masculine capability and feminine compassion." Neither side could imagine any other construction for gender and sexuality than that which would "fit new forms of patriarchy" (Oza 2001, 1069, 1090, 1069, 1091).

The *Burqa* and *Purdah*

Many Muslim women today concur with their fundamentalist Muslim rulers on wearing the *burqa* and living in *purdah* because they are devout and believe in the Qur'an without question, as all good Muslims are supposed to do. They voluntarily veil themselves as a means of achieving respite from the unwanted gaze of strangers, especially males, and even including females. Or in other words, these women veil primarily to assist males in their goal of not being distracted from their focus on the spiritual. In "Attar of Roses," in *Attar of Roses and Other Stories of Pakistan* (1997) by Tahira Naqvi (?–), a schoolteacher falls in love to the point of mad obsession with a strange woman in a *burqa* because of the brief, passing glimpse he gets of her beautiful sandals, the glass bangles on her wrists, and the smell of her perfume—attar of roses. Although he follows her, he loses her trail and ends up buying sandals, bangles, and Attar of Roses perfume for his own wife. The message here is that veiling women cannot ultimately enable men to concentrate on working to achieve higher thoughts, that most men cannot be distracted from their animal urges. Nevertheless, many women disagree with this position. They still believe that the *burqa* will help; that veiling women would refine and purify the best and highest, most spiritual elements of men's nature. But, as Rokeya Sakhawat Hossain wittily quipped: "Veiling is not natural, it is ethical. Animals have no veils" (quoted in Jahan 1988, 52).

Many women also don the *burqa* voluntarily as a public announcement of their religious, social, and political position, as a statement of cultural solidarity with nationalism, as a sign that they desire to continue to perpetuate their own cultural traditions and as a gesture of total rejection of the West and all its corrupt and corrupting innovations (Harlan 1995a, 12; MacLeod 1992; Pfeil 1994, 216). Or they do it to save money, because then they do not have to worry about changing fashions. Or to be able to move around more and talk more openly so they can socialize with men publicly without worrying about their reputations, or they can critique men and their irrational rules and regulations in their own private space. But many other women find that the price they pay for such protection is to be subjected to the oppression of family rules and regulations (Feldman 2001, 1112; Harlan 1995a, 12).

In Hossain's time—the late nineteenth and early twentieth centuries—as well as currently, it also was believed that *purdah* (confinement to women's quarters in the home) was designed to protect women from the dangers of the world outside the privacy of the women's quarters in the home. This may not have been the real reason for *purdah* customs. They may have been designed primarily to "assure that a wife maintains a respectful social distance from and subservience to her husband and his senior relatives. Although the customs are justified by reference to the necessity of protecting women from seduction or rape, they are designed primarily to protect the consanguineous extended family from disruption by affinal wives" (Minturn 1993, 92–93). The earlier Indian social reform movements of Hossain's time had ended *purdah* but not its ideology and societal foundations (A. Basu 1992, 108, 252, fn. 1).[5] These foundations contributed to traditionalists' strong resistance to ending *purdah* because of their conviction that female sexuality made women "vulnerable" and at the same time a source of danger to the society. Therefore any woman who would (attempt to) express her sexuality had to be policed and controlled. Secluding women protected "their modesty, guarded them against shame, and minimized the risks of 'wanton' behavior" (Ramusack 1999, 27). The "prestige of a man" is located "between the legs of a woman. . . . A man secures his status . . . by controlling the movements of women related to him by blood or by marriage, and by forbidding them any contact with male strangers" (Fatima Mernissi, quoted in G. Devi 1993, 127).

These basic rationales for seclusion impact gender relations to this day, to this moment (A. Basu 1992, 111). As a typical comment reveals: "The only time a woman who was in *parda* [*sic*] should leave it is 'feet first,' that is, on her way to the funeral pyre" (Harlan 1995a, 223, fn. 18). Even communal riots, although not part of "the daily dose of violence against women" (R. Menon and Bhasin 1998, 60), exemplify "savagely and explicitly familiar forms of sexual violence." Such riots comprise "part of the continuum" and, alas, "part of the consensus." Like other forms of violence they symbolically expose how "women's sexuality" is perceived. "In an all-male, patriarchal arrangement of gender relations, between and within religious or ethnic communities . . . women's sexuality symbolises 'manhood'; its desecration is a matter of such shame and dishonour that *it has to be avenged*. Yet with the cruel logic of all such violence, it is women ultimately who are most violently dealt with as a consequence" (R. Menon and Bhasin 1998, 41, 43, emphasis the authors'). The cause of all these forms of violence is "deep and wide-ranging" patriarchal "consensus" that sanctions the solution of violence to the issue of "women's sexuality and sexual status—chaste, polluted, impure" while imposing "silence" on women by attaching "shame and stigma to this very profound violation of self" (R. Menon and Bhasin 1998, 58). Thus women have to "learn the trick of silence, of female invisibility. How else could women protect themselves?" (Alexander 1993, 106). Especially when the state does more than "sanction" violence; when it "participates" in it by reinforcing "patriarchal control in the private and conjugal domain." Furthermore, its "anxiety" and "preoccupation" with women's "sexual conduct" and "sexual trespass" reflects the male fraternity from the private family level out to the public, community level (R. Menon and Bhasin 1998, 252).

Kamala Markandaya (1924–), through her Hindu heroine Ruksmani in *Nectar in a Sieve* (1954), exposes sympathy and compassion for the situation of Muslim women still in *purdah,* although tinged with a superior and discriminatory attitude toward them:

> The women—well, they were a queer lot, and their way of life was quite different from ours. What they did in their houses I do not know, for they employed servants to do the work; but they stayed mostly indoors, or if they went out at all they were veiled in *bourkas*. It was their religion, I was told; they would not appear before any man but their husband. Sometimes, when I caught sight of a figure in voluminous draperies swishing through the streets under a blazing sun, or of a face peering through a window or shutter, I felt desperately sorry for them, deprived of the ordinary pleasures of knowing warm sun and cool breeze upon their flesh, of walking out light and free, or of mixing with men and working beside them. (1954, 51–52)

Child Marriage, Treatment of Widows, Widow Remarriage

> *In all the "lore" of widow remarriage, it is the [caste-Hindu] father and the husband who are applauded for their reformist courage and selflessness.*
>
> GAYATRI CHAKRAVORTY SPIVAK

Early activists were essentially seeking to improve conditions for themselves and for women from their own high-status castes. In 1856, the Bengali Hindus ended polygamy, permitted women to emerge from *purdah,* permitted widows to remarry and to take part in the weekly congregation, and raised the age of marriage for their girls to twelve years, although this change was not yet in effect in more orthodox quarters. It also should be noted that their continuing refusal to allow women to work outside the home, to divorce, or to remarry are all indicators of upper-class status and caste, of luxuries the lower classes and castes did not have (Gopal 1999, 327–328, fn. 26; Minturn 1993, 7). The British outlawed child marriage, passing the Age of Consent Act in 1891 that raised the age from ten to twelve and made sex with underaged girls illegal, defining it as "rape," even if the men were married to them, and imprisoning them for a maximum of ten years or being "transported for life" (Burton 1998, 194, fn. 15). The Hindu Marriage Act of 1949 sets the age of marriage for girls at fifteen and for males as eighteen (M. Basu 2001, 62; Minturn 1993, 321). Elsewhere, Monmayee Basu places the age for girls under the Hindu Marriage Restraint Act of 1955 (Clause 5) as sixteen years and eighteen to twenty-one years for males (2001, 110). Nivedita Menon, however, claims that although the age of eighteen is the minimum age for marriage under Section 375 of the Indian Penal Code, the age of fifteen is accepted (2000, 88).

From 1850 to 1930, the English-run Privy Council ruled in case after case against women's having property rights so that Hindu widows eventually had no control over their property that reverted to their husbands' heirs because traditionally widowhood was tantamount to "civil death" (Agnes 2000, 122; Burton 1998, 214, fn. 126). Sonil, the heroine of Indira Ganesan's, second novel, *Inheritance* (1998), is only fifteen years old, yet she begins to question the institution of widowhood: "What was so bad in being a proper widow? 'A widow is nothing in our society. Unable to remarry, unable to entertain, always an eyesore, a begrudged extra plate,' one of my teachers had lectured in class. . . . But was that always the case? Why did she need to entertain anyway?" (1998, 133). There has traditionally been a stigma attached to being a widow, and widows lead even more constrained lives than they had as wives (Sangari and Vaid 1999a, 431, fn. 83). For widows without money, it is dreadful. Greedy relatives and others surrounding the widow often desire her inheritance for themselves. They suddenly become very religious, trying to talk a widow into committing *sati*—not always without success—in order to deprive the widow of what they themselves want: to privately control and oppress women; to inculcate into them an unquestioning belief in patriarchy; to keep widows dependent; to aid and abet the agendas of priests and other influential male community members so that the family will, in turn, be aided and abetted through profitable business ventures involved with *sati*. This despite Manu the sage, who was the most prestigious, the most influential "spokesman . . . of the Brahmanical

Sanskritic tradition" (Erndl 2000, 96). He warned that "[f]riends or relations of a woman, who out of folly or avarice live upon the property belonging to her, or the wicked ones who deprive her of the enjoyment of her own belongings, go to hell" (quoted in Agnes 2000, 113).

Ruth Prawer Jhabvala (1927–)[6] ironically describes a common predicament for a rich widow—relatives who suddenly become "orthodox" and who suddenly claim that they want her to follow traditional customs (that many widow still widely practice) that require her

> to shave her head, to reduce her diet to stale bread and lentils, and deprive her from ever again tasting the sweet things of life: to condemn her, in fact, to that perpetual mourning, perpetual expiation, that was the proper lot of widows. That was how they saw it and how their forefathers had always seen it. . . . There was no other way for widows but to lead humble, bare lives; it was for their own good. For if they were allowed to feed themselves on the pleasures of the world, then they fed their own passions too, and that which should have died in them with the deaths of their husbands would fester and boil and overflow into sinful channels. (1986, 41, 56)

As late as 2001, Divakaruni, in her short story "The Lives of Strangers" in *The Unknown Errors of Our Lives,* describes the following conversation about a widow, a "bad-luck woman" (2001, 75):

> "Her husband died just two years after her marriage, and right away her in-laws, who hated her because it had been a love match, claimed that the marriage wasn't legal. They were filthy rich . . . hired the shrewdest lawyers. She lost everything—the money, the house, even the wedding jewelry. . . . She had to go to work in an office . . . forced to work with low-caste peons and clerks! That's how she put her son through college and got him married . . . And now the daughter-in-law refuses to live with her. . . . So she's had to move into a women's hostel. A women's hostel! At her age!" (2001, 58)

In Mukherjee's *Jasmine* (1991), her eponymous heroine is widowed at around the age of eighteen. In the United States, in Queens, New York, in a community of Indian Hindus like herself, Jasmine is not allowed to participate in matchmaking with the rest of the female members of the family with whom she lives because she is a widow. She does not tell us, but this is because her presence at any celebration would bring bad luck (Harlan 1995a, 13). Wives are responsible for preventing their husbands from dying before them and those who do not have therefore failed to do their duty in a variety of ways. Because wives were supposed to safeguard their husbands' lives through their conduct and by performing various rituals properly, the prevailing opinion was that widows should be consigned to hardships such as extreme fasting, praying, severe clothing restrictions, and service to other family members. Another reason given for subjecting widows to great physical and mental hardship is that this is to prevent widows from ever appearing in such a way as to arouse men's lusts. When relatives did not provide homes and shelters for them, widows without recourse often became prostitutes. As Jasmine's experience reveals, for most widows remarriage was considered impossible long after this custom was thought to have been extinct in India (M. Basu 2001, 76; Humes 2000, 142; Mukherjee 1991, 130). Manu prescribed "patience for a widow . . . self-control, and chastity. She should also nearly starve herself by living on pure flours, roots and fruits" (Erndl 2000, 96). This was why, traditionally, young daughters-in-law themselves cooked the desserts for family widows (M. Basu 2001, 5). Furthermore, the widow has to remove anything connected with her prior marital condition such as her jewelry, can only wear simple clothing, sit in a dark corner for two weeks after her husband's death, and can only move around at given times of the day (M. Basu 2001, 67; I. Sen 1999, 411).

The prohibition against widow remarriage was widespread throughout India, as was shutting widows away in order to prevent unattached women from expressing their sexuality or tempting men to do so. But (re)marriage outside the faith and caste was considered even worse. Pandita Ramabai [Saraswati], the great, early feminist (ca. 1858–1922) and author of *The High-Caste Hindu Woman* ([1886] 1888), was herself a young widow who had married outside her caste and became a prominent doctor in India. She was famous, among other things, for her campaign for widow remarriage and for her exposé of the sufferings of married Hindu women. The reformers in the nationalist movement reacted especially adversely to this exposé because they attempted to situate the home as the spiritual source of Hinduism's deepest "values" (Burton 1998, 81). In contrast, Ramabai's definition of the home as a place of relaxation and pleasure for all family members was Western-influenced. She believed that India could not number itself among the great nations of the world unless "the Hindu *zenana* is transformed into the Hindu home, where the united family can have pleasant times together" (quoted in Grewal 1996, 178).[7]

Ramabai's feminism and nationalism also provided an alternative to those Western feminists who habitually spoke about Indian women's issues as if they were speaking for Indian women. Of Ramabai's familiarity with Sanskrit and Hindu ideology, as well as with the Christian scriptures, Kumari Jayawardena remarks: "For a woman to be well-versed in theology, in a society where religion is all-pervasive, has always been an advantage when challenging social evils that are disguised as religious orthodoxy; and Ramabai used her knowledge in the cause of women" (1986, 91). In addition to her involvement with schools for girls, orphanages, and homes for widows, Ramabai was one of the very few female delegates to the session of the Indian National Congress of 1889.[8] Yet despite this, Ramabai's conviction that women are unified because they are united in suffering oppression at the hands of males, has been charged with extending only to high-caste Hindu Brahmin women being oppressed at the hands of high-caste Hindu Brahmin men (Grewal 1996, 184). But, given her extensive travels, her breadth of intellect and learning, and her service in the Congress, such a charge of parochialism would make Ramabai as ethnocentric as Western Christian feminists—her contemporaries—who are notorious for having carried the baggage of their prejudices with them wherever they went.

Sati

> As in the case of war, martyrdom, "terrorism"—self-sacrifice in general—the "felicitous" sati may have (been imagined to have) thought she was exceeding and transcending the ethical. That is its danger. Not all soldiers die unwillingly. And there are female suicide bombers.   GAYATRI CHAKRAVORTY SPIVAK

Kumaran Asan (1873–1924), a male writer who fought againt women's oppression, depicted Sita in a controversial poem "Chintavishtayya Sita" ("The Brooding Sita") published in 1919 as protesting her being put to an ordeal by fire to prove that she had remained true to Rama: "Does the King think that I should once more go into his presence and prove myself a devi? Do you think I am a mere doll . . . my mind and soul revolt at the thought" (quoted in Jayawardena 1986, 87). Sally J. Sutherland Goldman views Sita's various predicaments as forcing her "to act" like "empowered males in patriarchal discourse" such as by making decisions, interacting with strange men who were not members of her family, "and even the mere fact of being heard" (2001, 224). Other Indian feminists also link Sita to the custom of *sati*. They reinterpret long-suffering Sita who finally requested (successfully) to be swallowed into the earth, her mother,[9] as in reality being "murdered by society . . . for how voluntary are voluntary deaths, and was it bliss hereafter or earthly hell that drove *sati*s to climb their husbands' funeral pyres to be burned alive?" (Sahgal [1986] 1988b, 67). In the 1980s, however, the traditional interpretation of Sita was still being forwarded in a television series "that dominated the Sunday morning schedule of millions of Indians" (Ramusack 1999, 26).

Many voices have been heard on *sati*—the sacrificial burning of widows—including the voices of Western feminists, early reformers, nationalists, the British, and Indian/Third World feminists. But the voices of the subjects of *sati* themselves, the women undergoing *sati* have not been heard (L. Mani [1989] 1998; Spivak 1999, 287). The Hindus and the British abolished *sati*—or attempted to do so—since the practice continues on in rare spurts to this day. Traditionally, only widows—and then only in rare circumstances—were reserved for *sati*, which Gabriele Dietrich calls "the supreme logic of housewifization" (1999, 85). *Sati* is one of the primary bulwarks of the patriarchal system (Sangari and Vaid 1999a, 385). According to Kumkum Sangari, some of the patriarchal constructions that *sati* perpetuates are the extended family, Hindu traditions, nari-dharma, patti-bakthi, sectional group identities, a fundamentalist yet cross-caste Hinduism, and that "spirituality" which is the mark of our "Indianness" and which distinguishes us from the materialistic West. *Sati* will manage the ideals around which our social order coheres, it will not only ward off the fear of death but feminists as well. (Quoted in Narayan 1997, 79)

A widow who immolated herself on her deceased husband's funeral pyre also would get a *sati* stone on the site where she had immolated herself to eternally serve as a reminder of her self-sacrificial deed. The site would attract pilgrims, which, in turn, would bring money to the male members of the family, to the townspeople, and to the temple functionaries and leaders (Ramusack 1999, 31). And what would the *satt* get in return? She would bring good fortune to three to seven generations of her husband's and even her own natal family. She would earn bliss for herself and her husband for thirty-five million years. In eternal ecstasy she would sport with her husband in heaven while being the object of praise-songs from "groups of apsaras [heavenly dancers]" (Spivak 1999, 299). Spivak points out that the presence of British police during *sati* to determine whether or not it was legal (i.e., whether or not the widow had exerted free choice in the matter as the proponents of *sati* claimed), caused some nationalistic backlash. Despite the two different views regarding the widow's freedom of choice, the constituent elements of female subjectivity while she was alive were entirely subverted by structuring *sati* as part and parcel of male domination and argued over and debated endlessly by both patriarchies (1999, 235, 298).[10]

If there were no such ideals of devotion and self-sacrifice prescribed for a *pativrata* [husband worshiper] the concept of *sati* would lose its power. When in the course of Sangari and Sudesh Vaid's study of rural villages local women were queried about *sati,* they responded that widows without means of support were being victimized. Local men, in contrast, saw *sati* as proof of a woman's "virtue." Immolated widows thus become icons of glorious "Indian womanhood." They are ideal wives upholding their family's honor because they are heroic and self-abnegating in sacrificing their lives. Sangari and Vaid, in contrast to these men, define as "aggressive Hinduism" the use of spiritual discourse for the purpose of regulating female sexuality by severely restricting women to the confines of domestic life within the home and to one husband even after his death (1999a, 396, 397, 405). These patriarchal values are part and parcel of nationalist ideals. Pro-*sati* campaigns in the late twentieth century pitted many presumably pro-*sati* nationalist women against Indian feminists, but "widows were conspicuously absent" from their demonstrations (1999a, 367).

Most Indian writers and critics discussed in this text agree that *sati* was/is the most barbaric practice of Hinduism and that it was/is a travesty of religion (L. Mani [1989] 1998; Saghal [1977] 1988c, 120). However, a very different concept of *sati* is illustrated in the definition given by *Sati* Mata, reputedly "of royal blood" who turned ascetic after being thwarted when she attempted self-immolation:

"The title *sati* should not be given to a woman who burns herself, but to a woman of virtue. And the greatest virtue is endurance. I am called the *Sati* Mata because my gurus are the Five *Sati*s, those five virtuous women who refused to burn themselves on their husbands' pyres. The true *sati* has the will to continue when the familiar world fragments around her." (Quoted in G. Mehta 1989, 125, 128)

Uma Narayan does not justify *sati* but, rather, attempts to put it in perspective by reminding us that by contending so long and hard over *sati,* both the British and their learned Hindu opponents failed to notice other crimes against women that caused just as much continual suffering, such as the deaths of untold millions from diseases and famine (1997, 65). However, the best arguments against *sati,* in my opinion, are those of Jotirao Phule (1827–1890) when he "speculated about whether any husband would become a *sata* by being immolated on the funeral pyre of his wife"(quoted in Jayawardena 1986, 84).[11] In recent remarks made to a reporter by village women during an interview, their response to *sati* was similar: "When I inquired if any of them were likely to commit *sati,* they said, 'Only if our husbands agree to burn themselves on our funeral pyres if we die first'" (quoted in G. Mehta 1997, 245).

Many Indian feminists deplore the linking of *sati* to daily religious rituals as a means of further legimating patriarchal oppression because it makes it easier for women to accept and agree to *sati*. That is, *sati* thus becomes naturalized as another element among many within traditional and time-honored Hindu religious practices. Family members and others who participate in *sati,* including those who justify *sati* on religious grounds, are viewed by these Indian feminists as creating a mystical aura around the act that is criminal. Such a faith depends on a whole series of constructions around *sati* that serve to obfuscate the fact that it is an abomination (L. Mani [1989] 1998, 1999; Sangari and Vaid 1999a, 325, 437; Spivak 1999, 284, 294). Widows inherited property only in Bengal during the Raj, and this was the underlying motive for Bengal's stringent enforcment of *sati* (Spivak 1999, 294, 300). Spivak rarely, if ever, uses the term *sati,* probably because the concrete and vivid term she does use—"the self-immolation of widows"—is so much more effective in its descriptiveness.

Narayan feels that the British, the West, and Western feminists have an obsession with *sati* that is not based on moral revulsion for a horrifying crime so much as on the need to construct themselves as civilized and superior to the barbaric and inferior "natives" (1997, 66). I would argue here that all of us globally, whatever our cultures, have a right to be repelled by *crimes against humanity, by human rights violations* wherever and whenever they occur, no matter what cold-blooded, unconvincing, specious religious, legal, and national pseudo-spiritual stonewalling discourse (jargon) is deployed to justify them. Human rights are beyond and above "identity politics," "cultural relativism," "cultural sovereignty," and "national boundaries."

Bride Burnings/Dowry Deaths

Many Indian women writers and critics discuss the abuses associated with the dowry system, which lead to brides' deaths when in-laws complain about the insufficiency of the dowry, such as a typical one that Amrita Basu describes. A woman who had a small child committed suicide by taking pesticides, and her friends maintained that she had actually been murdered by her in-laws because of the small dowry (1992, 163).[12] Such murders are considered by-products of urban life because of the anonymity provided by a large city (primarily Delhi); the employment of professional matchmakers; the increase of rampant consumerism; and the easy availability of second wives for grooms and their families (and another dowry) even when first wives have been murdered (Minturn 1993, 111; Raheja 1995, 58). Hypocritical politicians denounce the dowry system while themselves participating in it, and especially abuses associated with it (A. Basu 1992, 73–74). Furthermore, in the lowest classes there will be mortality because of poverty, but in the middle classes girls are kept from working so that the dowry that the bride's in-laws receives makes the bride into "a commodity." Such an "economic transfer, demanded and driven by" the bride's in-laws leads "to [female] culling" because families then strive to have the number of sons sufficient to offset the sum of any dowries occasioned by their having daughters (Harriss-White 1999, 142–143).[13] Radha Kumar states that until 1979 kerosene deaths had been considered suicide and had not been connected to "dowry harassment" until "Stri Sangharsh, a fledgling feminist group" demonstrated on behalf of a woman murdered by her in-laws because they were dissatisfied with the dowry. As a result, "feminists reversed the indifference of decades, linking death by fire with dowry harassment and showing that many official suicides were in fact murders" (1999, 350). In "Pigeons at Daybreak" in *Games at Twilight* ([1978] (1983), Anita Desai depicts a woman reading the news to her husband:

> "Floods in Assam." "Drought in Maharashtra." When is there not? "Two hundred cholera deaths" "And woman and child have a miraculous escape when their house collapses." "Husband held for murder of wife." "See?" she cried excitedly. "Once more. How often does this happen? "Husband and mother-in-law have been arrested on charge of pouring kerosene on Kantibai's clothes and setting her on fire while she slept." Yes, that is how they always do it. Why? Probably the dowry didn't satisfy them, they must have hoped to get one more. ([1978] 1983, 100)

It is considered a curse to bear a daughter because it means that the mother was being "punished" for having sinned in previous "incarnations." Intelligence in a girl is deemed wasted, a sign of God's cruelty. A female could not enter heaven if she did not marry, dowries bankrupted families for "generations," and if she is unfortunate enough to be abused and beaten by her husband and his family, a bride becomes "a powerless victim" (Mukherjee 1991, 34, 36; [1977] 1995, 228). Her only recourse under such circumstances is to commit suicide or return to her natal home. Wives who had no dowry, who rebelled, or who were childless were somehow subject to misfortunes such as falling into wells, being run over by trains, or burned to death while cooking on kerosene stoves "*supposedly* because of an accident while cooking" (Ramusack 1999, 69, emphasis mine). One of Mukherjee's major female characters, Dimples, believes with good reason that an acquaintance of hers in India was set on fire by her husband's family in order to get her dowry. Her husband's callous response is that, when working at the stove, women should wear cotton and not saris made of flammable material such as nylon. Then there is Alexander's caustic, heartrending response to such a claim of accident: "An exploding stove here, a burst can of kerosene there, matches that mysteriously caught flame when held to a *dupatta* or *sari pallu*" (1993, 209). Veena Talwar Oldenburg comments on these "accidents" that kerosene is always present in the kitchen, that victims can easily be doused with it, that consumer reports have shown that commonly used "pressurized kerosene stoves" tend to explode, and that bodies that are burned "with 90 or more percent third-degree burns" cannot provide evidence as to whether or not there was a struggle beforehand (quoted in Narayan 1997, 102). Yet, despite the Dowry Prohibition Law of 1961 and amendments in 1984 and 1986, M. Basu grieves that dowry deaths are "still prevalent in our society in a frightening way" and increasing "with depressing regularity" (2001, 96).[14]

Son Preference, Female Infanticide

In 1795 the Hindus made female infanticide illegal, but to this day Indian couples still prefer to have boys, especially as their first-born. In *The Fire Sacrifice* ([1989] 1993), Susham Bedi's heroine Guddo recalls that in India, *havans* (fire ceremonies) were performed only on her brothers' birthdays but forbidden on girls' birthdays. Once when she asked for a *havan* on her birthday, she was informed that if *havans* were performed on girls' birthdays, "then afterwards only girls will be born. In the future we must have fewer girls born in this family" ([1989] 1993, 75–76). In contemporary India, there is an epidemic of women's use of ultrasound sonograms and amniocentesis for the purpose of having "sex-selective" abortions if the fetus they are carrying is female. Ninety-nine percent of these abortions are performed on female fetuses, and this is responsible for the decline in the sex ratio (John 1999, 105; Narayan 1997, 144; Ramusack 1999). In 1988, in Maharashtra, feminists succeeded in getting legislation passed against amniocentesis, but it has not helped. Feminists are still concerned about advertisements by clinics, the focus on lower–class women in the government's family planning program, its experimentation with "controversial contraceptives," and the recent preponderance in the advocacy of sterilization procedures weighted for females, not males (Ramusack 1999, 71). In fact, Indian women did not even have to struggle to obtain the right to an abortion. It was made legal "and available on demand" in 1971, because it was seen as more of "a population control measure than a women's rights issue." Limiting family size is seen as a legitimate motivation for abortion by most of the population (Kishwar 1999, 85; Kishwar and Vanita 1984, 25–26).

In *Nectar in a Sieve,* Ruksmani, after giving birth to her first child, turns away "and, despite myself, the tears came, tears of weakness and disappointment; for what woman wants a girl for her first-born?" (Markandaya 1954, 19). In Sahgal's *Mistaken Identity* (1988a), a lawyer describes to the protagonist how this preference for boys is assured—through female infanticide. From 1879 on, "the disposal of female children had definitely been on the decline. . . . Regrettably, one had to do away with half one's infant daughters. [Here the lawyer is hinting that the protagonist's mother was involved.] It was custom-ritual" (1988a, 62). Women "dispatched" these babies by strangling with the umbilical cord or by "a pill of *bhang* [opium]," or by live burial after first filling "the hole up tenderly with milk" (1988a, 63). In Divakaruni's "The Ultrasound" in *Arranged Marriage* (1995), the author illustrates this situation through the simultaneous pregnancy of two cousins—Runi in India and Anju in the United States. After observing certain rituals at the temple of Shashti, goddess of childbirth, after making Runi put on "a good-luck amulet on a copper chain around her waist to appease the angry planets" (1995, 217), and after having an exhaustive physical examination to ensure she was in good health, Runi's in-laws discover that she is going to have a girl. They immediately order her to abort the fetus because it is inappropriate for the oldest child in their Brahmin household to be a female.

"Did her husband go for a checkup too?" Anju in America demands of her mother in India, who responds by asking her if she has forgotten how they "do things" in India? Anju then complains to her husband about why in India the woman is always blamed for everything they do not want or desire. He shrugs and informs her that it's because "[i]t's a man's world in India" (1995, 217–218). If Runi refuses the abortion and leaves, her husband and in-laws may not take her back, while her parents argue that her place is with her husband and his family and that otherwise people will conclude that she was thrown out because she was having "a bastard" and will not be able to remarry. Stigmatized by her neighbors and community at every opportunity, she will become a pariah, an outcast in her world. At the end of the story, Anju decides to ask Runi to seek shelter with Anju's mother. She also plans to ask her husband to sponsor Runi and her baby daughter on "a student visa." Such an ending is ambivalent because it depends on whether Runi will indeed have the extraordinary courage to make what are daring moves in India in contradiction to custom, especially since she has no obvious educational skills with which to support herself and a child. Thus, the author is claiming a wide chasm between the Indian woman in the United States and the Indian woman in

India, even in contemporary times. Other authors and critics do not see such freedom as Anju enjoys as possible in tightly controlled Indian communities. Perhaps Anju and her husband are living as a nuclear American(ized) family on their own and away from the Indian community.

Traditionally, unfeeling mothers were blamed for female infanticide; however recent evidence reveals that, although mothers murder the infants, they do so as a result of pressure from their in-laws or from males in their family who give them two choices: either murder the female child or become battered and tortured victims themselves (Goldman 2000, 394–395, fn. 42; Panjabi 1997, 159). But more than one hundred years ago it was Pandita Ramibai in acid words dripping with Swiftian sarcasm who made the most telling comment on female infanticide:

> After considering how many girls could safely be allowed to live, the father took good care to defend himself from caste and clan tyranny by killing the extra girls at birth which was as easily accomplished as destroying a mosquito or any other annoying insect. Who can save a baby if the parents are determined to slay her, and eagerly watch for a suitable opportunity? There are several . . . nameless methods that may be employed. . . . There are not a few child thieves who generally steal girls; even the wild animals are so intelligent and of such refined taste that they mock at British law, and almost always steal girls to satisfy their hunger. . . . The census of 1870 revealed the curious fact that 300 children were stolen in one year by wolves from within the city of Umritzar, all the children being girls. (Quoted in Chakravarti [1989] 1999, 69)

Pativratadharma (Husband Worship)

> *The only people who benefit from the behaviour of typical Indian wives are typical Indian husbands.*
> MANJULA PADMANABHAN

Indian women writers have held an array of positions on the topic of husband worship. In the 1880s, Nagendrabala Saraswati linked *pativratradharma* with the project of improving and modernizing India, of bringing India up to Western—specifically English—standards. She maintained that this could only be done by improving the home and family first. Saraswati argued that educating women was not for the purpose of making them better mothers and homemakers—or to become independent—but for the purpose of women's rededicating themselves to the ideals of obedience (quoted in Chakrabarty 1997, 377). Such an ideology for women has been contemptuously dismissed by contemporary Indian feminists. As a result of Indians' fanatic insistence on disposing of all girls in marriage, women are made into dolls, or marionettes, to be moved around as others wish (M. Kapur 1998, 85; Sahgal [1977] 1988c, 95). The contemporary writer Anjana Appachana, through the meditations of a traditional woman about marriage and motherhood, reveals what she believes to be the source for this conviction (as a result of relentless religious and social propaganda and brainwashing) that a woman can only be a wife and mother, and not also pursue an education and career:

> A woman should command respect for her resilience, for her fortitude, for her integrity and for how she brought up her children. . . . For a woman to sustain her intellectual abilities meant neglecting the home and children; to sustain the home and children meant neglecting the life of the mind. The choice was clear. Intellect got you nowhere in the kitchen. Contemplating one's life meant burning the rice. Thinking about relationships meant starving the children. . . . Subsume your needs to His. Silence . . . is all that is needed, that is all. (1998, 345)

As late as the 1930s Maitreyi Devi recorded that the custom of viewing the husband as "the ruling deity" in the Indian home was still widespread. The position of Indian men is still that of Manu [ca. 500 B.C.], that working for and serving her husband is woman's reward and how she acquires "virtue" (apparently, however, without there being any reciprocity on the husband's part, or the slightest feeling of "gratitude"). Qurratulain Hyder (1927-) describes "contradictory statements about women" by Manu and other sages in her epic *River of Fire* ([1959] 1999), through the musings of one of her male characters, a contemporary of Manu's, whose attitude is clearly that of his feminist creator:

> Woman could never be pure, she was the root of all evil, she was shallow. Women of good families envied courtesans for their dresses and ornaments. Evil came into existence because of creation. Woman gave birth, so she was the origin of all sin. Woman was hungry for love, and therefore unreliable. And yet, despite her weaknesses, she could be immensely virtuous, faithful and self-sacrificing. She should be respected. She symbolised Shakti [essential female energy inherent in women]. . . . And there were all those wives who were burnt alive with their dead husbands. . . . What is wrong with women that they should be shunned like lepers? ([1959] 1999, 21)

Elsewhere in *River of Fire* another male character cites Manu sarcastically, "with finality: '*Na stri swatantram*—there should be no freedom for women. Thus spake Manu Maharaj'" ([1959] 1999, 137). And in another scene where Hyder may be playing on Freud's famous query as to what women want, a contemporary female character, the wife of the family's driver, reveals that the situation remains today as it was hundreds, thousands, of years ago:

> "You do not know what men are. We do. They are happy as long as you go on adoring them, and they want enormous sacrifices from us. Otherwise they're unhappy. How can I explain . . . that girls are always in a weaker position? . . . What is a mere woman, after all. . . . She is a man's personal servant as a wife, and even as a mother. In her youth she is tormented by her in-laws, in her old age she is bullied by her daughter-in-law, as a widow, if she is poor she is ignored by everyone. All her life she has to serve, serve, serve. And even then men are not satisfied. What do they want? Complete submission, like God." ([1959] 1999, 267)

Devi likens husbands in their homes to all-powerful kings with "absolute" dominion over their subjects ([1974] 1995, 104–105). Her observation is borne out by the way in which Manu describes female life cycles: "Marriage is her *upanayana* [ritual that makes a man twice-born], cohabiting [with] and serving the husband [is tantamount to staying with and serving the guru], and *grihakarma* [household work] service to agni [the fire god]" (quoted in Chakrabarty 1997, 391). Even later, in 1954, the heroine of Markayanda's *Nectar in a Sieve* tells readers that "in all the years" of her marriage to her husband she never used his given name, "for it is not meet for a woman to address her husband except as 'husband'" (1954, 10). Somehow the treatment husbands accord wives is irrelevant to the reasoning behind *pativratadharma*. The worse husbands conduct themselves, the more of a challenge it is to "the wives' self-motivated commitment to their 'devotion'" (Courtright 1995, 188), as is revealed through comments from contemporary Indian women that Lindsey Harlan collected on this topic. The worship of husbands still goes unquestioned: "It is better to be a *pativrata* (a devoted wife) than a *bhakta* (a devotee of God)"; "A woman's husband is her god"; and "A woman should ask her husband to worship other gods." One respondent went a step further and said: "A husband is higher than a god: you can defame a god, but not a husband." Harlan concludes that many Indian women to this day still rank "selfless obedience to their husbands and their husbands' families . . . as the most important rule of female behavior" (1995b, 206, 209–210). They still believe in "self-sacrifice on behalf of a husband," and that "[a]ll women should sacrifice their own welfare for the good of their husbands" (Collins 2000, 57).

Feminist Indian writers and critics always question this belief, however, as can be seen over time—from Hossain's outraged report about the woman who let her child burn so that her husband could remain sleeping, to the present day, when Mukherjee depicts her heroine Jasmine as rebelling against this "caregiving" tradition by leaving her disabled protector in his wheel chair to run off with another man. Mukherjee herself, after a return to India in 1973, is assured by the wife of an advertising executive that the lesson of self-denial and self-sacrifice in the Ramayana is not sexist because worshiping a husband is tantamount to worshipping God. This woman believes that the inscription on a nineteenth-century poster that she owns contains injunctions in Bengali from which Western women could benefit. When a husband is "pleased" then God is also. The husband is for a wife her "life," "pride," her "only jewel" ([1977] 1995, 234). Amrita Basu writes that "The major life-cycle rituals associated with birth, marriage, and death, as well as the wives' daily *bratas* (resolutions or vows) all assign structural superiority to men" (1992, 112), and Spivak tells us that this is the case because women are not permitted to join their husbands in their final stages of purification. She also sharply questions those who smugly question the validity of feminists who dare to critique ancient texts: "The real question is, of course, why structures of patriarchal domination should be unquestioningly recorded. Historical sanctions for collective action to-ward social justice can only be developed if people outside the discipline question standards of 'objectivity' preserved as such by the hegemonic tradition" (1999, 301, fn. 160).

The narrator of Deshpande's *The Binding Vine* ([1993] 2001) believes of her mother-in-law—who had died giving birth to the narrator's husband—that her tragedy had been to be forced into a marriage by *her* mother with "a man who tried to possess another human being against her will." She cites an angry poem by the dead woman recalling what her mother had told her before her marriage: "Don't tread paths barred to you/obey, never utter a 'no';/submit and your life will be/ a paradise"([1993] 2001, 83). And, in Divakaruni's short story "Clothes," in *Arranged Marriage* (1995), when the bride's future husband plans to take her to the United States, she protests about traveling so very far to marry a man she had never seen. Her mother responds that every woman is destined to "leave the known for the un-known. . . . *A married woman belongs to her husband, her in-laws*" (1995, 18–19), em-phasis the author's). Ironically (perhaps influenced by Mukherjee's depiction of the idyllic relationship of Prakash and Jasmine in her novel *Jasmine,* which was brought to an abrupt end by Prakash's violent death), Divakaruni's bride falls deeply in love with her supportive husband, Somesh Sen, the co-owner of a *7–Eleven* store in New Jersey. Like Prakash, he, too, comes to a violent end, not at the hands of religious fanatics, but while working on "the graveyard shift." Instead of returning to India with her in-laws, Sumita intends to go on to college and into an open-ended American future, as her modern and Westernized husband (again, like Jasmine's Prakash) had intended for her when he told her: *"I want you to go to college. Choose a career"* (1995, 31, emphasis the author's).

Lakshmi Persaud, born in a Hindi community in Trinidad and now living in London, critiques the material in *Ramayana* and the *Mahabharata* from a far more blunt and open feminist perspective—as being unfairly used to indoctrinate girls in chastity, purity, obedience, patience, humility, into "the ideal wife syndrome"; into acting "as the moral anchor in a marriage . . . unswerving in loyalty and right-eousness, no matter how ill-matched her husband's response" (quoted in Kishwar 2001, 286).

Expatriation, Immigration

> *Even within economic migration, women often remain exilic.*
> GAYATRI CHAKRAVORTY SPIVAK

For those few Indian woman who did travel abroad in the nineteenth century, the act of travel was dangerous mentally and emotionally because it challenged basic cultural and Hindu belief systems. "For high-caste Hindu women [travel] was considered desexing and heresy and those women who went to the West primarily for education were the objects of condemnation, believed to have defiled themselves, their families, and 'Indian womanhood' itself—the most sacrosanct and cherished institution" (R. Kapur and Cossman 1999, 224). Such females became "public women" in the most disreputable sense, exposing themselves to physical danger, to being beaten, or worse, to contempt, insults, and mockery because they were at odds with some of the most basic cultural codes of nineteenth-century Indian civil society. By the time that I discuss this topic in Chapter Three, however, the issue is no longer a question of what impression(s) traditionalists had of Indian women like Ramabai or the Sorabji sisters who traveled abroad but, rather, the impression(s) that Indian women had of the societies and cultures to which *they* traveled. They continued to travel, still for education, as with most of the authors represented in this text, or as tourists with their families or spouses. After Partition in 1947, giving rise to communal rioting that has never ended, and especially after 1965, when the United States opened immigration to Indians (because of its shortage of doctors), the question ever hovers in these writers' minds as to whether or not they would migrate out of India, come and go forever in the limbo of never belonging anywhere, or emigrate to the West for good.

Indian feminist writers display a variety of perspectives on these issues, but only one united response—of outrage—against the West's assumption that because they were women of color they lacked an education and were uncivilized. The authors write eloquently on the issues that arise either for them or for their characters in the West. Some of the writers in this chapter are no longer tourists or visitors, or even immigrants. They are first-and second-generation Indians born in the West, and, like Divakaruni, they write of the irrational chasms between Americanized Indians and traditional Indians with obvious compassion and full understanding for Indian women who go West as visitors to members of their family, or the first generation of immigrants who attempt to impose Indian ways on the next generation. The traumas some of them experience in the United States and the clashes with their kinfolk are caused by their obstinate clinging to and vaunting of Indian traditions. Without self-examination or self-reflexivity, they display contempt for or misunderstandings about Western culture. Others are enchanted by Western culture, like Feroza's cousin Manek in the Pakistani writer Sidhwa's *American Brat* (1993). In a quarrel between Feroza's cousin and his wife, the wife expresses her longing to return to Karachi and her husband argues against it. Here Sidhwa provides readers with so vivid and so real an example of contrasts between the two cultures that Westerners, male and female, cannot possibly misunderstand her points.

Manek asks his wife Aban if she could get so many TV channels back home? She would not even be able to get two. In the United States, she has her Thunderbird, her washing machine, and dishwasher, and many other appliances. She also has baby food and disposable diapers for their baby who would get asthma in Karachi because of the pollution, as well as diarrhea from the water. Aban would be busy giving medicine to the baby day and night and washing her diapers with soap. Even if Aban had all the appliances, she would be unable to use them because of chronic electrical outages and water shortages. Aban responds that, although Karachi has a population of nine million, very few have asthma. She would not care how many dishes and diapers she had to wash if only she could be with her family and friends once again. And, besides, she would have servants. Manek reminds her that she should forget about servants. She would have to screech at them all the time. Once she is used to doing things her own way, she would no longer be able to put up with them.

Still other authors such as Bedi, for example, depict Indians as going West to make money sufficient for them to return to India to live the rest of their lives, caring for nothing else. Feeling like "a guest" in the United States, Bedi's heroine Guddo in *The Fire Sacrifice* ([1989] 1993) is a widow with three children who does not identify with the American worldview, whereas she does, with the Indian one. She is motivated only by her goal of earning a sufficient amount of money to enable her to pay for her children's schooling, to assist them in finding suitable employment, to see them marry, and then finally be free to return home to India where she would "live in splendour in her house in Chandigarh" ([1989] 1993, 70). She thinks of herself as a temporary visitor in the United States and that other Indian emigrés had even more selfish motives than hers. They only cared about fulfilling their own ambitions for success and upward mobility. They were not interested in politics or social issues, nor helping the powerless and impoverished. Some sent funds to their own relatives back in India, but this was as far as their worldview extended. "Nothing mattered but to work like the very devil and acquire one new convenience or luxury item after another. After all, that was why everybody came to this country! To emerge from the restrictions of class and caste, society and family, to lead a life free of responsibility" ([1989] 1993, 71). Then there are other Indians who remain in the West, happily or unhappily hanging on, always with the intention of eventually returning to India, but never doing so. Others, like Pramila Jayapal who was born in the United States, are continually taking stock, finding some good things and some bad things to say about both cultures.

Suppression and Denial of Female Sexuality

> *The perception of sex as a secondary attribute—a property or an adjective that one can add or subtract—to woman is a perception that still dwells in the prevailing logic of acquisition and separation.*   TRINH T. MINH-HA

For South Asian lesbians living in the Western world—we have one foot in a culture where people structure identities from sexuality and the other foot in a subcontinent culture where women are not seen as sexual beings.   SURINA KHAN

The hardest struggle for me has been, in general, to be a sexual being as a woman, and particularly so growing up in India, where women (at least those from the middle class) were not supposed to be sexual at all. In India, homosexuality is closeted for sure, but hell, even heterosexual sex before marriage is a big deal.   K. CHAUDARY

Younger feminist writers' and critics' responses to gender oppression, especially in terms of the "common erasure of female sexuality" (Grewal 1996, 207) are no different from those of their foremothers because the situation has not changed much. Writing about what she believes are "limitations" in contemporary Indian feminism, Grewal lists its assumption of "normative heterosexuality, its silence on female sexuality, and its dominant Hindu ideology" (1996, 180). Judging by the feminists' voices that extend back to Lalithambika Antherjanam (1909–1987?), such "limitations" are not altogether the case, and the younger generation's solutions to the problem of the suppression and denial of female sexuality does differ from those of previous generations in surprising, unexpected ways, as readers will discover. The works of the writers throughout the timeframe covered in this text— from the middle of the nineteenth century to the beginning of the twenty-first century—reflect the trajectory that Radhika Balakrishnan describes: a movement from public and private repression to alternative choices. An individual's "sexual pleasure," especially a woman's, is still not an acceptable topic for public (or, in many cases, private) discourse.[15] Nevertheless, the media is beginning to influence and expand women's sense of choice in sexual matters. This is the case because sexuality is socially constructed, and what they see in the media enables women to strive to free themselves from a society that has enculturated them into a repressive idea of what female sexuality is (2001, 54–55),[16] to "decolonize their minds" (Spivak 1999, 399) and bodies. Balakrishnan's definition of women's sexuality also accords with the way in which the authors discussed in this text describe themselves and/or their major characters over time: first as evading/avoiding sexual discourse altogether and focusing on other issues; then as struggling to achieve a consciousness of themselves as sexual beings; then as seeking sexual proactivity and becoming more open to "sexual knowledge": to have experiences that will enable them to construct their own individual identities sexually without endless "surveillance and constriction" (2001, 46–47).

As for constraints against "ordinary women," the ideal of "ordinary housewives, mothers and grandmothers" as always devoted, housebound caregivers effectively robotizes them, eradicating them as sexual entities possessed of individual needs. As late as the year 2000, Appachana, through the thoughts of a woman whose husband has retired, describes the current situation in India: "Her husband had retired a year ago . . . And all he did was talk . . . expound on South Indians and Bengalis and God knows who else. When did *she* get to retire? Was there ever any retirement from cooking and cleaning?" (2000, 67, emphasis the author's). Mukherjee reinforces this disgust with the ideal of caregiving in two of her characters, both immigrants to the United States. Dimples and Jasmine learn this lesson much earlier in life than Nanda Kaul, Desai's heroine in *Fire on the Mountain* ([1977] 1982a), who is a disillusioned great-grandmother: "The care of others was a habit Nanda Kaul had mislaid. It had been a religious calling she had believed in till she found it fake. It had been a vocation that one day went dull and drought-struck as though its life-spring had dried up" ([1977] 1982a, 30). Similarly, in the case of Mukherjee's Dimples in *Wife* (1975), after realizing that "her life had been devoted only to pleasing others, not herself," she then goes on to conclude: "Individual initiative, that's what it came down to" (1975, 211). Jasmine also has a sudden illumination that she has had enough of caregiving. Dimples' individual initiative takes the form of murdering her husband.

Although there is no excuse for her conduct, the [Indian] Supreme Court in a 1986 decision, reveals that her husband has provided her with one. According to the court it is "unthinkable . . . in social conditions presently prevalent" for a husband to refuse "to consent to his wife's working outside the home and thereby preventing her from being independent economically just for his whim or caprice" (quoted in R. Kapur and Cossman 1999, 226). This is an impressive statement; however, the Indian Supreme Court is a masculinist court whose decisions routinely fail to differentiate between sex and what is "implied by sex" in relation to females and how gender is socially constructed and organized. The court justifies treating women differently from men on the basis of stereotypical notions of gender that disadvantage women—limiting their individualities to sociocentric roles "embedded in family structures as daughter, wife, sister, mother, and so on" (Humes 2000, 143). The court fails to analyze how and in what ways the stereotyping of women's roles have contributed to reinforcing gender asymmetry (R. Kapur and Cossman 1999, 231). This has traditionally been the case in the Western world, as well. Like the female poet of Desai's *In Custody* (who turns for justice for herself to the patriarchal custodian of great patriarchal literature), whenever Western and Indian feminists turn to the law to modify sexist laws, they turn to a patriarchal state that conceptualizes the citizen as a male (N. Menon, 1999, 267).

Many writers describe their heroines as emerging, only after great difficulty, pain, and suffering into clarity about the gap between the multitude of external expectations and demands on women with which they are enveloped and stifled and the very different reality of their sexual needs and desires. This is illustrated in the description of a woman's feast, a celebration for newlywed young women, when the women stay up all night partying, venting their *shakti* (women's energy):

> The all-night revelry of the women, the songs, the husband's name-taking ritual pep-
> pered with jokes, some of them bordering on the obscene. And there were the games
> they played, the "*phugdis*", [*sic*] which even the older women took part in. Agile and
> skilful in spite of their age and size, each pair, hands linked, twirled in eye-blinking
> speed, hair coming loose and flying behind them, breasts bouncing, feet thumping. The
> ribald jokes the women made and laughed at until the tears poured from their eyes were
> equally astonishing. The women were a revelation to me. There was something uncon-
> trolled about them, a kind of wildness, a volatility, an energy, as if these, finally, were
> their real selves, breaking through the masks of Aais, Maamis, Kaakis and Maais that
> they wore through their lives. (Deshpande 2000, 137)

By the end of the twentieth century, feminist Indian writers were beginning to describe their female characters as breaking through into the light of clarity about the unjust and oppressive cultural training, expectations, shibboleths, and taboos of their society—"a vast space of micropractices and cultural forms . . . consti-tuted and legitimated by men and/or in male-gendered terms" (Sassen 1998, 82) to which they are subjected all their lives. At this point, the characters in Indian women writers' texts are consciously attempting to live by their own wants, needs, desires, and wishes, instead of bending themselves to the necessity of conforming to repressive rules and regulations for women's conduct everywhere they turn. The authors make it abundantly clear that it is not natural(ized), not "second na-ture" (where on earth is it?) to their female characters in India to express their fe-male sexuality. In a painfully conscious process, they are always struggling to do so, and when they do, their insights always come replete with endless challenges for self-expression. This issue, the constraints on female sexuality, is perhaps the major topic of gender oppression in Indian women writers born before the mid-twentieth century.

The second issue that I would identify as the major focus of the writers of this generation (and all previous generations globally) is the overwhelming necessity the culture places on the young Indian female's attracting a man, so that it is no surprise that the "eternal female dream of finding happiness through a man" (Deshpande [1980] 1990, 123, 124) becomes an obsession. In *The Binding Vine* ([1993] 2001), Deshpande attempts to think through this issue. Why is it so impor-tant not only for Indian girls to get a man, to acculturate Indian girls to think about little else, but also for their mothers to be obsessed with ensuring that their daughters find a man to marry? "That's exactly what I can't understand. Tell me, is getting married so important to a woman? . . . One always hopes one's children will get more out of life than one has. . . . Security. You're safe from other men . . . It usually gives them that guarantee of safety. It takes much greater courage to dis-pense with a man's protection" [1993] 2001, 87–88).

On the whole, what Nandita Gandhi and Nandita Shah admire about earlier generations of Indian women activists can still be applied to later ones as well:

These women have . . . taken bold and unconventional decisions in their lives. They have overcome numerous barriers, displeased their families, defied social customs, opted for inter-caste or inter-religion marriages, and survived as political activists in a male-dominated party. Most of them have . . . internalized the very essence of individual freedom, and courageously implemented it in their lives. (1999, 335–336, 337)

Outsiders Within I

On Purdah, *Veiling, and Denial of Education and Property Rights*

Man craves to appropriate the whole world for himself, and in doing so he hardly leaves any room for woman.
                                                                SANGEETA RAY

Krupabai Satthianadhan

Krupabai Satthianadhan (1862–1894), a feminist reformer who was a "New Woman" in her youth, wrote on behalf of Indian women in *Saguna: A Story of Native Christian Life* ([1887–1888] (1998), the first autobiographical novel in English by an Indian woman. It was considered unique because it established a tradition of writing in English and was immediately popular. For Western readers, it is difficult to imagine what it meant for Hindus in the nineteenth century to convert to Christianity, the religion of their British occupiers. The repercussions for all those who converted, as with Satthianadhan's missionary parents, were enormous. They chose to retain their Brahmin beliefs but still lost caste, for once they became Christian converts they were persecuted, made "outcastes," were considered impure, ostracized, disowned by their family and friends, and denied employment except by the missionaries (L. Mani [1989] 1998, 150; Tilak [1934–1937], 1950, 129). It even meant death for orthodox Hindus to be in the company of Christian converts. According to Ramabai—herself a Christian convert—

"Brahmins will prefer death to living with people of other faith or race" because they believe that they will be doomed "to eternal perdition in the world to come" (quoted in Lokugé 1998, 173, fn. 52). Sattthianadhan records that her paternal grandmother even attempted to poison her only son, Satthianadhan's father, for converting.

Especially offensive to Satthianadhan was the term "Natives" that British missionaries habitually used to describe non-Westernized Indians. She preferred her parents' own small and simple home to the missionaries' much larger home, her Indian food to theirs, and her traditional Indian clothing to Western garb. But she did agree with the British missionaries about Indian religions, which she thought barbaric, as well as certain Indian customs, specifically those related to the oppression of women. Satthianadhan and her family also experienced racism from the same British missionaries who had converted them. But even as a young girl Satthianadhan had already internalized her inherited caste and class elitism, as well as her passionate nationalist pride in being an Indian. After being sent to board with two British missionaries, she boldly informed them that from her perspective as a Brahmin she was an aristocrat and therefore vastly superior to these women who were from a lower class than herself ([1887–1888] 1998, 115). Satthianadhan also objected to her British missionary teachers' hypocrisy with a self-righteous pride in her scrupulous honesty, demanding it of others as well as of herself at all times. When her missionary teachers once told her that they would consider time she spent with them in the evenings free time, but then insisted that she converse with them while doing "fancywork" like them, she promptly reminded them that they had not kept their word. When one of her teachers responded that her doing fancywork was only for the sake of appearance because she hated "laziness," she fell into Saguna's trap. (Saguna is the name that Satthianadhan gives herself in the autobiography). Delighted at having caught her teacher in a display of dishonesty, Saguna harshly castigated her for her hypocrisy. Doing something for appearance's sake only is to act "falsely," she argued. She then admitted to readers that throughout her life her "tongue" caused her greatest problems, not surprisingly, whenever she exposed the lies and hypocrisy of others to them. Despite the ill health that caused Satthianadhan to give up her medical training and despite dying early, she succeeded in her own life in living as a Christian both in her character and in her conduct. Perhaps in flaunting that quality, as well as her intellectual and caste superiority, Satthianadhan may have deprived herself of the possibility of achieving sainthood, as much as she thought she might deserve it.

Except that she never converted, Maitreyi Devi shared Satthianadhan's critique of the Hindu religion, but she outdid Satthianadhan in her preference for most things Indian. She refused to use anything "foreign," even "a mosquito net or a fountain pen." The English had only one outstanding quality in her opinion: their ability to adapt to the most difficult situations. Otherwise Devi thoroughly detested all the English she knew for eating meat and for being alcoholics and felt nothing but contempt for Englishwomen's penchant for wasting time with tennis, bridge, drinking, dancing, and occasional "flirtations with each other's husbands" ([1974] 1995, 179, 175, 182). Devi here reflects common stereotypes of the period about Englishwomen as lacking in shame, modesty, and as sexually promiscuous—stereotypes promulgated by the Indian patriarchy in order to keep Indian women under traditional discipline, to prevent them from expressing themselves sexually in unsanctioned ways (Grewal 1996, 55).

Like all Indian feminists, Satthianadhan ardently advocated educating women, at least of her own Brahmin caste. She courageously protested the "enslavement" of upper-class Hindu women "by repressive institutionalized Hindu ideologies" such as child-marriage, worship of husbands (*pativratadharma*), and Hinduism's "idolatry and superstition" (Lokugé 1998, 4). For some reason, Satthianadhan's mother did not seem to experience any duality between her traditional Hindu values and her Christianity. Rather, it appeared to be a seamless whole to her. Satthianadhan, like her mother, succeeds in infusing her work with "religious and cultural hybridity," but unlike her mother, combined it with a feminist perspective that resulted from contact with the British. Thus, Satthianadhan was neither a cultural relativist nor an integrationist, but "a hybrid" who deals with the same "major themes of post-colonial women's writing" as are current today (Lokugé 1998, 16).

Saguna was unavailable to the reading public for over a century, although it was widely read and reviewed when it came out. In it, Satthianadhan reveals her major purposes in writing—to proselytize for Christianity and simultaneously to influence her readers to continue to uphold, honor, and perpetuate what she believed were the finest aspects of Indian culture. Except that she writes in English and from a Christian perspective, like other Bengal women writers of the late nineteenth century, one of Satthianadhan's major goals was to "expose . . . the pretentiousness, cowardice, and effeminacy of the [British] educated male" (Chatterjee 1993, 70–71). She detested Indian men who displayed internalized feelings of inferiority to British culture, who indiscriminately embraced and imitated everything British. Before attempting to reinvent themselves as brown Englishmen by rushing to cast aside their Indian identities in specious attempts to assume alien identities, Satthianadhan urged Indian men to first get in touch with their own cultural identity as Indians. Only then should they identify those elements of British culture that they considered to be actual improvements over their own culture and worthwhile enough to emulate. Indians should never give up their Indian identity in the process of "modernizing" and "Westernizing."

Satthianadhan's intertwined critique of gender bias and assimilation remains most persuasive to this day, most memorably in a scene at her school's graduation party, where her persona Saguna is imposed upon by three young men in quick succession. Satthianadhan's aim here is not to intimate to readers that Saguna has

magnetic charms but, rather, to express her complex "hy
economical way, as well as to satirize these young men, m
Mukhopadhyaya had done in 1882 when she satirized a
"Bangalir Babu" who worked like a slave for the British all
at night, boasted and blustered about it (Banerjee 1999, 16
1993, 219).

The first intruder on Saguna's privacy is an Indian barrister ...ho affects an English accent. He is wearing an English "eyeglass up, his coat all loose, a rose in his buttonhole, and . . . dangling a gold chain." He unfavorably compares the party they are attending to those "at home." What does he mean by the word "home"? The barrister means his "adopted home, of course." But how can England possibly be his home when his mother and father are here in India? Moreover, how can he claim "as his home the home of others?" Beaten in argument, the barrister pretends to take it lightly by laughing at a mere girl who cannot possibly "understand" that after having studied in England he no longer has the slightest thing "in common" with his "crusty old" parents and their "unbearable" customs. No one should expect him to have patience "with all their crotchets and old-fashion [sic] notions" ([1887–1888] 1998, 147).

Like Satthianadhan, although more than a hundred years later, Dipesh Chakrabarty blames this unfeeling, disloyal response, this "waywardness" of the barrister and other young men like him, on the English education that influenced them to neglect "their duties toward their families and the elders" (1997, 373). But this English education was strictly for upper-class Hindu men who were neither reformers nor early nationalists but, rather, opportunists whose goal was upward mobility for themselves under the British. They hoped and expected that when they returned to India after being educated in England they would get employment, advance within the British bureaucracy, become wealthy, and gain respect, as has the barrister in *Saguna* (Grewal 1996, 141). More than one hundred years later, the context is the same, only the content different. Bill Gates, bringing Microsoft to India in late 2002, was welcomed enthusiastically by the technological elite. And it is no different with Indians in the West whom Robert Reich (former Secretary of Labor in the Clinton administration) calls "the New Immigrant[s]"; who live "the real-time, hard-copy life-style"; who "want to enter the white or white-clone cultural enclave, the pool that largely supplies 'top level managers, professionals and technicians' who can 'secede from the rest of society . . . and communicate directly with their counterparts around the world'; whose dream is to be part of a 'community of [Internet] images,'" (quoted in Spivak 1999, 393).

What does Saguna know about it anyway, the barrister demands. After all, she is a girl who has never left India. She cannot possibly understand the feelings of a young man who after living in England now finds India "so awfully dull" that he no longer feels that life is "worth living" in India. The barrister here exposes the what Saguna sees as the chief flaw in Anglicized Indians: their abject mim-y of the envied colonizing power, its supposedly "superior, advanced civilization" ([1887–1888] 1998, 147). Indeed, according to Homi Bhabha, this was the aim of the British colonizers: to make Christianity "a form of social control" that would "induce" Indians like the barrister to imitate "English manners." For, once this was achieved, Indian mimics of their colonizers, like the barrister and his kind, would wish "to remain under" British "protection." Bhabha describes these men as Indians who replace their own reality with "the product" of their "desire—that repeats, rearticulates the English 'reality' as mimicry" (1997, 154, 158; See also Lee 2001, 564). This is precisely the ambivalent situation of women under global patriarchy—"in a consensual relationship" with the source of their "resistance." Women everywhere are outsiders in their communities—religious, ethnic, national—and can only belong according to whether these communities certify them as acceptable and legitimate. They are accepted as members of these communities only when they conduct themselves according to the community's standards and rules of "sexuality, honour, chastity." Inside India, women are in reality outsiders because they are not considered really "full-fledged" citizens of their own countries and because their "individual rights as citizens can be abrogated at any point *in the interests of national honour*" (R. Menon and Bhasin 1998, 199, 201, 251, 253, emphasis the authors').

Saguna suggests to the barrister that he could resist yielding up his Indian individuality to the British. He could make his life meaningful in India. After all, men are not born merely to enjoy and amuse themselves. "Enlightened men" should work—on behalf of India. The barrister agrees with her that there is indeed a great deal of work to be done, "but not in this stupid place." Then how would India achieve enlightenment if he and others like him find everything in England and nothing in India, if the best and brightest leave India? Above all, Saguna insists again, it is not possible to believe that someone else's country is one's own. Before Satthianadhan expressed these concerns, they were already widespread in the reform movements both at home and abroad for some years, and these concerns have lasted to the present time. In 1887, in the same year as Satthianadahn's *Saguna* was first published, Ramabai, one of the most famous of many other concerned reformers on this issue, wrote about her unwillingness to leave her own daughter in England. She feared that if Manomar were brought up in England, she would become "an Englishwoman." Then, even when the mother and daughter would be reunited in the future, Manomar would seem foreign to Indians who would then never relate to her "as . . . one of them." Above all, Ramabai fears that her daughter might try to pass as English if she stayed too long there; that she would then "blush" with shame if she had to admit that she is Indian, "as too often happens when Indians make their homes in foreign lands" (quoted in R. Menon and Bhasin 1998, 107).

Unwilling to admit that Saguna has vanquished him in argument, the barrister departs the scene of combat, but not before falling back on sexism, laughing derisively at Saguna and other young women like her who are incapable of understanding because they can only indulge in sentimentality ([1887–1888] 1998, 147). This is a particularly sore point for Saguna who, perhaps more than any other quality of hers, takes pride in her intelligence and learning. Desai, in *Clear Light of Day* (1980), provides a more recent twist to this exploration of the schism between reformers and those who would be Westernized/modernized. Bimla has remained home and dealt with her life at home—and with all that symbolizes. Her brother-in-law Bakul is an ambassador who represents the facade that many "mediating" Indians prefer to present to the Western world. According to Thomas Macaulay, the aim of the English in educating Indian men was to create a group who would serve as mediators between the English and the Indian masses. Such young men would become mimic men of the English: "We must at present do our best to form a class who may be interpreters between us and the millions whom we govern; a class of persons, Indian in blood and colour, but English in tastes, in opinions, in morals, and in intellect" (quoted in Bhabha 1997, 154; see also Spivak 1999, 369, fn. 78). Bakul is a perfect example of such an interpreter, such an Indian "ambassador" as was Satthianadhan's barrister over one hundred years ago. And the beat goes on. Arundhati Roy has created a similar character Chacko in her novel *The God of Small Things* (1998). The spoiled scion of *zamindars* (large landholders) who has been educated at Oxford and married an Englishwoman, this younger man's attitude is much like that of the barrister and Bakul:

> "But we can't go in," Chacko explained, "because we've been locked out. And when we look in through the windows, all we see are shadows. And when we try and listen, all we hear is a whispering. And we cannot understand the whispering, because our minds have been invaded by a war. A war that we have won and lost. The very worst sort of war. A war that captures dreams and re-dreams them. A war that has made us adore our conquerors and despise ourselves."
>
> "Marry our conquerors, is more like it," Ammu [his sister] said dryly, referring to Margaret Kochamma"[Chacko's English wife]. (1998, 52)

Satthianadhan's barrister, Desai's Bakul, and Roy's Chacko all fail to work to effectuate improvement at home. The difference between them is that the barrister believes in British superiority to India in every way—he has internalized his master's perspective—whereas Bakul and Chacko are merely hypocritical and selfish. Bakul claims it as his "duty," his calling, to be his country's ambassador and expands his claim to include all Indians who live abroad as serving as ambassadors from India in one way or the other. When abroad, Bakul will talk "only of the best, the finest" of India, such as "The Taj Mahal—the Bhagavad Gita—Indian philosophy—music—art—the great, immortal values of ancient India" (1980, 35). He is unwilling to talk "with foreigners" about Indian problems such as "famine or drought or caste wars . . . political disputes" or "election malpractices, Nehru, his daughter, his grandson" [Indira and her son Rajiv Gandhi, also prime ministers, and both assassinated]. These issues, Bakul insists, are ephemeral, insignificant "when compared with India, eternal India" (1980, 25). Narayan confesses to the same pressures to remain on safe ground with Westerners to which Bakul yields. She feels that her critiques of India have made Westerners uncomfortable because she did not conform to the appropriate role they expected her to play "as Ambassador and Emissary of my culture, vaunting its virtues, and thus providing an antidote and corrective to Western arrogance and cultural superiority. . . . Encountering such mandates to be an Emissary are unpleasant" because they make her feel that she and her "'Cul-ture'" are not respected, but censored with "a condescending form of moral paternalism" (1997, 132). As an Indian/Third World feminist, she also objects to being put in the "Emissary position" because it then impedes her feminism. Most importantly, such an attitude ignores the reality that women as outsiders have no reason to be loyal to any or a number of current "civilizations" (1997, 135).

Bim's response to Bakul, as caustic and critical as Saguna's to the barrister, is that because he feels as he does, Bakul might be better off living "abroad" altogether, because if he did live and work in India, especially since he is in government service, he would be unable to "ignore bribery and corruption, red-tapism, famine, caste warfare" (1980, 35–36). He "would be too busy queueing up for [his] rations and juggling with [his] budget, making ends meet" (1980, 36) to expatiate to Westerners on the glories of India. Similarly, when Alexander is tempted to return to India, a friend queries her caustically as to why she would assume that she would be better off back there. In his opinion, it would probably be more difficult, what "with kerosene and gas out of stock, with lines for sugar." When Alexander responds that she would just remain at home and have someone else do all that tedious work for her, her friend retorts that then she would have to supervise someone else. Alexander then changes her mind and begins to feel "enormous relief, at the sheer fantasy of return to a life I had never led" (1993, 175). As for Roy's Chacko, he does return home to India to take over his mother's thriving pickle business as well as everything else she owns, including her home, and promptly runs everything into the ground. He calls himself a Communist and his workers "Comrade," while doing nothing to improve their lot. He does nothing except to indulge himself in his vices—laziness, filth, overeating—and raping the wives of his male workers or the female workers who attract him.

In the next two enforced conversations that immediately ensue after the barrister leaves Saguna, Satthianadhan conveys her ardent feminism and nationalism with the same passionate conviction in which she expressed her indignation at the moral shortcomings of the missionaries she lived with as a young girl and the "artificiality" of Indian assimilationists. As a "New Woman" Indian-style, she was "modern" but only in that regard. Whereas Satthianadhan's Saguna was representative of the optimistic ardor of the "New Woman" at the end of the nineteenth century and into the first third of the twentieth century, by the time we get to the feminism of Desai's Bimla in the last third of the twentieth century, we can see that it still comes hard, is uncomfortable, and unnatural to her: "How my students would laugh at me. I'm always trying to teach them, *train* them to be different from what we were at their age—to be a new kind of woman from you or me—and if they knew how badly handicapped I still am, how I myself haven't been able to manage on my own—they'd laugh, wouldn't they? They'd *despise* me" (1980, 155, emphasis the author's). Bimla still has to go down on her "knees" to her male relatives to assist her in financial decisions. Her difficulty with being feminist reveals what a hard battle her feminism is for her (as it still was and is for Second-Wave Western feminists who are her [and her creator's] contemporaries) "to shed their earlier patterns of thinking" (N. Gandhi and Shah 1999, 337).

To return to the "New Woman" of the 1880s in India, a doctor next imposes himself on Saguna and attempts to propose to her. Unfortunately, he, too, starts out by claiming that Saguna "can't understand" what he means when he tells her that she does not have to go to England to study medicine. After all, she can stay in India and not work and study. The only time girls have to do these things is when they are unable to attract "suitable husbands." Saguna rejects him summarily. By "suitable," he obviously means someone like himself, but even if he were to ask her to marry him, she would not have him, not "for all the world" ([1887–1888], 1998, 148).

A student then intrudes on Saguna, unaware that he had already aroused her ire at the beginning of the party. Thinking himself very clever, he had pretended that he was so superior to Saguna and her female classmates that he was unaware of their existence. Assuming a "learned air" and "a sneering look," he had glanced down the list of prizes with the attitude that for female students "the prize-giving itself was a farce" ([1887–1888], 1998, 145). The student, like the doctor, assures Saguna that she need not go to England to continue her studies. She could stay in India and get married. Again, Saguna becomes enraged and retaliates with brutal honesty. "Marriage is not the goal of every girl's ambition," she insists, differentiating herself from the norm. In doing so, Satthianadhan here reveals one of her own rare preferences for the British colonizers' ways. She believed that they had made possible Indian women's liberation from traditional Indian constraints on women. Like British feminists of the period she, too, perceived her mission as uplifting other Indian women because they needed it (Ramusack 1999, 49). In her view, the British reforms in India were based on the religion of the British—Christianity—which empowered females, allowing them to be independent and to serve society without having to marry.[1] Nationalists differ with Satthianadhan on this point. They view the British interests in reform as attempts to emasculate Indian men, to make them appear effeminate so that their control over their families would be weakened. Others, such as contemporary feminist Indian historians, view British reforms as rationalizations of their conquest and dominion over India, a country that in their opinion would otherwise have remained benighted and barbaric, especially in relation to the savage and beastly customs and rituals imposed on Indian women such as child marriage and widow burning (L. Mani [1989]1998; Ramusack 1999, 42).

Certainly, Satthianadhan's perspective and work reinforced the convictions of British feminists of this period, that the only way Indian women could achieve "political salvation" was for them to achieve Christian salvation. Like the British feminists, she believed that Christianity was a civilizing religion, a religion superior to all other religions, and "because of the special place [Christianity] accorded to women, British women felt even greater grounds for superiority to Indian women and to their religions" (Burton 1998, 211). Satthianadhan also felt the same superiority, but this superiority was directed toward most other Indian women, British women of lower class than herself, and toward Indian religions. Other Indian women of the time, for example, Anandabai Joshi, agreed with Satthianadhan and the British feminists on this point: "When I think over the sufferings of women in India in all ages, I am impatient to see the Western light dawn as the harbinger of emancipation" (quoted in Burton 1998, 211). Nevertheless, the publication and wide distribution of Indian women writers' memoirs and autobiographies of the late nineteenth century, as illustrated by the British response to Satthianadhan's *Saguna,* especially Queen Victoria's immense admiration for the work, is suspect. By publication and ensuing acceptance in the Christian West, not only was "cultural representation for the subject" secured, but also "the hierarchies of power inherent in trans/national relations of the translation, production, and consumption of Third World texts" (Fernandes 1999, 142).

Satthianadhan's motives are complex, however. Saguna may be a Christian "New Woman," but she condemns the superifical aping of British culture and its customs when she accuses the student, the doctor, and the barrister of being "disgusting" because they represent England-educated men and now prefer English "manners, dress and other superficial things." On the one hand, these mimic men are desperately intent upon imitating all things English, but, on the other hand, they have not succeeded in "imbibing their liberal spirit—that spirit which gives to a woman equal privilege with man, and credits her with noble and disinterested actions" (1887–1888] 1998, 149). Here Satthianadhan's passion exposes the fact that she may very well be speaking from her own experience in regard to her own traditional mother who could not see the value of her eldest son educating her daughter. Satthianadhan's mother would continually interrupt whenever she found Satthianadhan reading and writing in her brother's study and would demand that she do household duties, instead.

At one point in *Nectar in a Sieve,* Markandaya's heroine Ruksmani tells readers that her father taught her to read and write. His envious neighbors claim that he did it to make certain that his children would be "one cut above the rest" (1954, 16). Ruksmani's mother, again like Satthianadhan's mother, felt that there was no point in educating a girl: "What use . . . that a girl should be learned! Much good will it do her when she has lusty sons and a husband to look after. Look at me, am I any worse that I cannot spell my name, so long as I know it?" Ruksmani's interpretation of her father's taking the time and effort to teach a daughter to read and write differs from that of her neighbors. In her view, he did it "because he knew that it would be a solace to me in affliction" (1954, 16). If this interpretation of her father's decision to educate her is correct it would signify a heresy on the part of a traditional orthodox Hindu because it was believed at that time that if a woman were educated she would be fated to become a widow (Burton 1998, 210, fn. 16). However, such an interpretation seems to indicate that Markandaya fails to take advantage of this opportunity to convey to readers the political resonance of literacy for Indian women and for the landless and lower classes. There may have been another motive—a political one—to Ruksmani's father's achievement of literacy and his determination to pass it on to his daughter, despite his neighbors' disapproval. M. S. S. Pandian observes as a characteristic of a famous actor-politician's films, that "[t]he hero's use of *literacy as a weapon of struggle against oppression* is often contrasted with its use as a weapon of oppression in the hands of the elite. . . . [L]iteracy, hitherto a privilege of the elite, now becomes an instrument of subversion in the hands of a subaltern hero, a challenge to education as a sign of authority (1997, 377, emphasis the author's). Feminist Indian writers make it obvious to their readers that literacy is an important tool, not only for subaltern heroes but also for subaltern heroines. As Satthianadhan's brother—and, later on, her husband—so in *Nectar in a Sieve* are Ruksmani's father and husband proud of her ability to read and write. Ruksmani's husband is illiterate, but as she remarks of him: "I am sure it could not have been easy for him to see his wife more learned than he himself was, for Nathan could not even write his name; yet not once did he assert his rights and forbid me my pleasure, as lesser men might have done" (1954, 17).

In 1870, Dayamasi Dasi published *A Treatise on Female Chastity,* and her husband encouraged her to read and write. He even published her work posthumously, as did Satthianadhan's husband. Why were these men so unusually supportive? In nineteenth-century Bengal, men who wanted to think of themselves as modern, like the Brahmo reformers, took it as a source of pride to marry literate, educated women, and were even prouder of wives whose works they could publish (Chakrabarty 1997, 397). Such a pattern endured into the twentieth century, with Antherjanam's father and husband, with Devi's father, husband, and guru, the great poet-philosopher Rabindranath Tagore, and with Mukherjee's father, who expected no less than the Nobel Prize in Literature for his daughter.

Satthianadhan was justifiably proud of her intellectual accomplishments so far above those of the other girls in her class that when she entered the large *zenana* (all-girl private) school in Bombay in 1877, she was given a special curriculum—studying languages. During her last year in the *zenana* school, its female English doctor made Saguna her assistant, a transforming experience for Saguna in terms of her feminism. She vowed to cast off all the cultural constraints against women to which she had hitherto been subjected and become "independent." She burned with desire to prove to her world that "a woman is in no way inferior to a man":

> How hard it seemed to my mind that marriage should be the goal of woman's ambition, and that she should spend her days in the light trifles of a home life, live to dress, to look pretty, and never know that joy of independence and intellectual work. The thought had been galling. It made me avoid men, and I felt more than once that I could not look into their faces until I was able to hold my own with them. (1887–1888, 131)

In 1878, the school doctor recommended Satthianadhan to the school missionary society for an unprecedented scholarship to medical school in England, to which a wealthy woman donated half the amount. Satthianadhan may not have received this scholarship because of sexism. Indeed, Satthianadhan does seem to record the interview as sexist throughout, because the interviewer continually interjects his concerns about her health, worrying whether Saguna will be fit to enter into such a grueling course of study. It is not surprising, therefore, that Satthianadhan was denied a scholarship on medical grounds. Because she had achieved notoriety in certain circles as the brilliant female student who was going to study in England, this rejection devastated Satthianadhan. But, the rejection could well have been due to some negative data about Satthianadhan's health that appeared on her medical records, rather than to the interviewer's sexism as a result of what did happen at the end of the following year. In 1889, Cornelia Sorabji, who had planned to enter the medical profession, was told to give it up for sexist and racist reasons, but also for health reasons—the medical course was grueling and the cold, damp English climate equally so.[2] Another young Indian woman who had been studying to be a doctor in Philadelphia had died from pneumonia. At Madras Medical College which Satthianadhan entered as a consolation prize, she distinguished herself once again as an outstanding student, winning several awards. But, as a result of overwork because of her compulsion to always prove herself the best and brightest, her mental and physical health broke down so severely that she was unable to continue her education. Instead, she retreated to her sister's home in Poona to convalesce. At this point, she met Samuel Satthianadhan, the son of the couple with whom she had boarded while at college. He had been away in England and turned up on a visit—supposedly by coincidence.

As their relationship ripened, her growing love for Satthianadhan came increasingly into collision with her ardent feminism. She then began to suffer from a deep and severe crisis of conscience until she finally resolved the issue to her satisfaction by shifting her perspective away from the feminism she had modeled on the English "New Woman." Where she had once longed to achieve independence through education and where despite her culture's refusal to accept and permit such roles for women, she had dreamed of pursuing a vocation that would serve society in a publicly useful capacity with high visibility, she now saw herself as having been selfish, even hedonistic.

Alexander, a Syrian Christian Indian born in Allahabad in 1951 and married to an American Jew, sarcastically defines Indian marriage from her traditional mother's perspective, as "[a] feminine form of transportation and sanctioned well by culture" (1993, 210). After all, what other way was there for an Indian woman at that time to travel? There can be no doubt that Satthianadhan did indeed travel, but in a different direction after Samuel entered her life: choosing at that point to recreate herself according to the Victorian icon of womanhood—"the angel of the hearth"—popularized by conservative (middle- and upper-class) Western men and women and very attractive to Indian reformers such as Satthianadhan. As members of the upper–middle class this image aligned with their "definition of public and private spheres in opposition to the language, behaviour and culture of the lower strata" (Sangari and Vaid [1989] 1999b, 13).

As a middle-class married Christian Indian woman, Satthianadhan now conceptualized her highest calling as service to society through marriage and her family. This was also much like the middle class married Brahmin Indian woman writer of that period who, in order to be accepted into "the society of the *bhadrmahila,*" must conform to the "important pre-condition for a woman's literary apprenticeship . . . the *bhadralok* insistence on membership of the *andarmahal,* on the total dependence of the woman on the male head of the family, on strict adherence to the traditional responsibilities of a respectable home" (Banerjee 1999, 164–165). True, Satthianadhan conceived of herself after marriage as having been "selfish" in her younger days by imagining herself "doing great things" out in the world. But she now rationalized that such a vision of an easy, independent, and intellectual life had been flawed with ego because it left the thankless, hardest tasks in life to other people. Above all, such a vision was not that of the self-sacrificing, self-abnegating wife and mother that she valorized. Here, her indoctrination into the ideals of a Hindu wife, even to her choice of language, dovetails perfectly with the Western Victorian ideal.

Satthianadhan revealed herself in *Saguna* as a writer gifted with rare spiritual honesty, with sensitivity combined with passion, and with the rigorous thinking that made her writing successful. These qualities enabled her to make crucial distinctions between Christianity and Hinduism, between institutionalized sexism and feminism, between Indian and British culture and tradition. These distinctions empowered her Indian readers to locate their precise situatedness in the colonial scheme because so many of them were traumatized and torn between having to choose between their parents' traditional ways and the intimidating but tempting "modernity" of the alien colonizers from the West. Her distinctions also empowered her British readers to understand their Indian subjects better, especially as the British government claimed to be bound by treaties with India not to interfere with their (patriarchal) social or religious laws and customs, wherever possible.

In some cases, the British did interfere and improve the harsh conditions for women—"[w]hite men saving brown women from brown men," as Spivak has caustically and famously quipped (1999, 285). When they did interfere it was often, inadvertently, to serve their own agendas. For example, when the British realized that they received less revenue from less productive systems of agriculture under *purdah,* they then found *purdah* a problem and interfered with it. For the most part, however, the British laws reinforced traditional Indian laws and customs and thereby actually worsened conditions most of the time for most Indian women (S. Basu 1999; Grewal 1996, 52, 53, 77–78) by returning power to the *zamindars,* ceding property rights only to men by excluding women from owning property, and fixing and ruling into patriarchal legislating hitherto diverse and contradictory customs and practices relating to marriage and property inheritance (Mohanty 1991a, 19).

In discussions in Parliament in 1943 on what eventually became the Hindu Succession Act of 1956, Lalchand Navalrai blamed women's demands for the right to inherit property as having "plunged" Indians "into the ocean of Western ways," but that Indians do not have to "allow ourselves to be drowned" (quoted in M. Basu 2001, 136). Furthermore, Navalrai objected to the proposed right of a married daughter to inherit from her husband's side as well as from her parents' side, thereby enabling her to inherit twice to the son's only inheriting once. But he failed to note that sons already "enjoyed" shares that their wives brought with them from their parents. Another objection raised in 1949 to this bill was launched on the grounds that Western reforms were unnecessary for Hindus, and another letter writer responded to this objection to the effect that just because some of the reforms were "Western in character" and because the reformers were "saturated with Western education," it did not make any difference whether they were "Western or Eastern." Whatever was in the best interests of India should be used for India (M. Basu 2001, 140–141).

Rokeya Sakhawat Hossain

At the time of her death in 1932 at the age of fifty-two, Rokeya Sakhawat Hossain, the "first and foremost feminist of Bengali Muslim society" (Jahan 1988, 1) was condemned by orthodox Muslims as "a shameless woman, a misanthrop [*sic*], a radical misguided by the proselytizing propaganda of Christian missionaries, and a sexist." In addition, her published work was dismissed as "inflammatory . . . designed to stir up insubordination among women" (Jahan 1988, 53–54). The first accusations seem laughable today: figments of her opponents' inimical imaginations, especially in view of Hossain's carefully cultivated traditional appearance and manner in public, which she consciously designed to offset the controversy aroused by her caustic and witty writing on behalf of the education of subordinated and oppressed women and the elimination of strict *purdah*.

Hossain always took the same down-to-earth, practical, commonsense approach in her publications and her public activities. Both were of one piece and equally devoted to improving the lives of other women. The founder and administrator of the Sakhawat Memorial Girls' School, Hossain persisted tirelessly in making her vision reality. By the end of her life, as a result of an "eminently practical stand" combined with a "strong streak of pragmatism and a clear understanding of the realities of life," Hossain, despite her critics, succeeded in achieving both public recognition and "success as an activist" (Jahan 1988, 52). To illustrate the complexity of her character—both visionary and realist combined—Hossain, the ardent feminist who dared publicly to challenge the Muslim fundamental leadership and even the Qur'an itself, always wore the *burqa* in public. This was not only in order to throw her opponents off guard, but because she was genuinely willing to work within the tradition as it existed, while destabilizing it wherever and whenever it infringed on the attainment of her ultimate goal—education for women. For example, rather than agitating for an end to *purdah* altogether, she instead called for only the minimal amount of *purdah* that would enable women to attain an education—keeping schools separate while providing sufficient teachers. Hossain's definition of *purdah* was not confinement in seclusion, but only the covering of the female body so that it would be protected from public exposure, from the gaze of strangers, especially males. These were the elements in *purdah* that Hossain found acceptable because they were dignified and decorous. She approved of making women invisible for another reason, as well. It prevented them from "constant surveillance by men" (Jahan 1988, 52); from provoking lower thoughts in men. This could lead to their making unwanted intrusions on women.

In "Sultana's Dream" in *Sultana's Dream and Selections from The Secluded Ones* [1908] (1998), Hossain "conceived of a society [that] transforms [the home] into the very nation itself," "a critique of the values of its patriarchal society" "a "consciously feminist utopia" (S. Ray 2000, 91, 122, 123) ruled by women, where men were kept in strict *purdah* in male *zenanas* or *mardanas* [private men's spaces]. From Hossain's first line onward, "what she has in mind is the essence of being a woman, that being a woman is seen as an ontological state common to female persons across class, caste, and religion, but also in a political sense, as a position within society that is structurally open to oppression" (Grewal 1994, 243). I would add that Hossain sees men the same way, but "as a position within society that is structurally open to" oppressing women—until women put them in strict *purdah* in *mardanas*. It never seems to occur to Hossain that women might oppress men once they got the power—because she obviously thinks it impossible that any woman would ever do so. In "Sultana's Dream" they never, ever do. They are all *Viranganas*—heroic women warriors fighting always only for a just cause.

In conceptualizing Ladyland, Hossain used a seemingly complicitous discourse such as Jonathan Swift uses in *A Modest Proposal*. The surface tone of genial collaboration—the pro-Irish Swift, with the English conquerors, the Indian female Dreamer, with Indian men—increases the reader's overwhelming disgust and revulsion for the bestial aspects of men that made veiling women necessary. When the Dreamer fails to notice men anywhere on the streets she is told by her Guide that men are kept "in their proper places," exactly where they belong, "indoors" ([1908] 1988, 9).[3] The Dreamer, shocked and amazed, wonders why women are not kept in the *zenana* and why men are not permitted out in public. Her Guide responds that it would be unfair to immure "harmless women" while allowing dangerous men to roam free. The Dreamer protests on the grounds that because women are "naturally weak," it is unsafe for *us* to emerge from the *zenana*. If there had been any doubt before, her protest reveals that the Dreamer does not represent Hossain, but, rather, a typically traditional Muslim female who needs to have her consciousness raised as to the injustice of *purdah* through confrontation with a culture in which gender roles are reversed. The cruelty to men exposed by the reversal in Ladyland assists in providing the Dreamer illumination despite an acculturation which has hitherto made her immune to the outrageous injustice of the custom of confining women. Once the Dreamer perceives that confining men in *purdah* is unreasonable, then she perceives that it is equally so for women.

The Guide then engages with the Dreamer in a Platonic dialogue, first observing that the streets are unsafe in the Dreamer's country because dangerous, wild men are trusted to roam free in public like "wild animals," whereas "innocent women" are kept in the *zenana*. What would be done if the insane escaped from lunatic asylums? Would those who were sane be kept in the asylums and the insane allowed to wreak havoc? The Dreamer answers that in India women take no part in managing "our social affairs" because men rule as lords and masters in India, assuming unto themselves "all powers and privileges" ([1908] 1988, 9) while imprisoning Indian women in the *zenanas*. The bemused Dreamer cannot imagine a world in which women do everything, and wonders how men would spend their time. Her Guide responds that men should do nothing because they are fit for nothing. By using women's quicker brains, they could be rounded up and trapped in *mardanas* as in Ladyland. But the Dreamer cannot imagine how this would be possible, since men's brains are larger than women's. The Guide responds that an elephant has an even larger and heavier brain than a man and still the man can catch, chain, and put the elephant to work ([1908] 1988, 12).

What happened long ago in the country now called Ladyland was that women began to make technological improvements, whereupon in retaliation men began to increase their military power. During a bloody battle between Ladyland's warriors and invaders from another country, the Ladyland army was on the verge of a tremendous defeat when the women requested the remaining warriors to retire to the *zenanas,* which they gladly did. Then the Lady Principal of one of the universities marched with her students to the battlefield and aimed "all the rays of the concentrated sun light and heat" at the invaders, burning them all to a crisp. Since then, Ladyland has never been invaded. Soon a petition was sent from the *zenana* to the Queen of Ladyland by the highest ranking men of the country—Police Commissioners and District Magistrates—on behalf of the military, asserting that the warriors did not deserve imprisonment because they had always been dutiful and therefore urged her to restore them to their previous positions. The Queen responded that if she would ever require "their services" she would send for them, and that in the meantime they would remain in prison. The shrewd Queen had no hope that the men would ever change, would ever be "dutiful" to her if she freed them. Since then, "*mardana*" rather then "*zenana*" has been established, in which men are kept confined in the homes to care for children, to cook, and do housework. As a result, crime and sin have ended, so that there is no need any longer for police or judges. Trade with other countries has become limited, however, because the women in those countries were still in *zenanas* and the men who came to Ladyland to trade had questionable "morals." For this reason, Ladylanders prefer not to have dealings with such men. No woman marries before the age of twenty-one, and women do all the work in much less time because men waste time by talking a great deal about all the work they are doing, but actually doing very "little."

At the end of the twentieth century, Jayapal drove through Rajasthan on to the Udaipur-Jaipur Highway. There she observed that women were working everywhere—in the fields and on the highways—and there were twice the amount of women working on the roads as that of men. These women (mostly teenagers) often carried children, or children clung to them. They were also carrying mud and rocks and were digging up the road where it had potholes. And what were the men doing? Seated under a shade tree, enjoying tea and "laughing," the men were busy supervising the women, pointing places out to them to make the piles.[4] This situation is but one more reflection of India's universal "sexual division of labour, in the production process and in the labour market" (N. Shah et al. 1999, 162). Sadly, in India discrimination against women still remains universal, much as it was in Hossain's time, regardless of class and caste, whether educated or illiterate:

> The condition of women in India follows naturally out of the society's perspective that men are superior to women. Female infanticide, dowry deaths, poor nutrition,

less education for women all stem from the perception that women are the lesser sex, to be apologized for rather than celebrated. Emotional and physical violence against women is not only accepted, sometimes it is even enjoyed. Almost always, the perception seems to be that women must have done something to deserve this violence. (Jayapal 2000, 120)

Young and American-born, Jayapal expresses outrage at how unjustly Indian women are still treated: for example, after a woman gives birth, she has to go one hundred feet away from her home because childbirth has made her unclean. After Jayapal inquires how many children people have, she is told how many *male* children they have, thereby "discounting the lives of the girls before they have even been given a chance at life" (2000, 123). Unlike Hossain, Jayapal does not live in a world in which "group gynophobia" . . . is institutionalised in caste" (Natarajan 1999, 183–184, fn.18). Also unlike Hossain, she does not envision a world in which women "triumph over men." Instead, Jayapal envisions a world in which "both genders [would] be treated with dignity and respect" (2000, 123). Hossain's Ladyland is, however, technologically advanced, using solar heat and capturing water in fountains to stop rains and storms, but sprinkling the earth when necessary. Farming is done through electrical equipment. Ladylanders also travel by plane. All these technological developments are inventions of female scientists from women's schools, to which males are forbidden matriculation ([1908] 1988, 11). Here, as in the case of *zenanas* being turned into *mardanas,* the Dreamer has simply reversed India's "social relations of domination" (Sprague 2001, 535) by maintaining that women as a group should be in charge everywhere because of their superiority to males as a group. This situation only substitutes rulers, while the same but reversed inequities still prevail—male restriction to *zenanas* and lack of education for males, for example. Of course Hossain is joking. By reversing roles, she is asking male readers to project themselves into the constrained lives that women are forced to lead.

Hossain herself was spared having to endure the worst effects of *purdah* because she was uncommonly blessed with the protection of two enlightened men. Her eldest brother taught her how to read late at night while their father was sleeping. Later, he talked his family into arranging Hossain's marriage to a man he admired, Syed Sakhawat Hossain. A much older widower, her husband was enormously proud of Hossain's gifts, supporting her writing and her "lifelong and relentless *jihad* (holy war)" (Jahan 1988, 2, 3) to educate women so that they could achieve financial independence and freedom from their male oppressors. When he died in 1909, Hossain's husband left her a large part of his savings above and beyond her share as his widow to establish the Sakhawat Memorial Girls' school, which still exists (Jahan 1988, 41).

In Hossain's time, *purdah* (confinement of women in certain quarters of the home) and wearing of the *burqa* (a voluminous and tentlike covering from head to toe) ensured women's invisibility in public. In addition to the similar complex meanings it has today, *purdah* also was a symbol of higher status at that time. Only affluent families could afford the expense of delegating and ensuring private spaces *(zenanas)* to women that could not be transgressed by strange men both at home and in public. Bengali Muslims remained fixed in their traditional customs and beliefs toward women until Hossain took up the causes of education for women and the end of restricted *purdah*. Upper-caste men, such as Hossain's father, practiced polygamy because divorce was forbidden. Men could circumvent this by marrying as often as they wanted, although girls were generally married off by the age of nine and widows could not remarry.

In keeping with her practical outlook, Hossain fought resolutely for her cause wherever she was situated and with whatever means she found at hand. For this reason, she is viewed by some contemporary feminists as limited because she worked on behalf of her own class—middle-class women. Such critiques are anachronistic, choosing to ignore Hossain's very different culture, time, and situation from our own. But, for the sake of argument, let me accept the premise of Hossain's class "limitations," as does Roushan Jahan, the editor and translator of the 1988 edition of *Sultana's Dream*. Still, as she admits, "the substance" of Hossain's feminist perspective holds today, "especially in recent times when women, thanks to fundamentalist Muslim ruling groups, are back where they were" (1988, 54). Even if Hossain were in fact limited only to her middle-class perspective, even if she were in fact limited in her concern only to the best interests of her own group—Muslim women—where could Hossain possibly begin her consciously feminist work except within her own community? Actually, however, she not only attempted to improve the lot of Bengali Muslim women, to address their problems and those of Bengali Muslim society within which these women had to live, but she also confronted Bengali society at large. Her feminist perspective included Indian women as a whole: "Remember," she wrote to her sisters, "we are Indians first, Hindu, Muslim, Sikh afterwards" (quoted in Jahan 1988, 53). Even more remarkably, Hossain reached beyond these women, beyond "narrow sectarian feelings" (Jahan 1988, 53). Her reach extended even to observing the conditions of Western women. Hossain found commonalities beyond the surface differences, thereby exhibiting a "glocal" view; that is, both a local as well as a "comprehensive world-view" (Jahan 1988, 43). Not until 1919 could this be found enunciated by educated middle-class nationalist Hindu women, for example, when they called for regular features in women's magazines to include women's perspectives as well as evaluations and descriptions of women's movements globally (Talwar [1989] 1999, 208).

Hossain could have railed as an Indian woman against Indian cultural icons the way Muppala Ranganayakamma did when she summarized her motives for writing her three-volume anti-Ramayana novel, *Ramayana, The Poison Tree* (1974–76): "The Ramayama favors men; favors the rich, favors the upper castes, and the ruling class. It supports exploitation; it was never a progressive text, not even at the time it was written" (quoted in V. Rao 2001, 184). Hossain could have distanced herself from the colonial intruder's womenfolk, as well. Instead, her strategy of focusing on commonalities beneath the differences enabled her to perceive that Western women also were victimized, despite their seeming to be so free and superior by comparison to Indian women. Hossain concluded that, despite outward appearances, Western women also suffered oppression from their menfolk. She believed that just as in Bengal and in India and everywhere else, men ruled their cultures in the form of manmade legislation, so all women everywhere, Western as well as Indian, were subject to male rulers' exclusionary laws. Resources were not designed for "vulnerable women like us" (quoted in Jahan 1988, 52). Here, Hossain not only talks of Indian women's vulnerability to men under patriarchy, but that of all women under patriarchy globally, as many feminists, both Western and Indian, maintain is still the case universally (MacKinnon 1987, 152; Minturn 1993, 7; Panjabi 1997, 158).

Between 1903 and 1904, Hossain published fiery and impassioned essays in various journals. Representative of all her other work, these essays were later collected in book form as *Motichur* (1908). In these essays, Hossain maintained that women are not inherently inferior to men either in mind or in spirit. If they were permitted equality, this would become evident. Men consciously confine women to the home as their dependents and inferiors, thereby denying them the same rights as men have to work for financial and economic independence.[5] Men socialize women into being secluded through *purdah,* thereby perpetuating their control of and domination over women. Men prevent women from knowledge of their legal rights by manipulating existing laws, or making laws that benefit themselves to their own advantage at ignorant and vulnerable women's expense. Confinement in *purdah* means preventing women from full mental and spiritual growth because it makes women weak in mind and in body. In turn, their abilities are severely limited. This was not a new claim, but a strong one at the time in Hossain's world. In 1879, Mabel Sharman Crawford compared the condition of British women without the vote to Indian women in *purdah,* maintaining that "if the physical health of woman is admittedly impaired by confinement within a limited space, her mental health also suffers through legislative disabilities; and that it is unfair to deprive her . . . of political liberty, as in the Oriental mode, to shut her up within four walls" (quoted in Burton 1994, 231). Aware of what they are doing, men unjustly and immorally prevent women, who comprise fifty percent of the culture, from their deserved right to health and well-being, thus depriving the entire society of its fullest potentials and possibilities. Without this right, women cannot function effectively to full capacity, cannot carry out the duties that the culture has decreed for women: running homes and rearing their children properly.

Education is the primary and most significant necessity for those who would be mothers, because mothers are the primary and most significant teachers and trainers of children. First free women from *purdah* so that they can then attain an education. If this were done, the entire society would benefit immeasurably because educated women are an enormous benefit to their society. As mothers, they actively contribute to their society for better or worse. This also was not a new argument. Kailashbashini Devi, writing in the 1860s, argued that education will purge Indian women of their "disposition to quarrel" when they emulated the angry side of the goddess Lakshmi and thus make them better mothers (quoted in Chakrabarty 1997, 380). This argument seems odd, given the fact that men have never been chided about *their* "disposition" to quarrel. Conversely, other authors of the period felt that only obedient women who modeled themselves on the gentle side of the goddess Lakshmi could make good mothers (1997, 381).

Closer to Hossain's position, Anukulchandra [Atulchandra] Datta had argued in 1906 that poorly educated Indian women were ignorant of the fundamentals of childrearing, whereas well-educated women would be capable of ensuring their childrens' proper diets, regulating their periods of play and study, and teaching them proper manners and morals. Ignorant mothers were raising a poor citizenry. But given an education, well-educated mothers would improve and strengthen the Indian nation by raising good citizens. With these arguments, Anukulchandra and other nationalists attempted to play on the fears of Indian men, as well as on their nationalist sentiments (Chakrabarty 1997, 378).

In *Avarodhbasini* or *The Secluded Ones* (1929), originally a series of columns in *The Monthly Mohammadi*, 1928–1929, Hossain used the genre of journal reports to indict *purdah*. Each report is accompanied by personal, usually highly ironic concluding comments that are as hard-hitting as the reports themselves. Here, Hossain did not maintain the omniscient voice generally found in journal reports. She either could not contain her outrage or did not wish to do so in the face of religious law that made women incapable of understanding and comprehending the world "from behind the veil" so that they could not become "conscious of the ways it restrains, denies, and mystifies" their "understanding of it by presenting this denial as religious law" (Panjabi 1997, 161). For example, Hossain ended "Report Eight" with a harshly ironic outburst: "Long live *purdah!*" (quoted in Jahan 1988, 26) about the mistress of a house that had caught fire. The woman was escaping the fire when she saw that her courtyard was filled with strangers. This caused her to return to her room, hide under her bed, and refuse to come out.[6] She was burned to death. Similarly, Sumi, the heroine of Deshpande's *The Dark Holds No Terrors* ([1980] 1990), remembers a Sanskrit story she had read in school about a woman who would not interrupt her husband's sleep, although their child was burning. So "blessed" is the woman deemed to be that the fire god Agni decided to save the child. Sumi then asks herself who could possibly have written such a story? She concludes that only a man could do so. Only a man could tell every woman generation unto generation from time immemorial that "her duty to ME comes first" ([1980] 1990, 207). Most women, forever man's foolish and gullible dupes, believe him because they are not aware of their rights (A. Basu 1992, 111; Hossain [1929] 1988). Sadly, even in India today, this is still true for most women, as it is in the West (Hasnat 1998, 43; Humes 2000, 145).

Hossain vented her indignation at the end of another equally horrifying report ("Report Fourteen"). "What a gruesome way to die!" she exclaimed. A distant relative of her husband's, while boarding a train together with her maid, tripped in her *burqa* and fell down onto the tracks. Her maid refused to allow the male porters to assist her mistress because it would mean having to touch her. She tried to drag her mistress free by herself but could not. Despite the presence of many men at the scene, the woman was badly crushed when the train had to move from the station after waiting for a half-hour. She suffered excruciating pain until she died eleven hours later ([1929] 1988, 27). In "Report Eighteen," Hossain tells of a doctor who had to examine his patient with a stethoscope placed inside a thick blanket in front of the bed. After the patient's husband asked him what his diagnosis was, the doctor demands of the reader: "What the—did he expect me to be omniscient?" ([1929] 1988, 28–29). This prohibition against male doctors examining their female patients provided a strong incentive for young Indian women such as Satthianadhan and Ramabai to become "lady doctors" in order to be of service to other women. A convert to Christianity, Ramabai wrote in 1885, over twenty years earlier than Hossain, that "although I am poor and weak in body I have (thank God Who has given me it) a mind strong enough to resist all these meaningless social customs which deprive a woman of her proper place in society" (quoted in Burton 1998, 93).

Hossain's reports are all painful to read, made even more so by her end remarks, and they proved another powerful and effective weapon in Hossain's ultimately successful repertoire of word artillery that she deployed to end the practice of *purdah*. In going public, in campaigning for many years as an activist for the cause of women to destabilize the prevalent and widely accepted convictions of her world and time, Hossain also displayed awesome courage in critiquing the holiest and most sanctified of documents for Muslims—the Qur'an—which Muslims accept as divinely inspired without question. Fundamentalists believe that the superiority of men is inherent and divinely revealed in the story of creation in Judaeo-Christian and Islamic texts. And, like Hindus, they believe in the strictures of Manu in Hindu texts, which declare that women cannot take care of themselves; that fathers are legal guardians over women in childhood; husbands, later on, and finally, sons. "A woman must never be independent" (quoted in Erndl 2000, 95). Hossain dared not only to refute women's perceived innate inferiority in these texts but also to mock such a perception. She specifically addressed the Islamic law that decreed that two women were the equivalent of one man by arguing that if this were the case then God "would have ordained it so that mothers would have given birth to daughters" in half the time that it took them to bear sons and that mothers would have been allotted only half of their milk supply for daughters than that for sons. But this is not the case, for God is "just and most merciful" ([1929] 1988, 48). She is thereby insinuating that God is far more "just" and "merciful" than men are.

Hossain also argued that ending *purdah,* as the Hindus had done, although it was a first step, did not guarantee the capacity in a woman to think and reason on one's own. Women could be unveiled and move around in private and public spaces but could still remain mental slaves. Hossain harshly critiqued women who had been "dragged . . . out of *purdah* in a blind imitation of the Europeans. It does not show any initiative. . . . They are as lifeless as they were before. When their men kept them in seclusion they stayed there. When the men dragged them out by their 'nose-rings' they came out. That cannot be called an achievement by women" ([1929] 1988, 50).

Based on their belief in women's inferiority, traditionalists felt that there was no need to educate women because they were their men's dependents in the home. Men must get their education, must learn to read and write English in order to get a job to support their families. So why should women be educated beyond teaching them to recite the Qur'an and to read a few basic primers on how to conduct themselves properly as Muslim women? Hossain spent her life debating this view. She took great care, however, to argue and reason within traditional parameters and ways of thinking. She debated this narrow definition of education that is still common in India where most students are not interested in education *per se.* Their motivation is to get degrees that will enable them to qualify for given jobs and view their teachers' purpose as to provide them with materials and give them exams that match only those job requirements (Minturn 1993, 333). "Real education," Hossain argued, was about all human beings, including women, developing their God-given capacities to the fullest. Women especially needed to be educated, must be educated, in order to end their dependency on men. This argument did bear fruit, and Mukherjee is only one example of getting an education and then enjoying the benefits of economic independence that ensued as a result—exactly as Hossain had predicted. In contrast to her childhood friends, Mukherjee was considered "unique" in India because she never had "to please my husband or any other future male provider . . . was accountable to no one except myself . . . [and] was not afraid of what my husband would say if I spent money without consulting him because I would never become skill-less, destitute, and lonely, even if he decided I was un-bearably disagreeable" ([1977] 1995, 226). In contrast to Mukherjee's bold, forth-right, somewhat strident rationale for educating women, which perhaps inadver-tently came across as boasting to her conventional, traditional auditors, is Mira Kamdar's quiet assertion, although equally radical, that "[t]he education of girls is the country's best hope for curbing population growth" (1998, 64).

In addition to being the only feminist of her time who publicly denied the belief of innate masculine superiority over women, Hossain was the only reformer of her time who realized that "economic independence is the first prerequisite of women's liberation" (Jahan 1988, 49). She strove to make women understand that in her opinion only education could free women's minds to think for themselves. Education should be their first goal because education would ensure their freedom by leading to economic self-sufficiency, then to economic independence from men, and from that point on, greater freedom would follow. Sadly, almost one hundred years later, Deshpande depicts a female doctor who is lecturing to female college students about becoming professionals and does not have the nerve to tell them what she believes:

> "They will tell you abut economic independence and an independent identity. Forget the words. If Draupadi had been economically independent, if Sita had had an independent identity, you think their stories would have been different? No, these are things that have been voluntarily surrendered, consciously abandoned, because that is the only way to survive. And what, in the long run, matters more than suvival?" ([1980] 1990, 137–138)

Hossain urged women not to see themselves as passive victims, helpless, trapped in conditions of "unimaginable powerlessness" (Kamani 1996, 354) so that it was impossible for them to improve their lot. Through their silence, Hossain contended, women continue to collude with their victimization by failing to oppose it. Women must stop accepting oppressive treatment from their men and stop depending on men's economic support. Women must get themselves educated and go out to work. Even if they can only utilize their current skills in the home and with children, they must still go out to work: "If our liberation from male domination depends on our ability to earn independently, then we should begin. We should be lawyers, magistrates, judges, clerks. . . . The sort of labour we put in our household can bring us wages if we use it outside" ([1929] 1988, 49). Hossain also did not disguise her impatience with women who passively accepted their lot. "With tremendous anger and biting wit displayed without camouflage" (Jahan 1988, 2), Hossain burst out in "Sultana's Dream" in the persona of the Guide who demands of Sultana the Dreamer: "Why do you allow yourselves to be shut up? . . . A lion is stronger than a man, but it does not enable him to dominate the human race. You have neglected the duty you owe to yourselves and you have lost your natural rights by shutting your eyes to your own interests" ([1908] 1988, 9).

When she died in 1932, Hossain believed, not without justification at that time, that her attempts to gain an education for women, both in her eloquent writing and in her work in the schools she founded toward that end, had succeeded.[7] Hossain lived surrounded by controversy. Indeed, how could it be otherwise, even now, given her time and place? Since her death, however, she has been acclaimed and acknowledged in India, as she deserves to be.

Suniti Namjoshi

Suniti Namjoshi (1941–) often goes beyond escape from reality into a utopian fantasy land, but, unlike Hossain, the escape is into a lesbian feminist separatist fantasy land that always ends in a dystopia. A poet, fabulist, and essayist, Namjoshi was born to a life of wealth and privilege. Her grandfather was the Raja of Western Maharashtra and later became a minister in the Bombay cabinet. Namjoshi has written several works of fantasy, or fables, such as *The Mothers of Maya Diip* (1989) and *Babel* (1996), a cross between children's stories (which they claim to be) and "Sultana's Dream," in which a good deal of philosophy combined with biting satire is included. Namjoshi combines the strong social conscience of Hossain with a unique contribution to the struggle for women's right to express their sexuality, in her case to achieve recognition and acceptance for lesbians.

In *The Mothers of Maya Diip* (1989), a lesbian feminist separatist fantasy, Jyanvi and the Blue Donkey are invited to visit Maya Diip by its Ranisaheb, whose personality and character resemble Namjoshi's own grandmother. Indeed, the book is dedicated to "Ai, my grandmother, the Late Laxmi Devi Naik Nimbalkar." Through a debate that Jyanvi has with one of the Matriarch's daughters, Saraswati, who is Jyanvi's lover, Namjoshi attempts to show how brainwashed women are, how inequitable society is. In a wonderful passage, Jyanvi argues that "the more powerful mothers hire other women to care for their children . . . the more powerful the mother, the more privileged the child" (1989, 39). Saraswati cannot understand why this should make Jyanvi angry because it is "natural" for a mother "to want the best for her child." Jyanvi points out, however, that this "best" is "at the expense of other women" and that if being a mother is such a marvelous thing," then "why do they pass off the chores to others?" Saraswati babbles on about how mothers do the best they can for their children; that it is natural for mothers to love their own children "best," and anyhow all the mothers of Maya are "caring" mothers until Jyanvi loses her temper: "To be allowed to slave for a snivelling child is not a privilege, it's a bloody bore! . . . [C]an't you see that it's you I want, not your damn daughter!" (1989, 39). When in Canada for some years Namjoshi had a lengthy relationship with a woman with children, and it is possible that these remarkable comments—perhaps unique in the blunt breaking of two taboos simultaneously—are based on frustrations derived from her own personal experience of life with this family, with a woman who ultimately placed caring for her children above her relationship with Namjoshi. Deshpande's heroine, Urmi, in *The Binding Vine* ([1993] 2001), makes the same point as Jyanvi, but then waffles: "Sometimes I think . . . they brainwash us into this motherhood thing. They make it seem so mystical and emotional when the truth is that it's all just a myth. They've told us so often and for so long that once you're a mother you have these feelings, that we think we do." Amusingly, when her sister-in-law responds to this observation by challenging her to an exchange—if it is indeed true that any baby would do, then she would take Urmi's son and Urmi could have her daughter—Urmi "instinctively" clutches her son "closer" ([1993] 2001, 76).

Using brilliant reversal to show the idiocy of any kind of gender inequities, Namjoshi has Jyanvi discover that the mothers of Maya destroy most male children and keep a few "pretty boys" around because it would be "wasteful" to keep them all around. "[E]xcept for the semen the lives of pretty boys are perfectly pointless." When Jyanvi wonders why these "pretty boys" do not attempt to overthrow their mothers, she is informed that they are disorganized and have no arms, turning "most of their aggression against themselves." The mothers of Maya "don't regard them as their own children—just as necessities" (1989, 53). Princess Asha the Apostate, another daughter of the Matriarch, differs so strongly that she demands an immediate change in Mayan institutions for the "pretty boys," such as equal rights, education, and the right to "become mothers like everyone else" (1989, 80). Princess Asha the Apostate argues that if things were reversed, if the boys were "treated differently, they might be different. . . . they would never reach the stature of normal women, but that, perhaps within their limitations, they could be helped to grow up" (1989, 80, 53). Through Valerie, who has escaped from her country (a.k.a. India) where Ashans "enslaved" Mayans, two "pretty boys," Modhan and Madhu, do find out to their amazement and fascination that in her native country the reversal of the reversal prevails. What they have always known and considered "natural," that is, "social support structures" that comprise alternatives to "the patriarchal family" (Dietrich 1999, 89), is not the way it is in Valerie's homeland. Only Ashans "mattered . . . had all the power":

> Every Ashan thought of himself as a kind of farmer, and of every Mayan as a bit of land or a field which could be his property . . . which could be used for growing babies. . . . [The Ashans] have enslaved [the Mayans] in order to force them to have their babies . . . who then belong to a particular Ashan. . . . The babies are branded by his specific genes. . . . Because only his semen is used to impregnate the Mayan who belongs to him. . . . So you see why the exclusive ownership of a Mayan is so important to an Ashan in my society. (1989, 86–87)

As a result of Valerie's telling the "pretty boys" about her culture, "about the norms of a heterosexual patriarchy," they acquire certain awareness of other ways of living, other ways than what they have always known in Maya. Valerie is arrested and imprisoned for giving them "ideas" about "rape, slavery, and war," for describing a society in which there were male masters and female slaves. Meanwhile, the boys have begun to think about "artificial insemination and enslavement." Valerie, outraged and frightened, wants to know what can be done. Jyanvi responds that somehow they must convince "males that a male-dominated society" is not conducive to their best "interests" (1989, 97), but Valerie doubts that this would ever be possible.

Through witty aphorisms that build on and contradict one another to the point of rueful hilarity, Namjoshi also rages against gender inequality and the denial of individual sexuality which she considers entirely irrational. In *Building Babel* (1996), another lesbian feminist separatist fantasy, the Queen proposes to open the community of Babel built and populated entirely by women. "The immigrants will be 'men' till they have been assimilated into the society of Babblers, at which time, at least some of them will definitely be accorded the status of women" (1996, 132). Members of the Sisterhood immediately begin to debate the issue. Snow White argues on behalf of men. They should first be screened and tested and then, if they scored well, would become "a trained workforce" for Babel, which would not therefore have to undergo the expense of educating them. Solitude thereupon "roared" out that "MEN NEED EDUCATING!" and then makes her first and last speech in public during Queen Alice's reign:

> "Men . . . have diseased identities. No, I am not an essentialist. I mean that the identities on offer to men are diseased. I refer to men as they are at this moment, men with their mutated genes and memes, which have not mutated sufficiently. They are troglodytes still. They fight sabre toothed tigers when there are no sabre toothed tigers to fight. They worship power and find the victory of battle heroic. They batter one another, they batter piglets, parakeets and peonies, they batter women, they batter the whole of Crone Kronos's creation. This they perceive as the exercise of power; and when they exercise power, then they feel they truly live. They hate Babblers, they hate everyone whom they perceive as 'not them,' but most of all they hate themselves. Even they understand that they are diseased, and yet they battle for their diseased being. To be cured is too onerous. Besides, power is an aphrodisiac. Power is a pheromone. Sometimes they feel the intoxication of being in love with themselves. The smell of power makes their nostrils twitch. Why allow such creatures in?" (1996, 114)

Reminiscent of the dreamlike rational-irrational of Lewis Carroll's *Alice in Wonderland,* Franz Kafka's *The Castle,* and Joseph Heller's *Catch-22,* when Solitude loses this debate, Queen Alice turns her into a man. Then, because she became a man, Solitude is banished from the council, as are all those who speak up and offer the same opinion as Solitude. One of the Sisterhood does have the temerity to admit that she wasn't too crazy about women, either because they did "too much backbiting, struggling and striving" and that women were burdened with inferiority complexes. However, she cared even less for men who were "[u]nbiddable and awkward. They don't fit in. Always in a mess, and always in need. More trouble than they're worth, but useful to the production and propagation of genes" (1996, 117–118, 119).

Queen Alice, like many younger contemporary feminists, is contemptuous and dismissive of the Sisterhood (the Suffragette and Second-Wave Western feminist description of ourselves): "Your thinking is hopelessly counter-revolutionary. You are a pack of old women who have outlived your time" (1996, 116). But Namjoshi does not let the younger feminists have the last word. After Queen Alice's death, the narrator cat (Namjoshi herself?) leaves Babel, turned off by the younger generation (the group we call Third-Wave feminists in the West), their "roistering and rowdiness, the 'me! me! me,' the young blood and fresh blood, the angst and the ignorance. I don't like watching women—grown women—tearing each other to pieces, committing stupidities, committing crimes" (1996, 139–140). The vision of the Second-Wavers, that bright new world that we would some day run so much better than any other world had ever been run; that construction in the air of feminist theories (brilliantly called "Babel" by Namjoshi) that we had labored so long and so hard to erect; that place where we once lived in our hearts and minds eventually becomes "no longer distinguishable from any other city. Perhaps it would disintegrate, perhaps not. Who cared?" (1996, 140), the cat sighs.

Outsiders Within II

On Corrupt Governmental Policies, Environmental Destruction, and Oppression of Tribals and Women

It is commonplace for feminists all over the world to maintain that our concerns, our perspectives extend beyond women's issues: that as feminists, we seek equal human rights for women everywhere and at the same time equal rights for all human beings, as well. We seek the end of all discrimination by race, gender, class, ethnicity, etc., not just the end of discrimination against women alone. As feminists we indeed have many countries where the fates of a great many women and men call out for critical political perspectives and action for change.　UMA NARAYAN

Mahasweta Devi

The remarkable activist-writer Mahasweta Devi (1926–) has made her life one seamless whole through her commitment to obtain justice for all the downtrodden, most especially the tribals. She has focused in her writing and in her life on exposing the inhuman cruelty and injustice of powerful corrupt entities toward the tribals and the landless and reveals extraordinary unyielding determination, obdurate strength, and undying commitment in her activism and writing over a period of many years. In her conviction, like that of her predecessor

Antherjanam (who is discussed in Chapter Four) that creative writers as a group "should have a social conscience," Devi projects onto her colleagues her own motives for writing: to serve society. Additionally, Antherjanam seems to me to have influenced Devi in her life and her work, in her perspective and in the passionate, brutal directness of her writing style.

All of Devi's writing—both journalistic and creative—is strong, clear, graphic, and riveting, always reinforced by historic facts and raw data and has an exponentially increasing power to horrify, depress, and sicken readers. Many Indian feminist critics and writers make the same accusations as Devi as in the following satirical effort by Anita Rau Badami (1964–), which is in the form of a letter to the editor. But, like Badami, they critique in passing as minor elements of larger themes in their texts.

> *Dear Editor,*
>   *Recently there was an article in your esteemed newspaper about the new highlight at Dizzee World in Madras. Apparently, trained birds imported from Singapore astonish visitors to the park by answering the telephone, conducting polite conversations, playing basketball, riding bikes, obeying traffic rules and picking up trash. It is my humble opinion that we, the citizens of this country, might be better served if these birds were to replace our politicians, corporate thugs, the mafia who run police stations and other assorted crooks.*
>   *Sincerely,*
>   *Pro Bono Publico* [For the Public Good]. (2001, 155)

In her character Arun, whose life is given over to protesting injustices, Badami is again as serious and direct in her critique as Devi:

> "You [his father] had your independence of India and all to fight for, real ideals. For me and my friends, the fight is against daily injustice, our own people stealing our rights. This is the only world I have, and I feel responsible for it. I have to make sure that it doesn't get blown up, or washed away in the next flood, or poisoned by chemicals. . . . We are all part of nature. . . . If the natural world goes, so do we. All the industrial effluents being dumped into the sea are destroying the turtles, and soon they will destroy us. Before long the water table will be affected, and instead of drinking water we will be drinking chlorine or whatever poison is being unloaded." (2001, 239, 246)

Jayapal also includes elements in her text that show her as socially and environmentally conscious, as, for example, in her description of a once clear and blue lake that she views with disgust from her train window on the way from Madras to Varanasi:

> Today it is black, black with sludge, with harmful chemical by-products of nearby factories, of decomposed waste and piles of garbage. A lone fishing boat tries to find something that can survive these waters. Behind it, the sun sinks into the earth, turning the sky's gray into melting red and pink and purple. God's work this beautiful sun and sky. . . . And whose work is the horrifying refuse, the suffering children? How can beauty exist so closely juxtaposed with horror? (2000, 194).

Likewise, the critic Satish Deshpande writes:

> Jharkand contains five major steel plants or virtually all of India's steel industry; most of the major coal, iron ore and mica mines; and several large heavy engineering and chemical plants. Also located here is the nation's largest integrated river valley project for hydroelectric power-generation and irrigation. (All this does not even begin to account for the varied forest-based products of the region.) Yet Jharkand and its original inhabitants remain backward and extremely poor. (2000, 185)

In scrupulous detail, Devi describes the exploiters of the tribals and the various methods that unconscionable groups have devised to trap and destroy them. Her focus on outrages against the tribals is unrelenting. Millions of suffering tribals lack the assistance of their own movements that such movements might afford them, as well as of local and state governmental and administrative and police entities (who all too often collude with exploiters of the tribals), and worse. Like the intellectual elite, the mainstream society perceives the tribals as "uncivilized." Devi queries such an unfair definition for the tribals, whom she compares favorably to the mainstream society, because their customs traditionally do not include dowries, *sati,* denial of divorce and widow remarriage, nor orphanages (because neighbors take orphans into their homes and raise them). Devi also admires the tribals because, for them, the worst crime imaginable is to insult or rape women. In fact, rape is not known to them, and their women are honored. She also admires the tribals because tribal women do not consider their husbands gods. In fact, they laugh at the notion, perhaps because they are "economically independent, and can easily separate, divorce, and remarry" (Kishwar and Vanita 1984, 137). They also have a custom of planting a tree at the birth of a child, thereby "forging a relationship between child and family because that tree is uniquely the child's. The trees are all slow-growing, and by the time the child reaches adolescence, his [*sic*] tree has just come into fruit, commencing its life as provider to the tribal and the tribal's life as guardian of the tree" (G. Mehta 1997, 254).

Whenever a tribal attempted to repay a loan, the *zamindars*[1] added huge (often-new) sums of interest to the principle of the loan. Over the years the interest keeps adding so that the debt often goes on generation after generation, although this is illegal (Devi [1997] 2000, 12–13). "In our India," Devi remarks with dripping sarcasm, "acts are for enactment and not for implementation" ([1997] 2000, 17). She angrily condemns capitalists in the forests for operating and expanding at India's expense, while only the tribals who cut down the trees for them are blamed ([1997] 2000, 148; see also Kishwar and Vanita 1984, 178; Spivak 1999, 380). Devi fears that tea gardens will deprive the tribals of their traditional food sources, which are valuable precious herbs for medicine, as well as water. Which class, she wonders rhetorically, gains from the planting of eucalyptus trees and from all its related activities? "Social forestry for which society? Not for the poor and downtrodden. For the rich then? . . . But at what national cost?" (66).[2] In the mid-1990s, the government of West Bengal finally reversed its policy and "announced that henceforth, fruit-bearing trees would form half of all trees planned under the social forestry programme." Furthermore, "if implemented, it would vindicate Devi's years of campaigning" (Ghabak [1997] 2000, xxv). Indeed, some radical groups, such as the Chipko movement, composed of women, have wrested control over the forest districts from the forest officials (Shiva 1999, 70). Because of a variety of "so-called government projects" such as factories, dams, "industries, sanctuaries and national parks" (Ghabak [1997] 2000, xxvi), and huge industrial, irrigation, and mining projects, millions of tribals have been displaced from lands that once belonged to them and have become migrant laborers. Gita Mehta quotes one such laborer who was forced to migrate to New Delhi:

> "We managed to feed ourselves by working on building sites. Carrying bricks. Mixing concrete. We lived in huts made from things that other people had thrown away. Then the country's bosses decided Delhi must look beautiful. From 'Remove Poverty' their slogans changed to 'Remove the Poor.' The government had bulldozers raze our huts, we were herded into buses, driven thirty miles out of town, where there is no work. No water. No food. Nothing to protect our children from the weather." (1997, 51)

After a massacre of tribals by the Bihar Military Police in 1980, large sums of money began to pour into the area from a variety of venues, including the World Bank, and this money was then "misspent for want of specific plans."[3] Arundhati Roy describes the results more specifically for the village of Emeneyem: "The banks of the river smelled of shit and pesticides bought with World Bank loans. Most of the fish had died. The ones that survived suffered from fin-rot and had broken out in boils" (1998, 14).

Anita Desai

In *The Village by the Sea* (1982b), Desai (1937–) describes these events uncompromisingly. Unlike Devi, who describes only the massacred marchers in Bihar led by women, Desai describes an all-women march in Bombay in which they hold up banners, make fists, and yell "Bring down the prices! We want oil! We want sugar! We want rice at fire prices!" and "Long live Women's Society for Freedom and Justice!" Marching in front is an old woman waving her "rolling-pin in the air." Other marchers beat on "cooking pots" "with long-handled cooking spoons," which, to their delight, made a deafening noise.[4] Hari and the other all-male members of his procession gape with amazement at this sight. It had never occurred to them to have women join them because they thought that men "could manage it all on their own" and that including women "would only be a nuisance." But these city women apparently "did not trust men to manage for them" and organized "their affairs themselves." The other males laugh and joke about this strange notion, but Hari does not, although it seemed like "a very strange new idea" to him. Instead, he wonders how his mother and sister would have responded to this all-woman march (1982b, 76).

Hari has joined this march to Bombay after witnessing the response by his fellow villagers to the news that the government is about to illegally buy up their land. When one of the villagers protests that their land cannot be taken, that it belongs to them and that they will not sell it, they are told by the representative of the factory whom Desai significantly titles "the stranger," that the government is callous and unfeeling. When it tells the villagers to sell, they must do so without asking questions because this area has been selected as the right site on which to build factories. Although the villagers argue that the government should rather choose to build on land where "nothing grows but stones and thorns," the stranger replies that the government has used "experts" to select this site because it is near Bombay, and "a railway line" can be laid here because there is a preexisting road that only requires widening. Additionally, transportation is fine, there is sufficient land for factories, "housing colonies," and "markets" that will become necessary because so many new workers will be attracted to the place (after the farms and homes, abundant trees and their wildlife are removed). And, the most chilling attraction of all about the village, which the stranger adds, apparently without a qualm, is that the future factory site will be "near the sea and the wastes can be pumped into it" (1982b, 60). When the villagers ask the stranger how many people will then come to the small village, he tells them that the numbers will rise into the thousands. But what then will happen to the villagers? There will be factories to replace the village that will produce gas and fertilizer and this will create many jobs but only those requiring engineering and mechanical skills. Workers will therefore be recruited from elsewhere "to run the factories." Nothing will be done for those who live on the land, nor will they be given jobs. They will have to leave the village and go a long distance to find work. They will be displaced and become migrant workers.

At the doomed procession of the fisherman and farmers in Bombay that Hari joins, an environmentalist from the city who is sympathetic to their protest addresses them and tells them that the residents of Bombay have just as much reason to be concerned. As a by-product of manufacturing fertilizer, the factories "will pump deadly chemicals into the air. . . . Sulphur dioxide, ammonia and dust will . . . pollute the region . . . for miles around." Although the government decreed that no fertilizer factory would be built less than fifty miles from any city, the site selected is less than ten miles away from the "heavily industrialised, crowded and polluted" city of Bombay. "How much more pollution can we stand?" (1982b, 77), the environmentalist cries. Later, homeless and hungry, Hari buys a coconut from a coconut seller who discusses the unsuccessful march with him, sarcastically wondering why the villagers came and what demands they want the government to fulfill for them. He tells Hari that their most practical requests, such as the easing of their hunger, are no different to the government than if the villagers had requested jewelry and mansions. They could make all the demands of the government that they liked, but did they imagine for one moment that the government can either see or hear them? He likens the corrupt government to "a mouth" that "eats . . . our taxes, our land . . . the poor." He advises Hari to listen to his warning and stay away from the government. Never "ask it for anything, don't depend on it for anything" (1982b, 85).

Similarly, in Badami's *The Hero's Walk* (2001), an inveterate letterwriter to the local Hindu paper complains "about the heavy-water plant that had opened on the outskirts of Toturpuram and was dumping its waste directly into the sea" (2001, 15). Also Sahgal, in *Rich Like Us* ([1986] 1988b), condemns the Nehru government's "rising technocracy, the professional-management class, intellectuals and top bureaucrats . . . a truly secular, modern elite" that advocates "the modernist idiom of secular nationalism, scientific technology and economic development" (Satish Deshpande 2000, 186). Sahgal shows up this exploitation for what it is in a discussion between a bureaucrat and his host about a piece of land that the bureaucrat had believed to be his host's until he is told it was actually a rural village area takeover for which the villagers had been paid and given jobs. The reader can imagine how well the villagers had been paid for the loss of their property and what jobs they would be hired to perform. At this point, Rose, a Cockney who has been resident for many years in India, intrudes into the all-male conversation with another consideration: "Jobs is all very well. What about their 'omes?" Again, the host repeats that the villagers have been compensated, whereupon Rose retaliates with fury that she supposes, then, that it wouldn't matter to him if *his* own house were levelled by a bulldozer "and you were given com-peng-say-tion. Compengsaytion! 'Ow do we know if it was enough compengsaytion?" ([1986] 1988b, 12–13).

Mehta's *Snakes and Ladders* (1997) refers to Indian women as suffering "social and economic disparity" (1997, 20). The vast majority of women are not unionized and are subject to homelessness because of "drought and debt" and "vulnerable to any exploitation," especially in the course of their "migration from the countryside to the city in search of work" (1997, 58). Lower–class women in factories do not earn enough to support their children. It is becoming increasingly rare to find them there because men are forcing out the small number who are hired in the scramble for the few jobs available. On this score, Devi indicts the criminal and corrupt factory contractors and their recruiters who cheat thousands of migrant contract laborers forced by poverty into working under contract for them. After being recruited by a chain of agents and subagents to labor in large government projects such as railroads, highways, and bridges, laborers work more hours than required by law and for less than legal minimum wages. They work only in the most difficult and menial of positions, even after achieving seniority, and all too frequently end up being cheated out of their earnings. After months of backbreaking, endless labor, they often receive nothing more than food sufficient for bare survival. Of course, even this is better than the conditions at home, which cause them to migrate in the first place. Adding to the men's plight is the plight of their womenfolk.

The same criminals also take advantage of young women whom they recruit and take to the brick kilns where they receive below minimum wages. Like the male migrant laborers, these women are also cheated out of what they should receive. And when women are hired as laborers it is only after the supply of men has been exhausted. They are sexually abused on all sides by the kiln owners, their employees, and so on down the line. Some of these young women never live to return home because of what Devi justly labels "the bloody exploitation of women" under the bonded labor system that forces them to go as contract laborers in the first place. Sahgal makes the same point in *Rich Like Us* ([1986] 1998b) about women workers in the kilns:

> Hundreds of brick kilns along [the Ganges] . . . open and swallow up women . . . Women labourers disappeared into the kilns where they worked and the pigholes where they lived, sometimes never to return, used . . . by the kiln masters and their men when they had finished carrying brickloads for the day. Some came back to the village when they were hard and old to recruit young girls for the kilns. ([1986] 1998b, 68)

In rural villages, as long as men only are defined as the sharecroppers and the women as their helpers, even though they do the same work women go "unremunerated." It is even worse when child care and housework are considered. Women laborers' lack of "independence" is not so much due to their lack of education but to their men's control over their "labor power." Such control can be traced in a vertical line out from the level of families, to the unions, to the employers, to the local community enforcers, all the way on up to the governmental level (A. Basu 1992, 137, 262; N. Shah et al. 1999, 151, 156). And not only in India. Sudha Deshpande enunciates a default position that in all probability represents that of women affected globally by the so-called feminization of the labor force. "We must remember for the present that to be exploited in the labour market is bad but not to be exploited is worse" (quoted in N. Shah et al. 1999, 151). Not only women. Child contract laborers are taken from the age of seven onwards to labor in carpet factories and then treated like slaves,[5] as in the case of two tribal girls living in a garbage dump in Delhi:

> The dense jungles that had once supported their community had been destroyed first by lumber merchants, then by stone quarrying, and they had been sold by their parents to a man looking for cheap labor to work on one of the city's construction sites. When the

building was complete, he had left them to survive on their own and they didn't know
where to find their parents, now working in some unknown part of India as bonded
labor. (G. Mehta 1997, 49)

The contractor who is paying them for rag picking is himself in flight from
having to repay a loan to his grandfather from a money lender that he and his father had already "repaid many times over" because the interest on the loan was so
astronomical that it was impossible to repay the loan. He now lives in a mud hut
"in a resettlement colony" (1997, 52).

Writing about the plight of quarry workers in *A Situation in New Delhi* ([1977]
1988c), Sahgal makes the same point with eloquence and passion:

> The outskirts of Delhi or the fringe of society or the edge of history, it was all the same
> thing. They were people who hadn't known they were people . . . [that] they need not
> work as many hours as they did, that they were entitled to more pay, that if a maraud-
> ing caste neighbor set fire to one of their huts or raped one of their women, they need
> not suffer it. The law provided redress. How difficult just to teach them they were
> human. The law, of course, said they were, and all their rights were on the statute
> book. But they couldn't read and those in authority had not taken the trouble to see
> that the laws were observed, and if they did, justice was slow and layers of sluggish pro-
> cedure clogged each step of it. The law of the land lay like disintegrated rubble in the
> quarry. ([1977] 1988c, 98)

Under such circumstances, is it any wonder that most tribals lose heart and
doubt whether there is any reason to become educated only to remain jobless? On
the rare occasions when tribals do receive an education and do find employment,
they are routinely harassed. One tribal, Chun Kotal, a Lodha, was a very rare sta-
tistic, especially in view of her being female. She succeeded in graduating high
school under the most difficult conditions, and then going on to college. She did
then receive employment, but she was harassed so repeatedly and so unbearably at
school and later on the job that she committed suicide (Spivak 1995, xxvii). Devi
writes about Chun Kotal at length in her report on the Lodhas and Kerias in her
collection of reports, *Dust on the Road* ([1997] 2000). This report, one of her most
powerful, can be considered the apex of her journal work, or from another perspective, the nadir, in terms of the damnable subject matter. The smaller tribal
groups of West Bengal—(the Lodhas, ca. forty thousand, and the Kherias, ca. fifteen thousand, according to Devi)—are separate groups, although both are recorded in the census as Savaras. They are in the direst of straits. Defined as a
group of criminals by the English colonizers, they have remained at the mercy of
this profiling to this day. At one point, Devi makes the sardonic comment that
the only Kherias one would ever see in Purulia were those in chains accompanied
by police on the way to court. They are routinely suspected and rounded up
whenever there is a crime, much as young black men in the United States, and
immediately after the terrorist attacks of September 11, 2001, as Indian American

men or other similarly dark-skinned men who were mistaken for Arabs were rounded up. Devi ardently defended both tribes from atrocities by continual appeals to the governmental administration, which eventually proved effective because the police began to prevent them once they were notified of the possibility of their occurring.

In her autobiography *Goja* (2000), Namjoshi describes her guilt-ridden love for her personal attendant, Goja, who cared for her and who slept on her floor. Namjoshi's strong feelings for this woman caused the author at a very early age to question the class system, "the set-up," as she puts it. All her life, through changing personal and political affiliations and fortunes, through dramatic changes in climate and culture, Namjoshi has continued to seek the answer to that question. Before she left India for good, Namjoshi proved her brilliance to her family and to other Indians when she passed the exams that made her a high-ranking officer in the prestigious IAS (Indian Administrative Service), the "successors" to the ICS (Indian Civil Service).

> The Service succeeded . . . in building up a tradition of integrity and professional competence that helped to impart to it a unique aura. . . . Its aura burgeoned and continued to attract young men and women . . . partly because of its continuing prestige and, also, partly as a means of serving the country without undue sacrifice. As Nehru once remarked, the IAS definitely became Indian; some of its members tried to be civil; and service was at least one of its motives. (Virthal 1997, 210–211)

Still, Namjoshi feels shame today about having "enjoyed" the "status this position gave her, with "people rising when I entered an office, the police springing to attention and presenting arms when I visited a subdivision" (2000, 63). What bothered Namjoshi most was "the gratitude of the poor" for only doing her job; for neither harming nor hindering them, even though she held "the power." That, she grieves, was the best that could be said of her. Namjoshi is still obsessed with her failure to resolve to her satisfaction why only a few human beings possess wealth and power and dominate millions of others who live in poverty. This perspective is like that of Sahgal's who is also high-born, yet who harbors

> an anguished awareness of the child at the back of a mud-walled village classroom sitting the width of six rows from the last row in the class [because he is a *harijan*], his drinking water in a separate vessel outside the classroom; a sightless beggar reflected in the glass show window of a shop displaying high-heeled snakeskin shoes; baby brides taking their dolls with them to their husbands' homes. ([1986] 1988b, 99)

In *Nampally Road* (1991), "a caustic critique of the emergency era in India" (S. Ray 2000, 155), Alexander's young Indian heroine Mira, whose perspective is that of the author's, joins the doomed Naxalite protests aginst the Indian class and caste system, as well as sexism. In perfect Sanskrit with "ferocity in her voice," she cites the Sankara second *sloka* which her godmother's *swamiji* had asked her to read:

"'For all beings a human birth is difficult to obtain, more so is a male body; rarer than that is Brahminhood; rarer still is the attachment to the Vedic religion.' . . . The point as far as I'm concerned is, what do you do with a woman and one who will never be a Brahmin?[6] What happens to her knowledge? Is she just mere pollution? . . . What of the Brahmin-hood part? That huge system of hierarchies, it chokes out life. Meanwhile people are being beaten and molested all around us. There's terrible social injustice." (1991, 85–86)

In Devi's story "The Hunt" in *Imaginary Maps* (1995), her mixed-race (Indian and Tribal) character Mary uses the day set aside for traditional women's hunting day to turn the tables. She hunts down as her prey her would-be rapist who has been harassing her at every turn with his unwanted attentions. However, such an ending in which tribal or lower-caste women enact revenge on their abusers and exploiters is not typical of Devi's work, both creative and journalistic. In "Douloti the Bountiful," the young virgin Douloti is contracted out as a prostitute by her father. Devi then exposes with breathtaking power the tragic inability of Douloti's father, like so many other fathers, to protect their young daughters from molestation and rape once they have fallen into the trap of taking loans from money lenders. Douloti is immediately taken away to a brothel as payment for the loan, but of course this loan can never be repaid because it "is calculated on compound interest" (Spivak 1995, xix; see also Pandian 1997, 377). Like all the other prostitutes in the brothel to which she is consigned, she is raped and brutalized without mercy, used as if she were a piece of dead meat by her captors. Douloti eventually becomes sucked dry and ridden with venereal disease. She is thrown out into the street to beg like the other prostitutes after they reach this stage, often accompanied by children from the men who have used and abused them. Douloti dies while attempting to return home.

In all that befalls Douloti she remains saintlike, fatalistic, passively accepting everything as is characteristic of tribals, according to Devi. However, Spivak contends that Douloti is "sweet, innocent, responsible . . . not a subject of resistance," not because she has internalized the fatalist spiritual perspective inculcated into her from birth, but rather because she (and by implication, many of Devi's other tribal women characters) has internalized the prevailing gender perspective in the form of "constraints" in terms of her "gendering." Sadly, Douloti perceives these gender constraints "as ethical choice . . . as responsibility and therefore the very basis of gender-ethics" which is "the hardest roadblock for women the world over" (Spivak 1995, xxvii, xxviii). Although Devi does not directly comment on Spivak's interpretation (Spivak introduces *Imaginary Maps* and has also translated it), she does protest the use of women as "merchandise" or "commodities." She also deplores the judiciary system for habitually ruling against women when they are raped on the grounds that only sluts or prostitutes are raped.

Douloti resembles Stanadayini in Devi's "Breast Giver" in *Breast Stories* (1997), in her experience of inhuman exploitation as well as in her character and terrible fate. Both women are treated as "merchandise," as "commodities"—Douloti for her vagina, Stanadayini for her breasts. Her husband uses her breasts entirely for his pleasure, and they are used as udders for all her employer's and daughters-in-laws' children[7] until they are eaten away by cancer. Likewise, Douloti's brutalized and abused vagina eventually rots away from venereal disease. I would include as parallels to Douloti and Stanadayini another of Devi's exploited and abused women characters in *Breast Stories,* Dopdi Mehjen, a Naxalite Santhal tribal woman whose breasts are "mangled" by her rapists—the police. However, she heroically refuses to internalize her treatment into a feeling of shame or humiliation. Instead, like the Draupadi of mythology, she handles herself in her "nakedness as an affront to their masculinity. . . . simultaneously a deliberate refusal of a shared sign-system (the meanings assigned to nakedness, and rape: shame, fear, loss), and an ironic deployment of the same semiotics to create disconcerting counter-effects of shame, confusion and terror in the enemy" (Rajan 1999, 353–354; see also Hiltebeitel 2000, 21).[8] Again, the character Gangor in Devi's "Behind the Bodice"[9] (also in *Breast Stories*), after being tortured by the police who also rape her, has her magnificent breasts mangled, but her raging spirit, like Draupadi's, can never be raped, for she knows what Nalini Natarajan does, that "the uncovering of women's bodies is related more to the politics of men's power relations than any interest in female subjectivity" (1994, 82).

In Chitra Banerjee Divakaruni's "The Maid Servant's Story," a tribal character, the beautiful, bright, and sensitive Sarala finds shelter as a maid in a middle-class family after having run away because her mother is forcing her into prostitution. Eventually her mother finds Sarala and attempts to retrieves her, without success the first time, and threatens her daughter's employer: "I know my rights. You might be rich, but I can get a hundred people from the *bustee* [slum] to come back here with me tomorrow. Make a stink like you won't believe. . . . Don't think I can't see the real reason you're keeping my girl on—that pregnant wife of yours isn't much good for anything else right now, is she?" (1995, 139). She then returns with a mob that breaks down the gates while demanding that "the girl" be handed over to them:

> "Her mother wants her back, and so does her man. You got no right to keep her. . . . Up to no good we hear, you folks. Taking advantage of a young girl like that . . . All you rich people, all alike, think you own the earth. . . . What's this about her not wanting? [to return to her mother] Everyone knows a daughter belongs to her parents, a wife to her husband. *Sahibi* [Westernized] talk like this is what's making our families fall apart." (1995, 150–151)

But, unlike Gangor, Sarala's spirit is eventually destroyed. She becomes hardened and embittered, spitting at her former beloved mistress. Despite her changed conduct, as well as her changed appearance, her former mistress still recognizes Sarala in the exploited prostitute. Sarala represents "the alterity of the subaltern," while Sarala's erstwhile mistress is deployed to represent "the domesticated and desexualized figure of the [middle-class] mother . . . the pious projection of the middle-class family as microcosm of the nation." Both women, in fact, represent the "exploitation of woman as metaphor" and are "a rebuke to the frank instrumentalism with which bourgeois nationalism mobilizes the image of Mother" (Mufti 2000, 29, 5, 17, 33).

Police brutality to Muhammad and Rameeza Be also has been recorded and protested by Devi and many others (Farooqi 1984, 186–188; Gopal 1999, 325, fn. 12; Kishwar and Vanita 1984, 34; Tharu and Niranjana 1999, 505). Also, in *Nampally Road* (1991) Alexander records an eyewitness description of the peaceful demonstration in which Muhammad, Rameeza Be's husband, was brutally beaten and murdered. Then Rameeza was taken into police headquarters and brutally raped. "As Rameeza's sari was torn from her body, a whole line of policemen still wearing their boots scrabbled among themselves for who should go first; how her wild fist-blows, her sharp cries for help had subsided as blood filled her wounds and ran down her bruised mouth, her blackened eyes" (1991, 89). Both Devi's and Alexander's stories are based on the same real-life situation. Alexander also uses tribal women's ravaged breasts as metaphor for the mistreatment of tribals in India, the way that Devi does. For Devi describes all her tribal women characters as more than just individual characters. They are not only suffering as individual tribal women, but as embodied representations of the condition of India. Just as Douloti's "bleeding, rotting carcass covers the entire Indian peninsula" (quoted in Spivak 1995, xx), so do Stanadayini's, Dopdi's, and Gangor's mutilated breasts. I would extend to all Devi's stories about tribal women what Devi herself states about "The Hunt"—that their tragic situations are "true for the rest of India" (quoted in Spivak 1995, xx). Devi uses her disfigured women mythically: as metaphors for India's plight in contrast to the nationalist metaphysical use of women as heroic "Mother Indias." And Alexander, in writing about Antherjanam in her foreword to the latter's *Cast Me Out If You Will* (1997), describes her as having made the connection between the suffering of her female characters and India, as Devi herself made in *Breast Stories,* namely that "The woman who must break loose is also India, which must break free of colonial domination" (1997, 190).

Devi also calls for rewriting Indian histories so that tribal contributions are included and integrated into them, especially their rebellions against the British. For example, she wrote a biography, *The Queen of Jhansi* (1956), about the Rani of Jhansi. When the British refused to recognize her adopted son after her husband's death in 1853 and annexed the state to themselves by applying the Doctrine of Lapse, she led Indian troops against them in 1857 in the first war of independence (the Indian Mutiny) and was killed in battle.[10] Further to the right, militant, even violent, terrorist Hindu women fighting against "colonial domination" were conceptualized as Devi does her tribal women. By projecting their actions as protective of the nation as family they could also be valorized as self-sacrificing on behalf of India (A. Basu 1992, 254, fn. 20; Gopal 1999, 311). The Communist Party made the same claim, only in terms of the drawbacks of the Congress party, namely that female "terrorist martyrs" had given up "normal nationalist politics" in favor of "terrorism," which they defined as "[a] still higher state of political 'maturity'" because they were frustrated by the Congress Party (Jayawardena 1986, 105). Dr. G. V. Deshmukh, a Member of Parliament at the time, also used Hindu women as an abstraction for India—devastatingly—when defending the passage of the Hindu Women's Right to Property Act of 1937 against orthodox Hindus. When they argued that women had no right to property because females were dependents for their entire lives, she responded that if this rationale were expanded to represent India it could be argued that because India had been dependent "for a thousand years" therefore "no Indian had the right to hold property" (quoted in M. Basu 2001, 130).

In "Witch Sabbath at Singbhum," and again in her report on witch-hunting in West Bengal in *Dust on the Road* ([1997] 2000), Devi offers many horrifying examples of murders of those who are accused of witchcraft, mostly women, but not always. Traditional tribal superstitions link the causes for illness, outbreaks of disease, and death of humans, cattle, and plants with witchcraft, never with germs, bacteria, and poor hygiene.[11] As in every piece of her writing, Devi questions whose benefit the oppression serves and rhetorically responds with sharp and penetrating conclusions. Her essays on witches, her explanations of the situations are the same explanations that make sense of the burning of witches in Europe, the Salem Witch Trials, and the actions of those Poles during the Holocaust who assisted the Nazis in mass round-ups and slaughters of their Polish Jewish neighbors whose property they then appropriated for themselves. Without police intervention, tribals are frequently manipulated to accuse and murder those whom they suspect of witchcraft by others who stand to gain by dividing and conquering the tribals, and/or by usurping accused witches' land and property, and/or using tribal superstitions to satisfy their own personal grudges against the so-called witches.

Desai's *Fire on the Mountain* ([1977] 1982a) illustrates this last point. Ila Das, an elderly, impoverished Brahmin woman who works as a government welfare officer, describes a "priest-man" whom she hates as responsible for the death of a little boy who "cut his foot on a rusty nail." Das, the welfare officer, told the child's mother to take him to the clinic for an antitetanus shot, "but she wouldn't hear of it. Or, rather, the priest-man wouldn't hear of it. Nooo, he said, Nooo, injections were the work of the devil and Maya-devi was *not* to take the child to the clinic" ([1977] 1982a, 128). Das also complains that if it weren't for that "*impossible* priest" the women would listen to her. "It's so much harder to teach a man anything . . . the women are willing, poor dears, to try and change their dreadful lives by an effort, but do you think that men will let them? Nooo, not one bit." She makes the same complaint in relation to child marriage. When she hears of one "in the offing" she goes to each house and threatens the parents with prison if they commit such "a social offense." Again, she believes the women would listen to her because "if anyone knows what it is for a girl to be married and bear children at the age of twelve, it's them, isn't it? But wherever I go, the priest follows me, and undoes what I do. He *hates* me . . . ooh, he *hates* me" ([1977] 1982a, 129).

When Das discovers that a family is planning to marry a seven-year-old girl to a widower with six children, "an old man in the next village because he owns a quarter of an acre of land and two goats," she argues with the mother and confronts the father, "a sullen lout" ([1977] 1982a, 129–130). This is the last time Das is ever able to perform her duty, for she is raped and murdered by the "sullen lout" for having the temerity to meddle in his affairs. Here Desai depicts a Dalit man viciously raping and murdering a defenseless old Brahmin woman. In doing so, she marks "the lower caste as the predatory male who becomes the legitimate target of 'feminist' rage" (Tharu and Niranjana 1999, 505).[12] In contrast, in 1992 a village level-worker *(sathin)* of the Indian government's Women's Development Programme was raped by two men in Bhateri village, Rajasthan, because she had reported their intention to hold a child-marriage to the district authorities. But, after the rape, the authorities colluded with the family and the district court judge decided against the *sathin* on the grounds that "upper-caste men would not even touch, let alone rape, a lower-caste woman" (N. Menon 2000, 82–83) and certainly not in the presence of her husband (John 1999, 116; A. Rao 1999, 243–244).

The money from fines against the witch or from the witch's land is taken by the *jangaru* (the witch doctor) who is the one who identifies the witch and the remainder is spent on alcohol and food. After ruling upper-caste village men in traditional councils put women on trial for sexual offenses of various kinds, or for performing witchcraft, there is a brutal misogynist practice of then punishing the women by stripping them and forcing them to march through the streets.[13] Most of the time it is because these women, usually widows without male family members to protect them, own property that these men covet. Their purpose in persecuting these women is to force them out of their property and the village, move them into bonded labor, and/or kill them in order to appropriate their property for themselves (A. Basu 1992, 144; Kishwar 1999, 40, 90–91; Rajan 1999, 343).[14] After indicting all those greedy monsters who take advantage of superstition for their own ends, Devi makes direct and specific suggestions for ending this form of persecution against women such as providing education, health facilities, timely intervention, or even prevention by the police who in most cases stand by detached from all proceedings—or worse, as we have seen.

Devi also appeals to the tribals themselves to change their ways in the most passionate language in the book, in the passage from which the title *Dust on the Road* is taken. She implores the tribals, especially the "privileged" ones, to ask themselves about whether their culture will be able to advance if they continue the practice of "witch-cults." The way things are going now, the tribals are "being destroyed, floating away . . . burning like red coals. . . . In the darkness of a dust-storm they are walking like ghostly slaves, walking behind the contractors, agents and touts, going to their end. They are being blown away like dust kicked up on the road . . . losing their lives, nationhood, language, and culture, identity—all that there is to lose" ([1997] 2000, 179).

Whenever Devi speaks of injustices by groups, she displays scarcely controlled rage. When she speaks of India itself directly she goes beyond that—to a heightened degree of impressive eloquence:

> India is still languishing in the mire of underdevelopment and antiquated feudal land relations. . . . In the real India there is lack of drinking water and water for irrigation. In the real India famine continuously stalks the countryside. . . . India is the land of massacres. . . . And there is a planned strategy to keep the real India in a state of perpetual deprivation. Millions are allocated for the development of the underdeveloped and tribal areas. If these areas attain real development, the wheel of the money game would come to a halt. ([1997] 2000, 174)

3

Outsiders Abroad

On Expatriation and Immigration

"You are believing that statue of liberty nonsense . . . ! This country has a thin veneer of hospitality. Underneath is a hard heart, turned against outsiders."
MARINA TAMAR BUDHOS

A rootless existence . . . forever the feeling of being outside. SUSHAM BEDI

Let me speak now, in this cold air, of the blisters of birth. My voice imprecise, my ignorance that of a perpetual immigrant, a woman with nowhere to lay her head. . . . I ask myself, am I a creature with no home, no nation? And if so, what new genus could I possibly be?
MEENA ALEXANDER

Anita Desai

Beginning with Anita Desai (1937–), Indian women's writing begins to focus on the fleeting quality of the present as filtered through the past, of the inevitability of change, the results of change and of displacement, often because of travel through time and space. Change is rarely willingly accepted by her major characters. They experience a feeling of being unwilling outsiders, of looking on at the culture into which they are born or wherever else they travel. As Desai has pointed out after living in the United States: "A screen has come between me and India. I can't simply ignore this experience abroad—it's too overwhelming, it demands to be dealt with, somehow grappled with. . . . [I feel] extremely isolated . . . removed to a society with which I have no natural link whatsoever" (quoted in S. Ray 2000, 128). Many Indian women authors have no allegiance to the way their society is ordered, especially in relation to societal issues such as caste and class, as well as to other issues such as gender roles and female sexuality. They never feel that they quite belong anywhere. They are uncomfortable, ill-at-ease wherever they are. Their sense of belonging, of a given situatedness in place has vanished, been severed by time's passage, or by expatriation. In Desai's *Clear Light of Day* (1980), Bimla remains in the crumbling family home taking care of her mentally deficient younger brother after the deaths of her parents and aunt, and after her older brother and younger sister have escaped. She says of both Old and New Delhi:

> Old Delhi does not change. It only decays . . . a great cemetery, every house a tomb. . . . *New* Delhi . . . is where things happen. . . . I never go. . . . And here . . . nothing happens at all. Whatever happened, happened long ago. . . . Here we are left rocking on the backwaters. . . . Anyone who isn't dull and grey goes away—to New Delhi, to England, to Canada, the Middle East. They don't come back. (1980, 5, emphasis the author's)

Except that she is not a nationalist, Desai's perspective on Old Delhi is similar to that of the "Indo-Anglian" writers whom Susie K. Tharu describes with unveiled contempt as distancing themselves or cut off from the reality of decaying cities and depleted, exploited countrysides:

> A note, I think, that marks nearly all Indo-Anglian writing today. Repulsed by the squalor and depravity they see around, a present reality that in no way matches the perfection of the recreated past, and disturbed, because for all their nationalistic fervour they are left clutching the bloated particulars of a decadent culture and remain as exiled as ever from the lives of the people, writer-intellectuals withdraw. They become cynical, engrossed in their interior landscapes and the oppressive lack of a future that defines their experience. Their work is proper, the themes small, their hands clean. The keynote is of disease, of graveyards inhabited by lizards, of backwardness, of decay. ([1989] 1999, 264)

Desai symbolically contrasts the New and the Old in Bimla's sister Tara's musings about the essential difference between herself and her husband and daughters: "She herself had been taught by her husband and by her daughters, to answer questions, to make statements, to be frank and to be precise. They would have none of these silences and shadows. Here things were left unsaid and undone. It was what they called 'Old Delhi decadence'"(1980, 13). Bimla and Tara are representative of many of Desai's characters in viewing their childhood as precious Edens lost forever despite their having had illusions of their world as secure and tranquil. They conceptualize time as a division between before and after some violent external event that ended their youth, the way they were, or by changes in relationships significant to them, or by a loved one's death, or Partition, or Mahatma Gandhi's, Indira Gandhi's, and Rajiv Gandhi's assassinations, or even by the Holocaust, as in Desai's *Baumgartner's Bombay* ([1988] 1990), which "aroused a great deal of curiosity and interest among Jewish readers" (S. Ray 2000, 127). The German-Jewish protagonist Hugo Baumgartner is the character who best represents this theme of displacement and loss. *Baumgartner's Bombay* is built around the technique of interlocking ironies. For example, Hugo's time during World War II in the British internment camp in which he is unjustly imprisoned paradoxically becomes the happiest in his life. Perhaps most ironic of all, Hugo is thrown into the camp because he is a German citizen. The English who run it are too stupid to realize the difference between a German and a German Jew and actually incarcerate the two groups together! This is like putting reptiles in with birds:

> They would see he had been arrested for no reason, being harmless, no enemy, merely a refugee from Nazi Germany who wished only to pursue his business interests in India. The papers were thumbed with expressions and gestures of rage and exasperation. "What am I to do then?" the man bawled when Baumgartner again protested at being labelled a German and "hostile". [*sic*] "Got a German passport, says you were born there—then what am I supposed to take you for, a bloomin' Indian?" . . . He retreated, baffled, wondering what magic word he might find that would release him from what was a monstrous mistake, or madness. . . . "They don't understand a thing," the small, sick-looking man with a beard told him, with bitter sympathy. "They don't even know there are German Jews and there are Nazi Germans and they are not exactly the same." ([1988] 1990, 106)

Sadly, and to his destruction, neither does Hugo understand this crucial difference. He cares for stray cats who symbolize adamant untamability. Human hospitality, concern, caretaking, nurturing, and compassion are irrelevant to their inherently savage, ferocious, and beastly nature. Desai describes Kurt, the German boy whom Hugo takes into his home as a human feral cat: "a bag of pale fur" that "might have been a cat," " a furred carcass before it disintegrated," and "not so different from a sick cat" ([1988] 1990, 12, 18, 143). Ironically, Hugo believes that his recognition of the derelict, drug-addicted hippie as a fellow German stems from instinct, the way one cat recognizes another. "He had sensed, he had smelt the German in him like a cat might smell another and know its history, its territory" ([1988] 1990, 21). But he is wrong. Kurt might be like an untamed stray cat, but he does not view his host as another cat, not even a tame cat. He views him as a mouse. Hugo's good deed, taking the homeless young German wanderer into his home, leads to Kurt's sighting and coveting the silver trophies Hugo and his deceased Indian partner had won at horse racing years ago: a brief time of happiness for Hugo. Yet it is with one of these trophies that Kurt murders Hugo, appropriately enough, in his sleep. For, in hosting Kurt, all Hugo's instincts had to be asleep.

Often Desai's characters are devastated and rendered inactive and ineffectual by seemingly irrational and sudden, violent change. But sometimes they embrace change, which, paradoxically can bring unexpected, indirect benefits, as happens with the boy Hari of *Village by the Sea* (1982b) after he leaves his tiny fishing village of Thul and goes to Bombay, where he survives and even learns a viable trade repairing watches. Faced with development and the building of a fertilizer factory that will replace his village and its timeless dependence on the sea and will obviously destroy the village's ecology and environmental purity, Hari plans to "give up" his "traditional way of living and learn a new way to suit the new environment that the factory will create at Thul so as to survive" (1982b, 155). Because Hari neither wants to fish nor farm, occupations that the arrival of the factory and the surrounding complexes will end forever, he plans to buy "some chickens, build chicken coops in my field, start a poultry farm, sell eggs in the village and chickens to the rich people who will come to Thul once the factory is built, and so we will live—for a while. Later I want to set up a watchmending shop" (1982b, 154–155).

No matter how Desai's characters perceive change and distance from their roots, it is these changes that change their perceptions of themselves and their world and that are usually depressing. Tara in *Clear Light of Day* escaped her home in Old Delhi where the quality of life appeared to her stagnant and unchanging by marrying a domineering, brusque, practical, can-do civil servant, currently an ambassador in the West who intimidates her and presumably has made her over into his image. But during Tara's visit to her ancestral home, she realizes that her husband has failed to make her over "into an active, organised woman" (1980, 21), that she has put on an act throughout her marriage. She has pretended to acquire and to prefer modernity, bustle, Westernization, to the traditional Indian way of life: "She had fooled Bakul into believing that she had acquired it, that he had shown her how to acquire it. But it was all dust thrown into his eyes, dust" (1980, 11–12).

Desai's multiple perspective can be traced to the double perspective initially offered by her sharply divergent parentage—a German mother and a Bengali Brahmin father. Western readers should be aware that Desai's major characters, such as Hari in *Village by the Sea* [1982b], a children's book, are insiders who critique what is happening in India where (traditional) culture and customs are disappearing, and being replaced by alien developments, generally technological. Desai also critiques Indians who have become outsiders, although born in India—expatriates who have chosen to live in the West and are no longer comfortable in India—like Bakul, the ambassador, and Tara his wife in *Clear Light of Day*. Tara, however, finds later on in life that she feels far more centered and at peace in her ancestral home in Old Delhi than anywhere else on earth. Desai also writes about outsiders who are literally outsiders because they are Western foreigners living in India. By this means, Desai cleverly offers readers acute and detailed insights into Indian culture as if through fresh eyes, while at the same time these European foreigners like Hugo Baumgartner have little to tell readers about their own supposed culture. This is also the case in *Journey to Ithaca* (1995), in which a European couple's experiences in India are far more real, detailed, and interesting than their experiences in Europe. Desai describes Indians as often contemptuous and disrespectful of foreigners, as Othering them, as in the case of Sofie, a former hippie, who is the German wife of an Italian member of an ashram. The Indian residents of the ashram manifest xenophobia based on their caste rules about purification and pollution, especially when it comes to bathing and eating. They force Sofie to wait in a line, sometimes for hours, just to get water. Once she only had a cup to fill whereas "the swami in front of her had a row of buckets and pots and jars" (1995, 76). Although Sofie kept repeating that she only has one item and finally puts her cup over his bucket at the tap, in a rage he grabs his bucket, pours the water over her feet, and shrieks "hysterically" that she has "polluted the water." Foreigners also are made to eat outside the dining rooms, their food served on leaves that were disposable so that what was left over could be easily thrown into the garbage and never used again. Thus the ashram's Hindu disciples could rest assured that nothing and no one had been polluted. Because she has not bothered to learn about Hindu customs and rituals, Sofie seems to have no clue as to what is going on. Actually, this same treatment is accorded not only to foreigners, but to other Indians of other castes, as Hyder makes clear in her description of a girls' school in Benares: "At meal times a dining-cloth was spread on the floor in a hall. A fat Brahmin cook trundled in, followed by his thin assistant who carried a brass pail full of curd. The chief Misra ladled out curd and poured it into the girls' brass cups from a great height so that he was not polluted, for the girls belonged to all manner of castes and creeds. Vegetarian food was served on banana leaves" (1999, 209).

Like the soulless young monster Kurt in *Baumgartner's Bombay,* Sofie and Matteo in *Journey to Ithaca* are among the thousands of Western hippies who overran India in the 1970s and 1980s. Desai has nothing but contempt for them, although she is ambivalent about their gurus. In contrast, Jhabvala devotes whole books to the duping and fleecing of gullible Westerners, especially Americans, in India and abroad, by their corrupt Indian gurus and their Indian hangers-on. Ameena Meer (1964–) also writes on this topic, but without Jhabvala's powerful irony and cynicism. In "I Want To Give You Devotion," Meer's narrator is the daughter of a wildly popular guru, "Ma-ji," whom she describes as riding "on the acceptance of most Americans that Indians had an innate knowledge of spirituality by virtue of their race" (1996, 92). Ma-Ji's ultimate fate is like Bhagwan Rajneesh's, who became enormously wealthy in the United States in the 1970s and 1980s and was ultimately deported.

One of Gita Mehta's characters sums up her perspective, much like Jhabvala's and Meer's, that the hippies are naive, ignorant, spiritual tourists and that Indians cynically take advantage of their gullibility and longing for spiritual enlightenment: "I think they should definitely have a quality control on gurus. A lot of my friends have gone mad in India"([1979] 1991, 18). In her introduction to *Karma Cola* and elsewhere, she writes:

> [T]hose days seem now an age of such innocence—when global escapism masquerading as spiritual hunger resulted at worst in individual madness, at best in a hard-won awareness that the benediction of jet-stream gurus was seldom more than skywriting, and that the mystic East, given half a chance, could teach the West a thing or two about materialism. . . . The trick to being a successful guru is to be an Indian, but to surround yourself with increasing numbers of non-Indians. If this is impossible, then separate your Indian followers from your Western followers in mutually exclusive camps. That way, one group accepts the orgies of self-indulgence as revealed mysticism and the other group feels superior for not having been invited to attend. . . . [Their gurus] were demanding not only complete and unquestioning obedience to their commands, but . . . also extracted payment for that privilege. And what inspired tithing. The price of abject servility could vary from paying a percentage of your income to handing over your whole stash. No rebates. No refunds. No questions. An outstanding example of Taxation Without Representation. Surely such a takeover owed its success to a general debility in the host body. Or else to the rumor that the streets of India are lined with miracles. ([1979] 1991, x, 38, 45–46)

The hippie in *Baumgartner's Bombay* is much like Mehta's Westerners in India, whom an English doctor, on duty for only a month, had described as casualties, "diseased, suffering from malnutrition, or trapped in inarticulate nightmares . . . scum. What is the point of taking them back home where they can infect other people with their lies and their dirty habits? I sometimes wonder why we don't let them die here in India, where it doesn't matter" ([1979] 1991, 22).

Hugo himself originally comes to India from Germany on business and never leaves because of World War II. He loses both parents to the Holocaust. His father commits suicide after the Nazis take his business and after a session with the Gestapo. His gentle, adored mother, the love of Hugo's life, disappears forever after being sent to a concentration camp. In the beginning of his life in Germany, Hugo is depicted as a child ashamed of his Jewishness while Christmas is being celebrated by the Christian teacher and the other students. They are all completely oblivious to the existence of any other religious belief systems in the world:

> What was the same? The sense that he did not belong to the picture-book world of the fir tree, the gifts and the celebration? But no one had said that. Was it just that he sensed he did not belong to the radiant, the triumphant of the world? A strange sensation, surely, for a child. He could not understand it himself, or explain it. It baffled him and frightened him even—as if he realized that at that moment he had wilfully chosen to turn from the step up and taken the step down. (1990, 36–37)

Desai here describes the Jewish boy's sense of himself as an outsider at Christmas by virtue of his religious and ethnic difference with the Christian Germans, and that this sense of himself is accompanied by a sense of being a failure. In reality, do Muslims or Hindus or Buddhists or Jews feel this way at Christmas? Most members of these religious groups have internalized our culture's festivals, rituals, belief systems, and customs inscribed into our psyches from birth. These buffers—of personal and group identification and affiliation—distance us in relation to *our others*. This is the way the Jews in *Bombay Time* (2001) by Thrity Umrigar (?-) are depicted—as comfortable in their Jewish difference while surrounded by Indians—Hindus, Muslims, Parsi, and others. When their would-be Parsi son-in-law brings them a Christmas gift every Christmas morning, "Abe and Emma, as gracious as ever," invite him in for tea. He always finds their apartment

> Bereft of a Christmas tree. It never occurred to him to question it. Soli knew all about Christmas trees and Santa Claus and mistletoe from the books he had read as a child. But he knew nothing about Judaism, and to him, Jews were just another kind of Christians. And Abe and Emma, touched as they were by Soli's annual gift, never had the heart to tell him that in some parts of the world, his innocent gesture would be enough to ignite a neighborhood. ([1988] 1990, 145)

Similarly, in *Goja* (2000) Namjoshi records that while she attended graduate school in the United States she was invited to an American friend's home for a weekend. The ethnocentric parents suggested that she call her family in India because it was Thanksgiving. After she informed them that Indians "didn't celebrate Thanksgiving," they were "hurt and puzzled and a little disapproving" (2000, 73).[1] Enraged, Namjoshi rightly defines their response as "wilful, unprocessed, unameliorated ignorance" and "stupidity," a luxury that is only possible as "a function of power. The powerful are stupid" (2000, 74), are guilty of "complacent ignorance" (Minh-ha 1989, 80).

Does not inculcation into their own religion and their own culture insulate, numb, distance, and protect most Indian children from such envious feelings as Hugo presumably has for Christians celebrating Christmas? Furthermore, after what happened to Jews in World War II and after Hugo's personal experience with Germans, no Jew born in Hugo's generation and still alive would be capable of being in the company of a German without acute discomfort, without the urge to run away, let alone bring one home. It is inconceivable to any such Jew that Hugo could bring himself to overcome his "revulsion" against the Aryan Kurt and extend hospitality to him. The memory of the decimation of our people is still too fresh, too strong in the Jewish generation alive during the Holocaust. What Desai is claiming as possible for Hugo to do is tantamount to imagining a family member of one of those who perished in the World Trade Center on September 11, 2001, or any of their immediate descendants, as capable in their lifetime of enduring the presence of, feeling kindly toward, or entertaining overnight in their home, a member of Al Qaeda.

Be this as it may, Desai is the first Indian woman writer who consciously illustrates the feelings in both her male and female characters of "the duality of belonging" (Islam 1996, 89), of not belonging at all, of homelessness, and of all the variations within that paradigm. She is the mistress of depicting Indians alienated in India; of depicting alienated outsiders from within—usually Indian women—of depicting alienated insiders without, as when Indians become expatriates, and/or return to India for visits, like Tara and Bakul; of depicting the feelings of outsiders who remain outside in India, as when foreigners from the West, like Hugo Baumgartner and his friend Sophie, settle in India.

Bapsi Sidhwa

An American Brat (1993) by Bapsi Sidhwa (1938–) is a delightful novel about a young Muslim heroine from Lahore, Pakistan, who comes to the United States, and her adventures and misadventures in the United States, which change her forever. Early on, Feroza visits the Port Authority bus terminal in Manhattan for the first time. She was used to filth and bad smells back home. But this filth, this bad smell "of vomit and alcoholic belches, of neglected old age and sickness, of drugged exhalations and the malodorous ferment of other substances she could not decipher" was something "alien" to her, something that symbolized for her the unfeeling quality of the wealthy nation that permitted "such savage neglect" (1993, 81). She rushes out of the building and vomits.

On the other hand, she apostrophizes "the enchantments of the First World" (1993, 103) in great contrast to common experiences at home. Phones work, water runs reliably, and electricity never breaks down or needs hours of "load shedding" every day. But Feroza continues to waver back and forth, next taking a negative note:

> Nevertheless, the schizophrenia she perceived at the core of America's relationship to its own citizens and to those in poor countries like hers continued to disturb her. She eventually came to the conclusion that it troubled her because America was so consummately rich and powerful, and the inconsistencies of its dual standards, the injustices it perpetuated, were so cynical and so brazen. Not that Pakistan or other countries were paragons, but then no one expected any better of Pakistan—it laid no claim as the leader of nations, the grand arbiter of justice and human rights. (1993, 172)

After some time, however, Feroza is grateful for no longer having to witness the terrible poverty, inequities, and oppression that she was powerless to ease in

Pakistan, such as the punishing of rape victims, and fundamentalists pressuring for more Islamic laws to be introduced. She realizes that if she returns to Lahore, the sense of "freedom" she experiences in the United States, the freedom to control her own life that she now believes is crucial to her to have as a woman, would immediately end. Feroza enjoys being anonymous, having her privacy, with no one interfering in her life. If she wants to, she can live however she pleases, in contrast to the wasteful demands on her time, the endless intrusions on her privacy in the fishbowl of Lahore. For these reasons, Feroza decides to remain in the United States after she completes her education. Furthermore, she finds benefits in technology that relate to her privileged, upper-class life in Lahore. Having servants, surrounded by servants, the responsibility of overseeing servants, all subtract from the time that in the West technological "gadgets" give her. Technology enables its user to be "sufficient unto one's self without the necessity of intrusive human contact" (1993, 312–313). The rest of the "jam-packed and impoverished" world might criticize the West as dehumanizing, as diminishing family values and "human contact" because of its consumerism, commericalism, reliance on technological gadgetry, and valorization of individualism and "privacy." But the rest of the world is hypocritical because it actually longs for all these things.

Guddo in *The Fire Sacrifice* becomes hopeless about the perpetuation of Indian rituals in the United States, where they are so irrelevant that they become merely rituals without meaning. They will become "neither Indian nor American" and the immigrant life "a rootless existence . . . forever the feeling of being outside" ([1989] 1993, 74). What Guddo mourns about Indian immigrant women's sense of rootlessness, of belonging nowhere, their insecure, fragile sense of self-worth as women originated in their treatment as outsiders in India. Should they return to India, they fear experiencing "rejection and nonrecognition" (Bhattacharjee 1997, 323) there as well as everywhere else, not least of all in the West. Sidhwa, Mukherjee Bedi, and Divakaruni agree with Bedi on the meaning of immigration. In the poem "We the Indian Women in America" (1996), Divakaruni reveals the Indian woman immigrant's predicament, the realization, with mixed feelings, that she/Indian women cannot return to India. On the one hand, these women are filled with nostalgic memories of houses of female relatives, servants, and neighbors that they did not realize they would miss so much when they left India. Their hearts were filled "with dreams of instant riches, Hollywood, or millionaire husbands." On the other hand, they have learned invaluable lessons in America: "to stand straighter, / speak up for what we want" because now they realize, like Feroza, that in this country "we can have it all, and are ready / to fight for it" (1993, 269, 270). This is why many Indian women cannot return to India permanently. They would have far more difficulty, it would be virtually impossible to act that way back home with impunity.

Bharati Mukherjee

Born in Calcutta, Bharati Mukherjee (1940–) was the privileged daughter of a brilliant pharmaceutical chemist who was always as supportive of her as was humanly possible, to the point of longing for her to win the Nobel Prize for Literature and requesting her to aim for it. In 1986, his daughter did receive the National Book Critics Circle Award for Fiction for *The Middleman and Other Stories*. Three years younger than Desai, Mukherjee's goals, aims, themes, methods, and especially her intention to "astonish, even to shock" ([1977] 1995, 299) are very like the more stylistically restrained Desai's. Mukherjee, like Desai, writes of insiders who are on the outside in India, as well as outsiders when they are outside India, and of Indians, especially women, who emigrate to the West from India. Mukherjee, like Desai, writes about India from the perspective of being an outsider in India and also writes about the West from being an outsider in the West.

After living in England and the United States, Mukherjee moved to Canada with her Canadian husband Clark Blaise and became a Canadian citizen. But she found Canada too difficult to bear in terms of its racism and sexism and was herself racially harassed in ways she had always hitherto associated only with the southern United States. In Canada, Mukherjee was forced to move to a back seat on a bus, refused service in stores, and was the object of racial epithets in a subway station. Similarly, even though she has chosen to remain in India, Kishwar complains that whenever she travels abroad, specifically in the West, she frequently experiences "racial prejudice and cultural arrogance" (1999, 251). As for Mukherjee, she returned to the United States for good in 1986. In "A Conversation with Bharati Mukherjee: A Reader's Guide" at the end of her novel *Leave It to Me* (1997), Mukherjee reveals that as a result of her own experiences in the United States she has focused her work on exploring "the making of New Americans and the consequent two-way transformation of America" (n.p.). From the beginning of her writing career, Mukherjee's Indian immigrant characters reflect her own feelings of displacement and alienation from India and of her "[n]ostalgia, for the way we had once been, and for the way the entire country had been" ([1977] 1995, 295), a feeling she fought. These mixed feelings about India coexist with her mixed feelings toward her host countries. One of her characters states that all Americans are emotionally crippled because they are only concerned with trivial things like their own trivial little relationships. Americans do not concern themselves about whether or not they are hurting the rest of the world. Another character states that the West is a place you would like to go for a vacation but not to remain. Yet another character agrees because she wouldn't want to be made to feel forever foreign (1988, 83). Mukherjee—and for the same reasons, and equally ironically—Diane Mehta (?–) both praises and criticizes her host country, indicating her loneliness, her torn and divided condition. Mehta asks herself whether she misses the monsoons, her "mother's hair in wet braids, sandalwood-scented" and simultaneously wonders ruefully what she really pledged herself to when she became a citizen of the United States: "Did you pledge allegiance to lawns and fences / better lives for us; the best western education?" where neighbors become substitutes for "extended families" and "freedom expires" (1996, 276).

In Mukherjee's *Wife* (1975), before Dimples leaves India, she queries a friend as to whether the dreaded feeling of foreignness would be assuaged if she arrived as "an immigrant." Her friend's response resolves Dimples' doubt. She could consider herself an immigrant all she liked, but what she will always be to the Americans "is a *resident alien*" (1975, 46, emphasis the author's). Burton cites an observer in England in the 1960s about the immigration "problem." This observer argues that West Indians or Asians do not become English by virtue of being born in England. They become citizens by law, but remain West Indian or Asian. The same is true for Hugo Baumgartner who remained a Jew, although he thought of himself only as a German citizen in India, and for Mariam Rubin in Umrigar's *Bombay Time* (2001) who was born and raised in Bombay. After Partition in 1947 and the formation of Israel in 1948, Rubin migrates to Israel with her family rather than remain with her beloved fiancé in India because of the mistake of Jews like Hugo in identifying with their host countries: "We were always raised to think of ourselves as Bombayites first, but . . . that's a mistake. That's how Hitler won . . . because the Jews thought of themselves as Germans, even when nobody else did. There is a new country being built for Jews and by Jews. I want to be part of it" (2001, 159). The same is true for Indian women writers who travel or immigrate to the West. Whether they retain their Indian citizenship or become citizens of other countries, they remain Indian so far as the Western population is concerned: "People on the move are under surveillance and their access to unmarked identities—which are most often apparently unfragmented national identities—is regulated" (Burton 1998, 191). Because of her unceasing perception of being Other as a woman in India and as an Indian woman writer in the West, Mukherjee always experiences anxiety in relation to her "visibility as a stereotype . . . [t]he pain and absurdity of . . . 'Third World art' and exile among the former colonizers; the tolerant incomprehension of hosts, the absolute impossibility of ever having a home, a *desh*" ([1977] 1995, 296–297).

After her return in 1973 to India for a year with her husband and children, Mukherjee recorded that she became a paradox to her birth culture. She was treated like an "honorary male" because she was "a career person." As such, she was granted the right of having independent thinking without being the object of disapproval in sharp contrast to her Bengali friends who were imprisoned in a narrow and provincial world of women whose only activities were "gossip and speculation" and whose permitted occupations were volunteering for charity work and teaching. The difference, Mukherjee concluded, between Indian women who had remained in India and Indian women who became emigrés was that the Indian women were miserable because they felt like prisoners in their constraining environment. This situation does not seem to have changed since Satthianadhan in *Saguna* had complained more than one hundred years earlier about assimilated Indian men and her classmates' parents who kept young girls superficial, silly, foolish, and ignorant by denying them an education. For this reason, the girls' "impoverished stunted, starved minds" provided them no source of nourishment other than "vain silly thoughts." And yet these girls "are the daughters of India whose lot is considered as not needing any improvement by many of my countrymen who are highly cultured and who are supposed to have benefited by Western civilization" ([1887–1888] 1998, 37). Likewise, Sidhwa's young Pakistani heroine Feroza in *American Brat* (1993) refuses to settle down anywhere "without a career." She wants to be independent of any future husband, not at at his "mercy." She believes that if she works at a meaningful profession "he will respect me more." The magic word to Feroza's mother is "respect" because she feels that although she has not been educated, her husband would not dare to disrespect her. Feroza then cuts to the bottom line, which had been Mukherjee's also; that traditional women who have never worked can never know what a thrill it is to make money themselves and to spend it as they wish.

Mukherjee's visit to India marked the turning point in her life in terms of her previous attitude toward herself as an "exile." Instead, after her visit she now views herself as an immigrant in the West. She would never again fantasy or exaggerate about India. She would consider herself in future visits as just "another tourist" who is "knowledgeable . . . but desolate" ([1977] 1995, 297). In future she would visit Calcutta, her birthplace, with her Canadian husband and two sons, much as Vandana Khanna (?–), a young poet who has lived most of her life in the United States visits India: "Like we didn't belong, a place I should call home / but as foreign to me as to you" (1999, 25).

Mukherjee feels happy about no longer living in India because she no longer has to assume "the crippling prudence that comes with living too close to imminent disasters" (1995, 296). In view of the events in New York and elsewhere in the United States on September 11, 2001, Mukherjee's rationale for giving up her Indian citizenship proves ironic. There is nowhere on earth where one can avoid such "crippling prudence," not even in the United States where Mukherjee, like so many millions of Americans, always believed that crippling prudence would never be necessary to exercise. One of Mukherjee's contributions throughout her career as an Outsider observer of American life has been her acute perception *until* September 11, 2001 that Americans were privileged to live in a kind of smug and secure assumption that the next day would be the same as the previous one and that new immigrants envied American certainty and wanted to share in it. Americans were oblivious to the fact that most new immigrants live always with terrible recent memories of sudden traumatic incidents continually repeated, of realized threats to their survival and that of their friends and families. In contrast to Americans, the conditions of new immigrants' lives seemed always contingent, hanging like threads. All this changed, of course, for Americans on September 11, 2001. For the first time in their lives, Americans forever lost their complacent sense of security when they experienced what recent immigrants have lived through before coming to the United States.

In her Epilogue to *Days and Nights in Calcutta* ([1977] 1995), Mukherjee revealed that she still abided by her 1973 illumination that her return to India had ended a cycle of nostalgia for her about India and about whether to leave home to live permanently in another country. She had begun a new cycle in which she would go from "exile to settler and claimant." Her most pressing subject would become that of successfully making a home in the "strange landscape" of the West, where a female of color was always surrounded by hostility when she was not invisible. After this visit, Mukherjee could admit to herself at last that it was impossible for her to return to India. Although she was now a member of a "despised minority" in a racist culture, she realized that she was unwilling to trade in "decision-making rights" that she enjoyed in the West for the luxurious, dignified life style of privilege that she and her friends enjoyed in India but had not earned. Like Namjoshi, who was a "victimizer" in India, Mukherjee was transformed into a "victim" in the West and, as a result, became "a relentless, fearless champion of freedom" ([1977] 1995, 302). However, this realization that "minority discourse empowered me rather than enfeebled me" took fifteen years for Mukherjee to make in the form of a final choice: to cross the border because she wished to do so; to experience a "homeland" that she herself had chosen and "not inherited" ([1977] 1995, 303). She no longer thinks of herself as an outsider outside, as "an Indian stuck in an alien country." She has traveled and lived in many places, but she now feels "emotionally and intellectually most at home in the United States" (1997, n.p.). For Mukherjee and many others of her generation, the salient question remains as to what makes an Indian woman who feels like an outsider in the West in so many ways—in terms of culture, race, religion, and gender—no longer feel outside, no longer need or want to "assimilate," to become "a *pukka* American" (Mukherjee 1985, 147). For Mukherjee, this moment finally came when she felt that she was an American because she had chosen to be an American.

Moving beyond Desai in this regard, Mukherjee focuses with great brilliance and clarity on the responses of Indian women to their host countries, on the responses of their host countries to them, and on the impact of each on the other. In the beginning, Mukherjee, like Desai, focused on Indians who chose to become expatriates, permanent residents abroad. In this stage, Mukherjee "tried to explore state-of-the art expatriation . . . attempting a mordant and self-protective irony in describing my characters' pain. Irony promised both detachment from, and superiority over, those well-bred colonials, much like myself, adrift in the new world, wondering if they would ever belong" (1985, xiv). Later, Mukherjee's characters make the "movement away from the aloofness of expatriation, to the exuberance of immigration": what the filmmaker Rajini Srikanth felt when she immigrated to the United States as a "chaotic nineteen-year-old . . . wondering if the confusion I was feeling was pleasurable or painful intoxication and only dimly suspecting that it was perhaps both and always would be" (1996, 23).

Mukherjee makes an interesting distinction between expatriates and immigrants. What she describes about her Indian immigrant characters in *Darkness*—their "broken identities and discarded languages, and the will to bond oneself to a new community, against the ever-present fear of failure and betrayal" (1985, xv)—is quite different from how she describes expatriates. The latter continue to "keep looking for signs," keep waiting, "surrendering little bits of a reluctant self every year, clutching the souvenirs of an ever-retreating past," and as a result "never belong anywhere" (1985, xiv). More than ten years later, Anannya Battacharjee added another distinction between the two states. Both involve "a deferring of commitment, an anguish over allegiances." The expatriate is a "deferred, but prospective" immigrant while for the immigrant returning to one's homeland "always remains a distant possibility" (1998, 165). Mukherjee does not see herself like Alexander who sees her "Indianness as a fragile identity to be preserved against being" obliterated . . . and "cracked by multiple migrations. Uprooted so many times she can connect nothing with nothing . . . writing in search of a homeland . . . no home, no fixed address, no shelter . . . a nowhere creature" (1993, 3, 4, 30). Rather, Mukherjee is positive about being "a nowhere creature" as a result of her multiple migrations. She celebrates herself "as a set of fluid identities" and her "Indianness as a metaphor, a particular way of partially comprehending the world" (1985, xv). Like Mukherjee, Alexander and other Indian immigrants find the United States problematic, eventually deciding to become "what I am—face the unbidden force of an ethnicity, here, now" (1993, 2000).

In a short story by Divakaruni ironically entitled "Silver Pavements, Golden Roofs" in *Arranged Marriage* (1995), a young woman leaves India to live with her aunt and uncle in Chicago. Her uncle is embittered because he has lost his business and been assaulted and scarred physically and emotionally by racists: "The Americans hate us. They're always putting us down because we're dark-skinned foreigners, *kala admi*. Blaming us for the damn economy, for taking away their jobs. You'll see it for yourself soon enough" (1995, 43), and Jayanti (the younger) does. Out on a walk, her aunt, the proud and elegant "Jayanti Ganguli, daughter of the Bhavanipur Gangulis" (1995, 51) is called "Nigger" over and over again by a gang of young boys who throw slush on their coats. "Can't they *see* that I'm not black at all but an Indian girl of good family?" (1995, 43) Jayanti (the younger) demands in shock and outrage, a query that exposes her as being as racist as the boys. Alexander shares

Jayanti's and her husband's bitterness and rage against angry whites. But, for her, these feelings of being "a special displacement, an exile" include Asians and blacks in packed cities as well as Indian immigrants who experience being stoned and murdered, "who live in fear of the Dot-Buster skinheads" (1993, 175), who are forced to wear Western clothes for fear of losing their jobs.

As Mukherjee began to realize herself living as an immigrant to the United States, her writing began to focus more and more on the topic of immigration to North America. Mukherjee's character Tara in *The Tiger's Daughter* (1971) is an expatriate, the state the author was in herself when she visited India after an absence of eight years. In this early novel, Mukherjee begins the movement outward that could only have been written by an Indian expatriate writer still coming to terms with all that she had left behind her. Tara, the Tiger's twenty-two-year-old daughter of privilege, returns to Bombay from the United States after a seven-year absence to study at Vassar, during which time she had suddenly married an American. For most of the seven years, she had yearned to return to India. Her relatives meet her at the airport. On the way to their apartment in the car, becoming aware that she has changed, they beg Tara to promise to shut her eyes "to everything terrible in India" and close her nostrils to its "smell." What bothers Tara most, however—and Mukherjee emphasizes this by making it the running thread in the book—are the disruptions to the life style of the upper-class Bengali Brahmins. For Tara, her father, the Bengal Tiger, symbolizes this group and reflects her fears for them. She likens him to "a pillar supporting a balcony that had long outlived its beauty and its functions" (1971, 30). Here Mukherjee, like Desai in *Clear Light of Day,* is conveying the fear and the terror of sudden death at the hands of rioters around every corner during the emergency declared by Indira Gandhi when she was prime minister.

Tara travels to Calcutta by train to be with her parents, thus shocking her Bombay relatives because she travels in a compartment with men, contrary to the custom that women should never be alone with them. This decision indeed turns out to have disastrous implications for Tara because, while traveling, she meets "a National Personage" with a face like a monkey who is spiderlike. In keeping with the analogy of a spider and a fly, the "National Personage" eventually rapes her, once again because she makes a disastrous decision to allow her maid to leave her alone with him.

The outsider within, Tara reminisces about New York where she is the outsider outside, an observer from another planet. To her, New York is Other, "exotic," but still "a gruesome nightmare" like Calcutta. In India, after Partition, refugees from East Bengal and Tibet poured into Calcutta. Riots broke out. Owners of businesses and factories closed them and fled. Students rioted over the shortage of rice,[2] or because of difficult exams, housewives could not make ends meet, makers of sweet meats committed suicide because of the lack of sugar, and *zamindars* were tortured and murdered. In New York where Tara is living with her husband, police accompanied by dogs prowled the subways and she constantly fears being mugged and going down side streets at night where young women like herself were stabbed and murdered, students rioted over the war in Vietnam, and people complained about "pollution."

In Sidhwa's *An American Brat* (1993), when Feroza attempts to talk to her friends in Lahore, Pakistan about conditions in the United States for blacks and Hispanics—including poverty and scarcity of jobs—they, too, like Tara's friends in Calcutta, India, refuse to identify with people in a wealthy country so far from theirs that had never been devastated by war. In its greed, it used up one quarter of the resources of the planet. Meanwhile, it added pollution to the air and water with nuclear testing and "poisonous pesticides that could serve as well to obliterate Third World pests like themselves" (1993, 238). Feroza understands how they feel. The local filth and poverty were like a cancer to which American poverty seemed comparatively minimal. Still, poverty is poverty, Feroza concludes. To her Pakistani friends, however, conditions in a Harlem ghetto where residents took for granted reliably running water, electricity, refrigerators, and cars could not be compared to "the rag-and-tin lean-tos [of Lahore] infested, stinking . . . without bathrooms or electricity" (1993, 238, 239).

During a Sunday picnic on the grounds of her father's factory, once the site of a beautiful mansion, Tara grieves over what the mansion has become because of industrial pollution of the environment. Across the lovely landscaping, beyond the elegant pond, chimney stacks were vomiting fiery fumes but the only pollution her group was concerned about in Calcutta was "caste pollution" (1971, 41). Jasmine, the heroine of *Jasmine* (1991), complains even more strongly—about the United States. The first thing she sees on the horizon when she reaches Florida by boat are a nuclear plant's cones with smoke rising from them. As she wades to shore, Jasmine passes what she sarcastically calls "Eden's waste"—bottles, fruit, wet boards and boxes, opened plastic garbage bags. Like Devi, Mukherjee in *Jasmine* also excoriates opportunistic, exploitative capitalist land-grabbing schemes in the United States with deft ironic use of chillingly heartless Americanisms. In describing an insensitive plan for adapting a bankrupt neighbor's farm into a golf course replete with all the amenities, Jasmine adds sarcastically that she is unsure about what plans the buyers would have with the existing pig shelter and its pile "of night soil" (1991, 8–9). She then remarks that she is gradually growing used to the continual transformation and fluidity of American character and American landscape, only occasionally feeling nauseous.

When accused by an aunt of despising Indian ways, Tara wonders when she had become an outsider in her own culture. Had it begun with her experiences at Vassar, with snow, with "new architecture, blonde girls, Protestant matrons, and Johnny Mathis" (1971, 45)? Or had it begun with her alienation from her childhood beliefs, from the Hindu religion which she had practiced with her mother in her mother's prayer room so many times in India in her childhood? When Mukherjee returned to India, as Tara does, she found that she could no longer forgive her culture; that what was terrible about Calcutta was that *"lives . . . have been sacrificed to notions of propriety and obedience"* ([1977] 1995, 217, emphasis mine). Tara is jokingly called an "Americanwali" by her aristocrat friends who are what she would have been like had she not received an outsider's perspective from having lived abroad. Calcutta, they tell her, is falling apart, turning Communist. *Goondahs* surround factories and allow no one to enter or to leave, which is what will happen later to her father's factory.[3] When one of Tara's friends, Pronob, imprisoned in this manner in his factory, requested water, the *goondahs* sent in a Coke bottle filled with urine, a word which he cannot use because in Westernized Calcutta any conversation about anything to do with bathrooms is prohibited. Tara's group sees no choice but to allow the hard-working, rich Marwaris, lower caste than Bengali Brahmins, to fight it out with the Communists. Tara views this group of young people with whom she had grown up as the last generation of the familiar, traditional Bengali Brahmin world and Pronob as its chief representative. He would like to see an end to factory unionization, but Tara is mainly concerned about what will happen to her group who had inherited their wealth and their weaknesses. Pronob refuses to immigrate because he refuses to be anonymous in New York like Tara. The anonymity would not adequately compensate him for its accompanying loss of the privileges and powers of his class and caste. Ironically, he loses both because he loses his life.

Tara had thought her marriage to an American was glamorous, that her friends would admire her for making such a marriage. Instead, they turn out to be racists, self-enclosed behind an inviolable fortress of arrogance that situates her as an outsider and bars her from reentry into their elite circle. They admire American movie stars and Englishmen, but disapprove of marriages such as Tara's with foreigners whom they call *mlecchas* (outcasts). As with Tara's friends, this characteristic is common to Hindus who look on everyone contemptuously "except their own *jati* (group) as *mleccha"* (Chatterjee 1993, 97). In their view, Tara's doing housework in New York like washing dishes, taking out garbage and cleaning bathtubs—in Calcutta, one servant was especially dedicated to the cleaning of bathrooms—were eroding all her fine and sensitive Bengali qualities. Tara's friends only want to hear about America the beautiful, about TV and cars, "fast foods and record players." They do not want to hear about poverty and student protests. New York was not at all like Calcutta, they insist. They keep plaguing her to teach them the latest sayings like "turn on" and "cool" (1971, 70). Dedicated only to trivia, Tara's friends neither know nor concern themselves about the protests, the riots, the revolutionary activity all around them. They spend their time sitting on the balcony of the Hotel Catelli fuming at the vulgar agitations. That is, until the rioters reach them one day when they attempt to leave the hotel. Leaving the car to defend an old

Brahmin man who is being beaten by them for being the very essence of the arrogant and unyielding old order that the rioters detest, Pronob, the old man's younger version, is himself brutally beaten to death by them. A similarly insensitve Brahmin like Pronob is the manager of a bank in Divakaruni's "The Maid Servant's Story" in *Arranged Marriage* (1995). When caught in a *michil* [march] with his brand-new "powder-blue Rolls Royce" he curses the union and those on strike for cutting off traffic, waving flags and screaming irrational "demands" that inconvenience "decent folks." He believes all the marchers should be jailed and taught "a lesson," as when the British ruled. The perspective of such snobbish, self-centered Brahmins and Pronob's fate at the hands of justifiably furious rioters reflects "a double bind" for India because it has not succeeded either in discarding the remains of "oppressive cultural traditions," nor has it succeeded in utilizing some of the more democratic institutions and traditions inherited from the British (Fernandes 1999, 134).

Tara does not relate to her friends' intolerant and obstinate caste perspective. In fact, she feels outrage at the sight of the homeless all around them and considers her friends callous for not sharing her feelings. She seriously considers an earlier return to New York than she had planned because of an incident that brings her such great pain that she feels hatred for Calcutta. Outside a fancy restaurant in which she had just dined with her friends, several children had eaten food off the sidewalk. Her friends had claimed that those children were used to such conditions, were strong, and not like them. What pained Tara even more than her friends' callousness was the fact that the children appeared overjoyed to be able to devour their filthy street treat. Eventually she comes to feel that the miserable conditions in Calcutta were beyond her capacities to improve. To engage in crusading for justice for these people was therefore pointless. Instead, it was best for her to do nothing, absorbing "all shocks as they came" (1971, 157).

Kamila Shamsie (1973–), a much younger Pakistani-born author who now lives in London and Karachi, describes her heroine in *Salt and Saffron* (2000) as coming to the same conclusion as Tara had more than twenty-five years previously: "It's not that we *can't* empathize with those on the lower rungs of society; the problem is that we *can*. We can imagine what it feels like to be so deprived, and it's our fear that we could, or our children could, end up like that which makes us keep our distance from the have-nots. Because at a distance we don't have to think about it" (2000, 183). In contrast, Jayapal suggests that one also can focus on making changes for the better. Both passive acceptance and activist views have validity, and the reality of the situation is incomplete without both. In America, the situation is such that it is easy to believe that individuals are independent and separate from one another and that if we are deserving we will experience good things in our lives. Not so in India, where it is clear and palpable that someone's enjoyment comes at the cost of another person's suffering.

Occasionally, Mukherjee likes to temper the terror and the tension in *The Tiger's Daughter* with ludicrous but hilarious satire. For example, Tara's friends become host families to Americans. Thinking that an exchange student named Washington McDowell had to be of Scottish ancestry, they insisted upon selecting him. McDowell turns out to be an African American basketball scholarship student at Berkeley, 6' 7" tall, with a foot-wide Afro, garbed in a colorful Indian shirt and beads and a peace symbol, and wearing jeans bearing messages. On the way from the airport, their car is waylaid by taunting rioters. McDowell gets out of the car, shakes hands with those gathered around him, and urges "you cats" to "get with it! I want some noise. I want some chanting, man. You guys gotta get a little class in your riots or else you ain't getting' nowhere." He then teaches them to raise their fists, to clench them and shout "Brown is Beautiful." The rioters applaud him hysterically. He then succeeds in deflecting the violence the rioters intend to perform on the car filled with his hosts and their friends, including Tara, by telling them to "cool it" (1971, 169, 171, 172). He was brought over from the United States in order to figure out how to aid and abet the rioters. True to his word, some weeks later he leaves his hosts and joins the rioters. Unfortunately, he is not with her when the book ends. Alone in a cab on the way to the airport for her return trip to New York, Tara is trapped once again in the midst of a riot. Helpless and unable to flee, her doom appears imminent.

In this early text, Mukherjee concentrates on observing the various differences that make it impossible for the immigrant and for those who remain in India to understand one another. Both sides are ignorant about each other. The Indians are only aware of superficial characteristics about the United States—its commercial and materialistic and technological wonders. Tara is called upon by her Bengali Brahmin group to be a bridge between the two cultures. When she tries to explain their "Other" to her group, however, whether their "Other" is the United States, or other castes and classes than their own, they are pathetically uncomprehending. They are unable to project their imaginations or their sense of humanity into other thinking, other ways. Mukherjee also sees India as being destroyed from within by heartless, crude, upstart politicians, like the "National Personage" who, after raping Tara, goes about business as usual. The rape symbolizes that this is what he is doing to his country, to all that is best and finest in India. Like Tara's friends, he is unfeeling, callous. Between the nouveau riche Mahwaris, like the corrupt "National Personage," the rioters, and the insulated, self-absorbed, traditional Bengali Brahmins, Tara is convinced that India is succumbing to chaos, anarchy, and destruction.

In "A Wife's Story " in Mukherjee's *The Middleman and Other Stories* (1988), an Indian woman has come to the United States on scholarship to get a Ph.D. Her mother was beaten by her mother-in-law when she dared to atttempt to take French at the Alliance Francaise and her grandmother, a wealthy *zamindar's* daughter, "was illiterate." This emigré is only one of a long line of female characters who make host countries abroad rather than their native India the background for their struggle to prove themselves. The emigré attends David Mamet's play *Glengarry Glen Ross,* in which Indians are insulted. Because of its communalism, racism, and antisocial perspective, this play would have caused riots in India. The audience never would have allowed the actors to continue. The actors would be put in prison, and the play would be banned. As for the American dream, she finds it tyrannical and frightening. First, Americans act as if immigrants of color are nonexistent, then invisible. Then they laugh at such immigrants, looking on them as objects of humor. Then they are disgusted by them. She is informed by Americans that when immigrants are insulted it means that they are accepted, more or less. In contrast, like Tara (and doubtless their creator), she can understand how both Indians and Americans feel. She would never have expanded her worldview had her mother not decided to study in the United States.

Jasmine, one of Mukherjee's later immigrant heroines, also comes to realize that Americans relentlessly Other difference. Immigrants must become a quick study, must become as "All-American" as they can. Relaxing their guard is never possible for them. They cannot wear Indian garb, nor reveal anything to anyone that would indicate that they were foreign. We have to "murder who we were so we can re-birth ourselves in the images of dreams. . . . Experience must be forgotten, or else it will kill" (1991, 25, 29). Here Fred Pfeil ignores or misreads Mukherjee's stark, bitter comments that reveal a highly critical perspective toward American cruelty and insensitivity toward immigrants to the point where immigrants must "re-birth" themselves into American look-alikes, American mimics, or else. Instead, Pfeil sees Mukherjee's bitter irony and sarcasm as jaunty acceptance, and Mukherjee as "the privileged, postcolonial emigré, for whom the pleasure of perpetual oscillation between dislocation and identification is as available as it is for her First World readership. . . . the Third World's appearance within the First supplies the pretext for the loss of any sense of stable identity, and the yielding to a giddy placelessness" (1994, 207–208).

In all her immigrant characters, Mukherjee speaks to those who, as Trinh Minh-ha describes herself, "understand the dehumanization of forced removal-relocation-reeducation-redefinition, the humiliation of having to falsify your own reality, your voice. . . . And often cannot say it. You try and keep on trying to unsay it, for if you don't, they will not fail to fill in the blanks on your behalf, and you will be said" (Minh-ha 1989, 80). And Lubna Chaudhry, like Mukherjee's characters and Minh-ha, follows "guerilla strategies . . . as an oppositional tactic to power structures" when oppressed. She practices what she calls "flexibility" as a crucial element of survival, taking up and discarding a variety of "identities for various lengths of time and in different contexts" (1998, 47).

Most other immigrants, even those as critical as Mukherjee and Minh-ha, are more positive about the United States. For example, Naheed Hasnat rejoices that because of the Constitution of the United States, she is allowed to practice Islam, a right denied her in India. Here she is permitted to "be a chameleon," to pick and choose as at a buffet what she considers the most desirable of the diverse "cultures and ideologies" that have gone into the construction of the United States (1998, 44). Anuradha M. Mitra also disagrees with the necessity for immigrants to "re-birth" themselves, or else. Her response to American rejection of difference is first anger and then pride in that difference: "I realize that my anger is mostly self-directed because I try so very hard to find my place. And I don't. Yet, in some un-defined corner of my self, I stand tall because of my difference" (1996, 5).

Mukherjee introduces the bizarre and violent suddenly into a text, directly and brutally, and her feminism is clearly integral to her work, which it permeates. She also routinely attempts to integrate or reference classics of Indian mythology and American literature into her works, always from a strongly feminist perspective. In the two works where she does this most successfully, *Wife* (1975) and *Jasmine* (1991), she integrates Indian mythology and her feminism into both characters and plots. Dimples and Jasmine combine the attributes of the goddess Kali, "the all-powerful mother goddess," both nurturing and violently destructive "in a feminist mould" (Kumar 1999, 357). As Rita DasGupta Sherma points out, females who identify "with powerful [goddess] models" can "subvert orthodox norms" whereas females who identify primarily with nurturing, "non-autonomous, submissive models" (2000, 26) tend to stay within cultural bounds.

By 1997, however, this formula no longer works for Mukherjee, even though she informs readers in a foreword that in *Leave It to Me* she will apply the story of the goddess Devi slaying the Buffalo Demon king into her novel, and her heroine Debi is obviously based on the nurturing, "all-forgiving" Mother Goddess Devi, who has several manifestations. One of them, Shakti, is wantonly sexual and the mother who not only creates life, but destroys it, as well (DasGupta and Das Das-gupta 1998, 116; DasGupta Sherma 2000, 24). Another manifestation of Devi is Durga who destroyed Mahisa [Mahishasura], the Buffalo Demon King because the gods could not do so. Her festival, the Durga Puja, is widely celebrated every autumn in Bengal (Ramusack 1999, 32). Similar to *Leave It to Me* is the sudden and shockingly brutal violence in *The Glassblower's Breath* ([1993] 1999) by Sunetra Gupta (1965–), which ends only after the heroine's husband without warning shoots three men in his kitchen who are involved with his wife in various ways, but without the mythological dimension of *Leave It to Me*. In *Jasmine,* Mukherjee's characters are more credibly motivated, better delineated, and more likeable, even when she describes horrendous actions similar to those in either *The Glassblower's Breath* or *Leave It to Me,* where I could find no sympathetic characters. Uniformly cynical, sleazy, repulsive, characters wisecrack and make sick(ening) jokes while performing disgusting, horrifying acts, including murder and beheading, as in the myths.

In this regard, Debi is not unlike Jasmine, who murders her rapist—with whom feminist readers around the world can identify—or Dimples of *Wife* who murders her husband in an act of quiet desperation/insanity/transformation into a *Virangana* or Kali because Amit has long refused to allow her free and full self-expression and constrains her entirely within the four walls of their apartment. Totally self-centered, insensitive, and demanding, Amit is following Indian tradition for husbands in never considering his wife's needs and desires, only *his,* and is preoccupied with *his* self-image. In control over his wife's wishes—"She needed his informal approval and his know-how for everything" (1975, 33)—he refuses to allow Dimples to leave the apartment, let alone go out to work. Had Amit been willing to moderate, to show some flexibility, Dimples would have adhered to the prescription that "[a] good Hindu wife had to maintain the pretense that her husband was supporting the family" (Badami 2001, 14). Instead, Amit makes all decisions about everything and leaves Dimples no room to express any opinion of her own, or have any self-expression, completely silencing his wife. Forcing his wife to "'unspeak' is also a species of silencing" (Spivak 1999, 429). At this stage, rather than reaching "the point when the censorship imposed by the family and society becomes [her] internal self-censorship" which would have resulted in "her final silence" (1999, 168), Dimples murders her husband, her censor. Here Mukherjee clearly advocates direct, violent retribution modeled on and inspired by the decisive and horrendous actions of the avenging goddess in her various manifestations against her oppressor enemies. Kishwar, however, who has experience with this situation in the course of her pioneering advocacy of women in domestic abuse and violence scenarios through *Manushi,* offers a less threatening solution for Dimples' predicament: "Unless women can struggle successfully against the bans imposed on their speaking against abuse that affects them most intimately, they are unlikely to have their voices heard on other important social and political matters or, for that matter, to act as full members of society They will remain socially and politically marginalized, thus facilitating their continuing subjugation" (1999, 168).

Indian children may delight in the clear binaries of good versus evil, can root for the goddess when she rises up against the powerful and destructive and cruel and murdering Buffalo Demon, as Mukherjee claims. But, unlike both Jasmine and Dimples, the character and actions of Debi in *Leave It to Me* are unconvincing, insufficiently motivated, and incomprehensible to Western readers. The mythology does not inform sufficiently. According to some accounts, the only way Durga (another manifestation of Devi/Kali) could kill the buffalo demon was to remove her clothes. "She stripped and within seconds of seeing her, Mahishasura's strength waned and he died under her sword" (U. Menon and Shweder 2000, 157). Durga then takes the form of Kali and rampages against everything alive in her path. But this mythological diminension is not evident in the final scene in which Debi's father, a mass murderer, based on a real-life, notorious mass murderer, escapes from prison. He then kills and beheads his wife's lover after murdering his wife, Debi's mother, who had informed on him to the police. Debi (at this point clearly in her Kali manifestation) then kills her father with a cleaver, after which there is a tidal wave. All this is terrifying, horrifying, and unspeakable because we believe in the reality of the scene, whereas its mythical properties are lacking for us or have insufficient resonance, unlike in the case of *Jasmine*.

By the end of the twentieth century, American-influenced greed, materialism, consumerism, and cynicism is so far-flung globally, so degraded, has become so meaningless, that perhaps Mukherjee could only attempt to give dignity and meaning to the sordid lives and actions of her characters by relating them to mythological characters who commit their brutal acts either in the cause of evil or good—except that no one is good in *Leave It to Me,* not even the heroine Debi. It is not for lack of trying on Mukherjee's part. From the very beginning of her career, she has always striven to present ample cause and motivation for justified violence on the part of her young Indian characters, always attempted to make readers identify with them. For example, Dimples' predicament in *Wife* (that of an Indian girl trained to become a traditional wife who immigrates to the United States with the husband arranged for her by her parents) is easily identifiable. For a long time, Dimples tries to love Amit, to fulfill her need for love and romance, a repetitive motif in Indian women writers' texts. Dimples is disappointed, frustrated, and feels like a prisoner in a cell with a husband to whom she cannot communicate. Vinita, another young Indian wife in Mukherjee's *Darkness* (1985) has the same revulsion toward her unromantic husband:

> Within reach, but not touching her, Sailen sleeps on his stomach. He is breathing through his mouth. She imagines his fleshy lips; they flap like rubber tires. But he is faithful and ambitious, so why then is she moved by an irresistible force to steal out of his bed in the haven of his expensive condominium, and run off into the alien American night where only shame and disaster await her? (1985, 153)

The cover of my copy of *Wife* shows a miserable young Indian woman in a cage to signify Dimples' predicament: first, as a girl child back home in India where her parents had dictated everything to her at every waking moment, and, second, with her husband in New York. Similarly, while simultaneously remembering the cage of an Indian woman's existence in India, Alexander describes her own experience in New York after her arrival. She wonders whether she is trapped inside a cage of some kind and then experiences a memory of a bride set afire with kerosene in Hyderabad because her dowry was not deemed sufficient "because a woman is nothing who cannot bring in money, property, new manhood" and because Hyderabad is "a city where women were raped in the communal riots, their veils shredded, mouths stuffed with stones" (1996a, 139). These constraints—what Alexander calls the tyrannical government, "the wheel of worlds into which a female body is cast"

(1996a, 142)—are what Mukherjee similarly defines as the overly inflexible and un-bending enforcement of "communal identity" as the sole permissible identity in India, its intolerance of any "individual quirkiness or rebellion" (1997, n.p.). As Krishnabhabini Das wrote one hundred years before *Wife* was published: "We too are human beings, and have eyes; / But we are blind and live in cages" (quoted in Grewal 1996, 169). And the situation has not changed.

Chief among a score of excellent works, the novel *Jasmine* (1991) is Mukherjee's most successful work. In her depiction of Indian and American customs, she com-bines the use of irony—both hilarious and tragic—with a strong feminist vision. Mukherjee also provides American readers with a new take on what the current gen-eration of immigrants from politically unstable, continually war-torn countries want: dullness, sameness, predictability from day to day. Her heroine Jasmine had been blessed in India with a wonderful husband whom she loved. She had married Prakash Vijh when he was twenty-four and she was fourteen without a dowry and for love. It was he who first taught her feminism and whose dream was to come to the United States to study in Florida and to found a business with her. Courageously defying custom, he forces her to call him by name, rather than to use pronouns in the traditional husband-worshiping way of wives, and refuses to allow her to get pregnant at fifteen. On the verge of their departure from India, he is murdered by members of the Khalsa Lions, a band of Sikh terrorists who demand their own "pure" state and an end to "all filth and idolatry" such as meat eating, tobacco smok-ing, drinking of alcohol, or the cutting of hair. Turbans must be worn at all times and women removed from public places. The leader of this group, Sukhwinder, goes further, calling every Hindu woman a whore and every Hindu man a rapist. He con-siders the wearing of a sari as "the sign" that the woman is a prostitute and that Hin-dus are all determined to commit genocide on the Sikhs whose only protector is Pa-kistan. One day, screaming "Prostitutes! Whores!," Sukhwinder throws a bomb into a sari shop where Jasmine and her husband are buying saris for her to wear in the United States. Prakash covers Jasmine's body with his and dies.

Previously, the Khalsa Lions had murdered Jasmine's teacher Masterji. After chopping off his beard and hair, they empty thirty bullets into him for not being a good enough Sikh. Masterji had wanted Jasmine to go on to higher education in contrast to most Hindu fathers such as Jasmine's, who is reluctantly willing to ac-cept her working as a bank clerk because in going out to work she will be in the presence of men unrelated to her whom she does not know. Jasmine goes far be-yond even this furthest stretch of his imagination to announce that she intends to be a doctor, and her father's response is to conclude that she has gone mad. Her grandmother, his mother, agrees, insisting that the madness must come from her daughter-in-law, Jasmine's supportive mother. As a result, the latter is beaten throughout the night. Nevertheless, she holds firm, and Jasmine is permitted to continue her schooling.

Mukherjee sees Jasmine as "innocent, curious," as embracing all she experiences, much of it bewildering, in "the New World." On her first day in the United States, having landed illegally in Florida, Jasmine is brutally raped in a deserted motel by Half-Face, a Vietnam veteran, now the captain of a fishing boat bringing illegal immigrants, including Jasmine, into the United States. He describes himself as "in the nigger-shipping biziness" and calls Asia "the armpit of the universe" (1991, 93, 99). Wandering away after murdering him, Jasmine meets Mrs. Gordon, who takes her in. Mrs. Gordon uses her home as a shelter before releasing illegal female immigrants into the American void. She trains them to never forget that if they act as if they are American—walking and talking like an American—then Americans will assume that they were born in the United States because Americans don't have the capacity to assume otherwise. Although Mrs. Gordon struck Jasmine and all those she rescued as the highest type of American, nevertheless she is later jailed because she would not identify "her contacts" or give out any information on the "army of illegal aliens" she had helped to enter welfare. When Mrs. Gordon becomes mortally ill, the government abrogates its charges of "contempt" against her and graciously permits her to die in her own home rather than in prison. A projected film of her life, perhaps starring Katharine Hepburn, is planned but then canceled because it lacked "the demographics." Americans were becoming frightened of as well as "positively hostile to illegals" (1991, 120, 121–122).

Later, in America, in the heartland—in Iowa—Jasmine finds that there are also extremist fanatics like the Khalsa Lions. The tattooed man who visits Jasmine is a member of the Aryan Nation Brotherhood. And there are Khalsa Lions in America, too. One day in a New York park, just as her employer is about to propose to Jasmine, she sees a hot-dog vendor in the distance. It is Sukhwinder, who knows that she is an illegal alien and is tracking her. Shortly after Jasmine arrived in New York, she was hired by Taylor and his wife as caregiver to their adopted daughter Duff. Jasmine fell in love with Taylor, a physics professor at Columbia University. He struck her at once as her ideal American, when, in the course of the interview, he smiles and jokes with her while serving her biscuits. Convinced that in Sukhwinder's attempt to reach and kill her, he will kill Taylor as well as Duff, Jasmine flees to Iowa because the little girl had been born there. Later Jasmine, although pregnant, suddenly leaves her lover Bud behind in Iowa. But she does not do so without providing Bud with another caretaker—his abandoned wife Karin who runs a suicide hot line and still loves him. He is now paralyzed in a wheelchair, requiring constant care after having been shot in the back by a berserk farmer in the erroneous belief that Bud, his banker, was the cause of the loss of his farm. Later, at a conference of bankers, a man comes up to Bud after he has presented a paper and tells him that when he shoots Bud he will kill, not cripple him, as Bud's previous assailant had done. He then tapes a pamphlet to Bud's chair titled "Jews Take Over Our Farmland" (1991, 140). Bud is believed to be Jewish because he is a banker.

Ultimately, the crucial issue for Jasmine in relation to the evil that Sukhwinder, the Khalsa Lions, and the skinheads represent is to accept the eternal coexistence of multiplicities of goodness and evil without either conquering the other, unlike Christians who attempt to stamp out evil *and* to forgive it (Humes 2000, 148). Jasmine's acceptance of evil is confusing to Westerners. As Mehta describes Westerners in India for spiritual reasons:

> The visitors do not have that profound Indian consolation of knowing that everything and every perception is a con, and worse, a self-induced con, a view enshrined in the Hindu concept of Maya. As a result, too many visitors take the masquerade as incontrovertible fact. The gurus, their Indian hosts and fathers, don't help them to acquire the tranquility that comes from the Oriental ability to see in a plethora of contradictions a literally mind-blowing affirmation. To go from the monomania of the West to the multimania of the East is a painful business. Like a sex change. ([1979] 1991, 35)

At the end of *Jasmine,* Mukherjee's heroine no longer wants to spend the rest of her life caregiving, caretaking, recipe giving, preserving food and lives. Instead, she wishes to experience life to the fullest, to achieve her own goals. Jasmine is going to express her love for Taylor sexually and with a passion that will be reciprocated by him, which no doubt reflects her creator's feminist demands in relationships with men. Jasmine simply will not settle any longer for nurturing and caretaking without passionate love and sexual fulfillment, as well. Instead of murdering Bud, as Dimples had murdered Amit, Jasmine leaves Bud, her disabled lover who wishes to marry her, whose love for her provides her with economic security—a home, food on the table, a decent life in an Iowa community. To him, she is the exotic, alien Other, dark, mysterious, inscrutable. The reason she leaves Bud is not because she chooses one man over another, although a life of caregiving is a good one, a noble one according to Jasmine. But, when confronted with the choice "between the promise of America and old-world dutifulness," Jasmine, a feminist version of Huckleberry Finn, lights out for the territory, for "Adventure, risk, transformation" (1991, 213–214), driving away with Taylor and Duff to a new life in California, "greedy with wants and reckless from hope" (1991, 214).

Sayantini DasGupta and Shamita Das Dasgupta, daughter and mother, claim that they differ from the generation following the first wave of immigrant feminist Indian women. As a result of patriarchs who run the Indian communities, the traditional notion of strong women emanating from the Indian myths "has been lost in the process of immigration and self re-creation" and therefore "for many Indian American women raised in the West, being 'Indian' and being 'feminist' are antithetical concepts" (1996a, 388). Nettled by Mukherjee's changing her protagonist's names in *Jasmine* from the names Joyoti to Jasmine to Jane to reflect her ever-increasing feminist feistiness of perspective, they angrily point out to readers that "Obviously, Mukherjee believes that only a 'Jane' could be a 'fighter and adapter,' as opposed to Jyoti, who is doomed to be the opposite" (1996a, 398, fn. 11). Moreover,

Jasmine claims that she owes the spark that first lit her feminist fire to an American role model, her employer, for whom she works as a caretaker. She admires this woman for her self-sufficiency and independence in leaving her first husband for another man when she falls out of love with him. Incensed by Mukherjee's crediting of Western feminism for Jasmine's growing feminism, DasGupta and Das Dasgupta tartly contend that Indian women immigrants did not need the Western feminist movement to free and emancipate them, although Indian American women are no longer influenced by Indian models of warrior women (*Viranganas*)—"the phallic feminine" (Hiltebeitel 2000, 20)—like the Rani of Jhansi or Indira Gandhi, or Rokeya Sakhawat Hossain, among others (DasGupta and Das Dasgupta 1996a, 390). Rinita Mazumdar disagrees with them, claiming that in Indian society the *Virangana* is still "a pervasive image that is widely accepted" (1998, 142). And does not Jasmine consciously turn herself into Kali after being raped? Doesn't she slit her tongue so that the blood drips down from it as in all the depictions of rampaging Kali and her bloodthirstiness before she despatches her white American rapist by stabbing him in his neck while he sleeps?

On the whole, however, DasGupta and Das Dasgupta are correct in arguing that Indian feminists do not need Western feminists to become feminist. Indian "cultural contexts" are just "as capacious and suffused with contestation" as are Western cultural contexts and Indians just as "often . . . criticize the very institutions they endorse" (Narayan 1997, 9). Even so, Narayan also cautions Indian feminist critics to remember that the term "Westernization" is nothing more than nationalist discursive attack strategy "of dismissal" and "delegitimation" (1997, 30, 36) deployed to squelch differing political perspectives such as feminism, nothing more than

> a rhetorical device, predicated on double-standards and bad faith, used to smear selectively on those changes, those breaks with tradition, that those with the authority to define "tradition" deplore. We need to ask forcefully what sets off our transgressions, our changes, the breaks we would make with "our culture" from all these breaks, changes, and adaptations that have been going on all along. . . . We insist that the choices and happiness of women should matter considerably more than the preservation of "Tradition" even as we call attention to the selective and problematic ways in which these "traditions" are understood. (1997, 29)

Das Dasgupta elsewhere has concurred with Mukherjee. In the West, both for immigrant and second-generation women, it is no different. If they differ in their thinking and conduct they are labeled "Westernized" (i.e., traitors to the culture/community) and reined in. If mothers do not raise and train their daughters to become traditionally good and obedient wives, and if daughters act independently, they are "psychologically exiled for their betrayal." The same rules apply for "lesbians, social change activists, and cultural critics . . . [who are] peremptorily dismissed from communities as non-Indian" (1998, 6).

When Jasmine has just arrived on American soil she has not yet been Westernized or met any American, except Half-Face, let alone a Western feminist. Clearly, in Mukherjee having Jasmine counterattack and murder Half-Face, this Ugliest of Ugly Americans, Mukherjee is referencing the Indian *Virangana*/Goddess tradition. My defense of Mukherjee, however, does not in any way diminish my respect for DasGupta and Das Dasgupta's insight that the full and free expression of Indian immigrant women's sexuality is not possible so long as the "dichotomous conceptualization of gender roles" (1996a, 397) continues. Here I would add that such an expression is not possible so long as their immigrant community is run by "imperialist nostalgia" (Renato Rosaldo, quoted in Grewal 1996, 151), so long as Indian women in their immigrant community are denied the right to include their views of what is culturally loyal/disloyal or what is respectful/disrespectful and to express their individual sexualities. They should not have to continually reference or privilege, or compare themselves to a masculine model of experience. Comparisons always keep the subject in an inferior position (Das Dasgupta 1998, 9; Minh-ha 1989, 96).

Suniti Namjoshi

In *Goja* (2000), Suniti Namjoshi (1941–) observes that Americans dislike her because she refuses to give them the kind of image they want of her. She likens Americans to Romans and wonders what it is that they want from her. She concludes that it is "confirmation" when they boast that they are the very best, always in the right, and deserve to be the rulers of the world because everyone else is "wrong" (2000, 49). Later Namjoshi imagines a three-way debate taking place between herself, the spirits of the Rani of Western Maharashtra (her grandmother) and Goja, her lowly maidservant, two unlikely allies who join in a powerful critique of the West, which sounds suspiciously like Namjoshi herself. She describes Americans as always describing Americans to other Americans and to other nations. Americans are absolutely certain that they are humane, but that no one else is, although they know nothing about other cultures and other people who, however, do know a lot about Americans. From the American perspective, "it isn't necessary" to know about anybody or anything else. "Servants," Namjoshi comments to her servant and her grandmother, "know a great deal about their masters—they have to know. Don't you find it significant that all three of us understand English?" (2000, 103).

When Namjoshi attempts to ask forgiveness of her servant for having exploited her, Goja informs Namjoshi that she is incapable of forgetting and forgiving. To do so would be to "collude" with the existing setup. Namjoshi then turns to her grandmother seeking forgiveness for having abandoned her, and she does so, to the reader's surprise. One wonders if this would have happened in reality. Back in India, Namjoshi's grandmother had demanded that Namjoshi live a lie, to pretend she was not a lesbian. Indian culture denies and conceals only male homosexuality while permitting it covertly, so long as the men marry and father children. But it denies, conceals, *and* suppresses female sexuality of any kind. Namjoshi refused to obey, to conform to her family's attempt to bargain with her, as well as to conform to her culture's values and norms. As a result, she was dismissed on the grounds that she was violating "an implicit [social] bargain" by not keeping to it on her part. From her perspective, however, her family and society would not "keep their side of it" because she "had thrown in" her "lot with the West; very well then, let the West look after me" (2000, 77).

Namjoshi does make one positive statement about Western culture. She feels that although they have an obsession about "suffering," at least they attend to it. Like Mukherjee, she views Indians as accepting suffering as an everyday part of life and passing it by, ignoring it "as though it didn't matter or didn't exist" (2000, 105). She does not believe it serves any purpose to be angry with the Indian government or the West; that anger is "a luxury" that only the rich and powerful can enjoy. She wonders what benefit there is for women and the impoverished and outcast in being angry because when "inhumanity reaches such proportions perhaps those who perpetrate it are not human. Would I be angry with a tiger that was eating me? Just afraid and in pain. What would be the point of anger? Of angry explanations to the man-eating tiger? No point. The tiger does what it does" (2000, 151).

As for her own experience as an immigrant, Namjoshi has found that her lofty caste and class ranking is ignored in the West. Like Mukherjee and so many other Indian immigrant writers, she has been routinely discriminated against because of her dark skin color, which Westerners connect with inferiority of birth and educational levels. In India, in contrast, Namjoshi automatically received respect wherever she went, although she is always acutely aware that "gender is like caste, which exists in a state of relational inequality" (Visweswaran 1994, 101). Namjoshi concludes that it makes no difference for women in any country because women's rank everywhere is always automatically lower than men's, always contingent upon their connection with their male rulers:

> [B]eing despised doesn't make me despicable. . . . If I'm a third-class citizen, does *that* make me a third-rate human being? I should like to point out to all the queens and princesses that ever there were that no woman is a first-class human being. She's second class. And anyway I was a lesbian, so presumably I would have been a third-class human being in any society wherever it was in the wide world. (2000, 110)

Susham Bedi

The heroine Guddo in *The Fire Sacrifice* ([1989] 1993) by Susham Bedi (1942?–) does not identify with the average American, or even the homeless on the street, as she would with the same element in India. Because she had not had any dealings with Americans, she had no feelings of identification with or compassion for them as she would in India. Bedi, like the other Indian writers, also condemns from an obvious outsider perspective the major qualities and goals of Western culture—in this case, American culture. On all sides, material objects were continually being invented to improve the quality of life in the eternal quest to attain happiness and make work easier through ever improved machines "and then one became a machine for earning money to buy one of those machines" ([1989] 1993, 53). It seems on occasion that Americans can do nothing right. In describing her neighborhood in New York, Guddo notices the piles of garbage bags on the sidewalk and their abominable smells. Each day she compares these sights and smells to "the filthy open sewers" of India with a sense of infinite superiority because no efforts are even undertaken for hygiene and cleanliness ([1989] 1993, 69). Mitra expresses the same caustic sentiments: "In this country of shining laminate and sparkling surfaces, the soul sees so much at the top that it shies of being scratched. I have noticed that the overpowering smell of America is Lysol: it cleanses, sterilizes, and purifies without affirming one's own idiosyncratic smell" (1996, 424). Guddo is also shocked—an odd response given the typical city scene in India—by the sight of crazed, hardly human, homeless peple on the sidewalks covered "in stinking rags" because in the United States, the home of such devotion to "wealth and humanity" such "disgraceful examples of unfortunate mankind" [*sic*] ([1989] 1993, 69) could yet exist However, Bedi later has Guddo admit to her son that it is a great deal worse in this regard in India than in America. Americans go to India to study its great music, to learn about Indian culture. Indians, in contrast, care nothing for Western music and culture. They are only interested in science, in computers, good jobs, and good incomes, with prospering financially while "boasting about cultural superiority" ([1989] 1993, 82). Guddo also notes sarcastically that being stylish and being aggressive were believed to be signs of "virtue" in the United States. There is a huge demand and supply for books on these subjects, with each author differing with the others. She sees Americans as just as restrictive in matters of clothing, conversation, and conduct as Indians. Despite their endless use of such formulaic mantras as "democracy and freedom" these words were just another confining element of the "restricting convention" of capitalism, which controlled every move, every aspect of American lives ([1989] 1993, 72–73).

In response to Americans' critiques of the outmoded Indian class and caste systems, Guddo—obviously Bedi's stand-in—brilliantly and powerfully argues that Americans have just as strong a class and caste system, as well as religious and ethnic divisions in terms of money and skin color. She likens WASPs to Brahmins, Jews to Kshatriyas, Asians to Vaishyas, and blacks to Shudras" ([1989] 1993, 73).[4] But not only Americans protest the Indian class and caste system, as Bedi makes it appear. Feminists do also. Without making the comparisons that Bedi does, and

unlike Bedi, many feminist Indian writers and critics highlight gender issues in relation to the Indian class and caste system. They believe that "the construction of
the boundaries of gender is always contingent on the politics of caste," which Dietrich astutely views as a "marriage circle." However, I would add that whatever the
caste and class, patriarchal marriage is used globally as "an instrument of control
over women's sexuality" (Alam, 1999, 454; Dietrich, 1999, 91; Fernandes, 1999, 139;
Kishwar 1999, 209).

On the whole, Bedi is not more positive about India than any of her colleagues. It is her aim, however, to view Indian shortcomings by comparing them
to American ones in order to put Indian shortcomings, so much more publicized,
into perspective. Guddo's daughter, a doctor who also emigrates to the United
States, rapidly realizes that she is being treated as "an outsider," that Americans
"minoritize," "Other" her and Indians like herself, Hindus, who had been from
the majority in India, as well as from the upper classes. Muslims, Sikhs, and
Christians were the minorities in India. She was shocked to discover that, in the
United States, she would never again experience being "in the mainstream" but be
separated from it. Guddo, her mother, does not believe that there is freedom to
express one's opinion in this country either, because school children are being
brainwashed by the government and "multi-national companies" about the Soviet
Union. They are being taught that it is a monster that should be hated and that
Americans should be prepared at all times to annihilate this monster. In sum,
Bedi's comparisons between the United States and India reveals that she is a powerful apologist for India in terms of leveling the playing field between India and
the West:

> While in India there lingered the ghosts of poverty, conservatism, social violence and ir-
> rational moral values, here [the United States] the ghosts of fierce egotism, exaggerated
> hedonism and loneliness were very much alive, and they numbered in the millions. . . .
> Even if we're seen wearing slacks or skirts, what we wear inside us stays the same. We
> don't change ourselves. Wherever we go we create our own India again, whether others
> think it's bad or good, even if where we live is called a ghetto or Little India, even if be-
> cause of our closed society later generations are kicked out of their adopted countries, or
> whatever price we have to pay. ([1989] 1993, 73, 177)

Gita Mehta

In marked contrast to the other authors' attitude of perennial outsider is that of
Gita Mehta (1943–). When an immigration official at New Delhi airport once
asked her how long she had resided outside India and why she still carried "an Indian passport," Mehta was unable to swear at him because in India females cannot
do this, but she wanted to scream back at him that India was her "damned soil"
and he should never forget that. Mehta proudly intends to retain her Indian citi-

zenship as long as she lives. She places the blame on conditions in India for emigrés like herself living most of their lives outside of India. No one had much hope for India's future, although Indians might be regarded highly for their past glories. Despite inheriting freedom, this generation of Indians had to face "grim" current statistics. The population is enormous. Illiteracy preponderates. Fifty percent of the population lives in dire poverty. There were disparities between the classes that seemed too "Herculean" a task to attempt reversing. A corrupt government on all levels is the "standard." In painful contrast, "these self-confident dwarfs from the First World only had to worry about what they were going to buy next" (1997, 21). Mehta also wonders how come there is such a large movement away from countries that have become free in recent years into those very countries that their ancestors worked so hard "to expel" (1997, 19).

Meena Alexander

Meena Alexander's maternal grandmother was Elizabeth Kururilla, who was active in the Nationalist movement, an ardent follower of Gandhi, and the first woman member of the legislative assembly in Travancore. Alexander (1951–), a Syrian Christian, was raised in Allahabad, Kerala and North Africa, and is a longtime resident of the United States. Alexander traded in her Indian passport for an American one and openly states the benefits of the United States, as well as its drawbacks. Laura, a character in her novel *Nampally Road* (1991), has three sisters who have emigrated to Canada, and she longs to emigrate there, primarily because her husband beats her viciously. Laura's sisters write her about shopping malls, describing them as "palaces of chrome and plastic, crammed with glittering things to buy, carts that you pushed through aisles as music rang in your ears." It is a source of wonder to Laura that "even the vegetables there are covered in plastic" (1991, 43). This is very hard for her to believe because in Hyderabad plastic bags are kept carefully, washed and dried as long as they lasted. Alexander's purpose here is to show the surreal difference between the world of materialism, consumerism, and overabundance and the enduring and familiar world of great poverty. In contrast, in *Pilgrimage* (2000), Jayapal stresses American environmental destruction, openly condemning their use of plastic bags—used once and then thrown into garbage piles.

As an immigrant Alexander finds that if she has her American passport on her she can travel freely across many borders and come to this country without a visa or a "green card." But, if she does not carry her passport, Alexander cannot even imagine taking a walk on a country road devoid of people of color. She dreads meeting "men in army camouflage, toting rifles to kill deer, all the xenophobia of America sitting squarely on them, or bikers on Route 23 with big signs pasted to their machines: '500 years after Columbus, Keep out Foreign Scum'" (1996a, 65).

Like Mukherjee, Alexander sees immigration as a border crossing that offers the opportunity to eradicate one's past life. "The shock of a new life" can change one completely. One can tear up one's "old skin, old habits" (1996a, 93). "The shock of arrival" in the West after traveling from one place to another, then arriving on these shores and of living here "crystallizes the jagged boundaries of . . . disjunctive worlds." A "painful" chasm forms between the brutal reality of being perceived "as Other" and the "desire" not to be so perceived (1996a, 152–153). This "shock" ultimately provides Alexander and other Asian American artists with their material.

Indian women in India have always been constrained by the power of the patriarchy, no matter what the time period in India, no matter what the movement— the so-called "Golden Age of Hindu Rule," the "Barbaric Muslim Rule" that followed, or the Raj that ended in 1947. As an Indian woman in the United States, Alexander has to deal with being a "racialized" female. The woman of color is burdened in the United States by having to learn to walk in this "dense irregularity" (1996a, 144–145). She has to learn how to forge the disparity of her experiences into the unified whole of memory. One can ultimately live successfully and even joyously in a present created from several "anchorages." From this complexity of so many jangling discordances on all sides of an Indian woman's life, with her past and her future so seemingly incongruous, comes Alexander's fragmentation theory that can also be expanded to include immigrants from all over the globe, as well as ethnic and racial minorities in any culture. The result of repressed desire in Asian artists, both male and female, is a disjunctive art in which fragmented or "mutilated" body images are created to express the artists' sense of "radical dislocation," of being Othered in the Eurocentric United States. Asian artists do not feel that they have traditions in this country. However, the dislocated, "disjointed" condition, which is the product of their memories of the past and their experiences in the United States, enables them paradoxically to reconceptualize, to radically reenvision the American space in their creative work.

Alexander, as well as other immigrants, also asserts that fragmentation can be positive (Costa 2000, 733; Mercer 1990, 54). That is, if the fragmentation emanates from the multicultural feminism prevalent in the United States. Such a feminism then forces the fragmentation of patriarchy and of racism. In turn, this multicultural feminist fragmentation opens up a possibility for women to express their "female desire/female sexuality." If such a possibility ever became reality it would disprove what the culture sanctions as "feminine" (1996a, 186).

Manjula Padmanabhan

The short story "Stains," in *Hot Death, Cold Soup* (1997) by Manjula Padmanabhan (1953–) has continued this trend through the alienation wrought by different cultural training in a story describing the cultural conflict that erupts between an African American woman, her Indian boyfriend, and his mother. When Sarah and Deep visit the widowed Mrs. Kumar at her home in Pennsylvania, Sarah begins to menstruate. Mrs. Kumar, a traditionalist gatekeeper, treats it as a shameful impurity to be concealed and sends Sarah down to the freezing basement to clean the stains separately. Deep is embarrassed by the mention of the topic and protective of his mother when Sarah complains to him. He informs Sarah that in India this topic is not discussed and that he knows nothing about it. That is, he wants to know nothing about it. In contrast to them both, Sarah realizes that she glories in her period, even the pain that it causes her. She even begins to question why she conceals her blood flow in a tampon and decides to use napkins from now on because she "no longer want[s] to hide my blood from myself" (1997, 205). Sarah also realizes that Deep will defend his mother at all costs, that "he would never be able to see it her way. It's clear enough to you, when it comes to world events, when it's Russia controlling the flow of arms to Uzbekhistan, or the US controlling patents in the Third World. But when it's your mother controlling the flow of my blood onto our sheet? Oh no! Then it's tradition! It's being polite!" (1997, 197).

Sarah suddenly leaves without their knowledge and returns home, whereupon Deep immediately calls her. His mother likes Sarah and would agree to their marriage. But Sarah realizes that the chasm between them is too great, as illustrated by their differing responses to menstruation. To her, as to feminists, menstruation is a life-affirming process marking the potential continuity of humankind. It should be a source of pride and glorified fully as much as masculine capability whose glorification is carrried to such excess that it becomes a virus or cancer of sexist *hubris* on a global scale, a case of testosterone poisoning that projects into every area of life, even including language that suppresses, omits, and denies the use of the female case in discourse. Given such circumstances, how can Deep defend sexist Indian customs that irrationally humiliate and isolate menstruating women as unclean?

He also has taken every opportunity he could to mock the United States as having no culture. In Deep's view, "the West is suffering from . . . a loss of meaningful tradition," whereas Sarah defends the West, arguing that "the only difference is, it's not old, it's not gilded with time. TV . . . K Marts and Hollywood . . . Star Trek and Superman, Freeways and credit cards" are just as much a "meaningful tradition" (1997, 201) as any of India's. The United States does have a culture, albeit a new one.

Moreover, Indian feminists, as well as feminists all over the world, are no longer permitting (Indian and other) masculinist traditionalists to define for their culture(s) what is significant and meaningful and what is petty, trivial, and irrelevant entirely from their own male-oriented perspective:

> "I've decided that the only level of culture I care about is the kind which makes my own life reasonable and intelligent. Listening to music and hanging paintings on the wall is all very well, but if at the end of the day someone wants me to hide my blood

underground and to behave like an invalid—forget it, you know? If that's what tradition means, then I say, take it off the shelf. Leave it out. My packet of ultrathin, E-Z wrap pads and what it represents to me about the journey my generation of women has made, is all the tradition I need. . . .

"Sarah," said Deep, "are you comparing five thousand years of civilization to . . ." he choked on the words " . . . feminine hygiene products?"

"Yes," said Sarah and put the phone down. (1997, 208)

Chitra Banerjee Divakaruni

Manjula Padmanabahan lives in New Delhi, India, and Chitra Banerjee Divakaruni (1956–), near San Francisco, California. Nevertheless, they are much alike in terms of illustrating the cultural and gender clashes metaphorically and literally within the Indian and Indian immigrant home through key incidents occurring there in the course of mundane daily chores. Additionally, as appears to be a major characteristic of younger authors, they both describe their major female characters as leave takers. They either return to India when they fail to adjust to the cultural divide, or they leave India, leaving their loved ones behind—or they leave their menfolk behind both in India and in the West when a yawning, immovable chasm comes between them.

In "Mrs. Dutta Writes a Letter" in *The Unknown Errors of Our Lives* (2001), Divakaruni writes of a widow who has given up everything to come to live in California with her only son, his wife, and their two children. She still gets up at five A.M. every morning because she had been taught by her mother-in-law as a bride that "*a good wife wakes before the rest of the household*" (2001, 2, emphasis the author's). In doing so, however, Mrs. Dutta wreaks havoc on the family's own customs because the noise she makes in the bathroom wakes them up unnecessarily early, and her grandchildren complain about her using their bathroom. She is shocked and infuriated by their lack of respect for her, compounded by her daughter-in-law's failure to rebuke them. By Indian standards, American(ized) parents are neglectful, allow children to treat elders disrespectfully, give them too much leeway, too many privileges and freedoms. Jhumpa Lahiri (1967–), in her short story "Interpreter of Maladies," in her eponymous Pulitzer Prize-winning book, makes the same point through the perspective of their Indian cab driver about an Indian American family who have come as first-time tourists to India:

Mr. and Mrs. Das behaved like an older brother and sister, not parents. It seemed that they were in charge of the children only for the day; it was hard to believe they were regularly responsible for anything other than themselves. Mr. Das tapped on his lens cap, and his tour book, dragging his thumbnail occasionally across the pages so that they made a scraping sound. Mrs. Das continued to polish her nails. She had still not removed her sunglasses. Every now and then Tina renewed her plea that she wanted her nails done, too, and so at one point Mrs. Das flicked a drop of polish on the little girl's finger before depositing the bottle back insider her straw bag. (1999, 49)

Mrs. Dutta also thinks the amount of TV the family watches is disgraceful, and the children horrify her again by talking back to her when she tells them to turn it off. She is critical of her daughter-in-law, as well, priding herself on using sugar in the tea because she is convinced it is better for her son than the "chemical powder" her daughter-in-law uses. Mrs. Dutta is unaware that her insistence on sugar and on cooking fried and fatty foods for the family is anathema to her daughter-in-law, while her grandchildren would rather eat frozen burritos. Mrs. Dutta also does not put the dishes into the dishwasher until it fills up because germs are bred that way. Instead, she does the dishes herself by hand after breakfast and throws away all leftovers. Her Hindu training has enculturated her never to mix contaminated food with unused food. Time and again Shyamoli patiently explains to her mother-in-law not to throw away food unnecessarily and not to do the dishes herself and leave them dripping all over the counter, to stop interfering with the children: to stop ordering them not to do certain things that she has given them permission to do. Shyamoli feels that her mother-in-law has appropriated the kitchen for herself, cooks whatever she likes, and smells the whole house up and even their clothes with the grease from her cooking to the point where she no longer feels it's her own home.

The children have hidden away the copy of the *Ramayana for Young Readers* that Mrs. Dutta brought all the way from India, and when she asks them to sit near her while she prays, they are reluctant to do so. When Mrs. Dutta reminisces about her childhood or the past, they do not want to hear her. In contrast, when they speak on the phone to their friends they chatter about alien matters incomprehensible to her, such as "Power Rangers, Spice Girls and Spirit Week at school" (2001, 13). She is horrified when one day her daughter-in-law asks her son—addressing him by his name, no less!—to do the wash. First, she had never throughout her marriage called her husband by name, and, second, it is shockingly inappropriate for a man to wash clothes. She will do the wash for them all. She cannot bear thinking of the possibility of her son's hands touching his wife's and her underclothes. Leigh Minturn explains the regulations for washing men's clothes, and in doing so, it does not seem to occur to her that she thereby inadvertently exposes the fact that men never wash women's clothes:

> The washing of men's clothes by family women is regulated by the status of the women, extensions of *purdah* and sex-avoidance rules. The avoidance of sexual contact with older men is extended to the washing of clothes men wear below the waist, and the status hierarchy and blood versus affinal kinship ties among women are extended to their washing customs. Thus, any woman may wash a man's shirts, but his pants, shorts, or dhotis, worn below the waist and in contact with the genitals, cannot be washed by a man's daughter or *derani* [daughter-in-law]. . . . In conservative joint families, wives avoid washing their husbands' pants, shorts, or dhotis. (1993, 140)

Shyamoli, a stockbroker, responds that in contrast to Indian customs that are responsible for Indian men's uselessness in the home, in America there is no such belief in the division of gender roles. She works all day, as does Sagar, and if he does not "help" she would not be able to run the home. The term "help," however, betrays Shyanoli, and perhaps her author, as still conceptualizing household duties as a woman's responsibility, even if she is a stockbroker. Instead of accepting Shyamoli's explanation, Mrs. Dutta attempts to end-run around her by secretly requesting Sagar to teach her how to use the washer and dryer, which he does. When she attempts to work them, however, she becomes frightened and resorts to doing her clothes by hand when no one is home. The climax comes when Mrs. Dutta hangs her wash over the neighbor's fence, enraging their American neighbor, who then waylays and humiliates Shyamoli that evening as she is coming home from work. Shyamoli finally blows up because she has been on her guard for so many years never "to give these Americans a chance to say something like this, and now—" (2001, 29).

At the end of the story, Mrs. Dutta feels that in this country of the young she is "alone" and irrelevant and intends to return to India as her best compromise. She is comfortable and at home in India, but she is deprived of family life with her only, beloved son and his family. She will forever be neither here nor there, as Alexander puts it, about this typical quandary of the unsuccessful immigrant who forever tries "to move between two worlds . . . I can't bear it, this here-there business" (1996a, 143). The title of Divakaruni's book—*The Unknown Errors of Our Lives*—reflects the fact that Mrs. Dutta's "errors" and those of her son's wife and children are "unknown" to them, as they are unconscious of why and how they occur. Therefore, neither side is flexible or accommodating, or rational. Mrs. Dutta is irrational because her actions are based entirely on her caste Hindu belief systems without any real attempt on her part to learn other ways, to modify her behavior. The Americanized Shyamoli does attempt from the very beginning to patiently endure all the stresses and strains of her now different customs and value systems from her mother-in-law's. Her neighbor's complaints against her mother-in-law, however, embarrass and humiliate Shyamoli to the point of venting her true feelings. In doing so, she exposes what Mrs. Dutta has not realized—how suppressed her daughter-in-law has been by her mother-in-law's traditional conduct. The gap is too much for all of them to close, except for Mrs. Dutta's son, Sagar, who understands where both women come from literally and metaphorically—one straight out of India and one, like himself, long resident in the United States. He is sympathetic to both perspectives, and therefore ambivalent—always torn between them, always uncomfortable.

In another short story, "The Names of Stars in Bengali," Divakaruni presents the "other" side of the gap—the Indian side—when a daughter visits her mother in India together with her two young sons. They can hardly believe that this new manifestation is their mother. Instead of jeans and t-shirts, she now wears a sari and a red dot on her forehead. She appears younger, foreign, and laughs far more than in the United States. She eats with her fingers, does not hurry any more, does not shake her car keys at them, yelling for them to hurry up because they were late for wherever they were going. "They hadn't laughed so much in their entire lives, they'd never thought India would be this much fun, they wished they could stay forever. When they said that, both their mother and grandmother grew quiet and didn't answer" (2001, 240). TV antennas stick out from the thatched roofs, young boys whistle American rock stars' songs without comprehending the meanings. The Indian relatives watch the news at night and know all about what is going on in America: about "O. J. Simpson, Madonna, Monica Lewinsky. How your president [Clinton] sent bombers to the Gulf" (2001, 267). Neighbors who come to visit are very curious about America, as were Mukherjee's neighbors, relatives, and friends when she returned for her first visit. They ask the boys' mother if machines really do all the housework, if everyone drives cars, even the elderly, and that when they can no longer drive are they then relegated to nursing homes by their children? She does tell them that she has two cars, but not about costly insurance, or being "road raped" by other drivers during rush hour, who blow their horns and shout at her: "Fucking Dothead go home" (2001, 254).

Their grandmother had visited them once in America, but she had become intimidated about what appeared to her daughter to be insignificant things like "the burglar alarm, the answering machine, the knobs on the dishwasher" (2001, 259). They had fought over trivial issues, and when her daughter had hinted that she had never enjoyed any "fun" times in her family, her mother had become incensed about such a silly American idea as families being for fun. They were set up to feed and clothe and teach children so that they could do the same in their turn.

Divakaruni once again reveals through home life the result of the inevitable gap between generations when one immigrates:

> Perhaps it was something all parents and children undergo as they grow older. But in their case, they had stepped into a time machine named immigration, and when they fell from its ferocious spinning, it was into the alien habits of a world they had imagined imperfectly. In this world, they could not inhabit a house together, in the old way. They could not be mother and daughter in that way again. (2001, 261)

Anjana Appachana

Although Anjana Appachana (1956–) now lives in the United States, her emphasis is not on cross-cultural critique, but on Indian situations. Still, Appachana does have something valuable to say about both India and the United States. On the one hand, she abhors about India the burning of brides for dowry, the rampant corruption, people slaughtering one another over religion, and Harijans still suffering discrimination. On the other hand, in America children were molested by their own fathers, husbands abused and beat up their wives as the men of the servant classes did in India, friends raped each other; the old were neglected. Whereas in India women were paid the same as men who worked at the same jobs, this was not the case in America where this was still fought over. A woman could never become a president, nor could African Americans. Americans were gullible about religious charlatans, and African Americans were the American untouchables. Several supposedly educated Americans asked an Indian visitor whom they thought learned the English she spoke in America whether there were roads in India and whether there were tree dwellers there.

Pramila Jayapal

In 1995, Pramila Jayapal (1965–), the director of an international loan and technical assistance program involved with health programs for women and children in developing countries, received a grant from the Institute for Current World Affairs to return to India for two years. Jayapal had left India when she was five and had lived in Indonesia and Singapore before emigrating to the United States. A good deal of the results of Jayapal's journey to India, published in *Pilgrimage: One Woman's Return to a Changing India* (2000), concerns Jayapal's penetrating and fair-minded assessments of both the West and India. She sees India as multidimensional, layered, full of complexity and contradictions (2000, 73). Originally emigrating to the United States as a teenager, Jayapal had only wanted to assimilate, to wear torn jeans. She refused to learn to speak Hindi or Malayalam, was not interested in India, but in America's "exotic amusement parks and enormous shopping malls, and, perhaps, most importantly," its "aura of freedom, defiance and worldliness" (2000, 16).

Before receiving her grant, Jayapal thought of India as "repressive and backward," while America was "creative and advanced" (2000, 18). Ultimately, however, like most of her traveling colleagues, Jayapal found reality far more complex. In India, she did find filthy conditions and impoverished people, which disgusted and depressed her, as well as made her feel guilty because feeling disgusted and depressed reinforced the stereotypes about India. She found poverty in the cities worse than in rural areas because in cities the slum dwellers had come from the villages seeking better lives. They had become displaced and found that their dreams were delusions (2000, 65; see also Umrigar 2000, 253). In contrast, Jayapal admired the fact that there was no concept of privacy in India. People felt connected to one another and aware that they were parts of larger family, community, and national entities, whereas in America private space was conceived as "sacred."

Behind her closed door in the United States she could shut herself up in her own private world of her choice and ignore any other reality. In India, as in other cultures globally, Jayapal found that injustices to women crossed class, race, and ethnic lines, and were experienced every day by women, publicly and privately. In India, Jayapal found that even educated women never had to support themselves, consequently fearing to do so. In India, financial independence is still hard to achieve for single women. If a single woman remains in India, she is disrespected by her culture. She is considered "fallen" and becomes a target for men on the prowl. It is enormously difficult for women to effect change in their societal roles because they then have to be prepared for ostracism by those who reject change, defining change as threats to "Mother India," to the traditional Indian way, and as depraved imports from the West and Western feminists. To be fair-skinned is highly desirable and improves one's chances for a good marriage and in attaining respect. Those Westerners who condemn India's caste system should be aware that the West has a caste system, as well, although at the same time Jayapal admits to being repelled by India's. She blames Indian belief in *karma* (destiny) and caste as permitting educated and wealthy Indians to convince themselves that to be privileged is a right coming to them, whereas the poor do not have the right to any privileges (2000, 97).

Jayapal's caste is the Nayar caste (landlords, farmers, professionals), part of the Shudra caste (laborers), about half of the population in Kerala, Jayapal's ancestral home. It is matrilineal, with property and family name traditionally passed down through the female line,[5] which accounted for their not committing female infanticide, not having a dowry system, child marriage, bride burnings, or "ostracism of widows" (2000, 30). After marriage, the woman remained in her family home and was not dependent on her husband. Her maternal uncle, not her husband, was responsible for her or their children. As with certain Native American tribes, when a woman tired of her husband, she put his shoes outside the door, and he left.

Brought up in a family with powerful women gave Jayapal an early grasp of her own sense of self as a female in addition to what she felt was possible for all other women. She always felt pain when Western feminists condemned India's oppression of women and would use Kerala as her "defense," but she had to acknowledge that the Western feminists were right. In India, she finds shelters for what was termed "problem girls and women" from all classes who had been "battered, abused, tortured or raped" (2000, 40), as if *they* were the problem. Moreover, the girls were stigmatized if they suffered mental illness and were not permitted to return to their homes.

The hardest thing to learn about many educated contemporary Indian women and men was that they still acceded to traditional "norms." Therefore, she concluded that the United States did better in relation to women's rights. Many people she met in India were privately in accord with traditional prescriptions for gender roles, while others questioned them, also privately. Ultimately, however, it came down to the need to live the best they could somehow in ways that were always exposed to pressure to conform in contrast with their private wishes. Jayapal discovered that she had been wrong to assume that educated Indian women would be activists, would fight on behalf of women's issues, would be full of self-confidence, and conscious that they possessed abilities beyond and above what was societally decreed. After six months, Jayapal's white American husband joined her for the rest of the time. Accustomed to equality with her husband in the United States, Jayapal, like Mukherjee so many years before her, was continually subjected to Indians who differed with the couple about how they performed their "respective roles" (2000, 50).

She did find Indian feminists, however, apparently in sufficient numbers to divide them into three groups. She defines as "bourgeois feminists" those Indian women who wanted "small reforms; as "radical feminists" those Indian women who blamed patriarchy for subjugating women, and as "socialist feminists" those women who also included other oppressed groups such as "Harijans, tribals and the working poor." As for those Indians who view feminism "as an 'ism'" brought in by the West and inappropriate in the Indian context, their arguments signify either ignorance or a conscious refusal to remember "that if feminism means fighting for women's rights, it is a struggle and a process that has been at work in India in large and small ways since the nineteenth century." Although it is necessary for men to become feminists, they must not take control of the movement. Women must in the end do it for themselves. For more than 150 years, the method of shaming and humiliating and ostracizing Indian feminists or would-be feminists in order to return them to the fold of sacred, traditional norms for women took the form of British bashing—those lying intruders who poisoned Indian women by importing the alien degeneracy of Western feminists. Blaming feminism as a Western "'non-Indian' idea" and therefore to be summarily dismissed is also a dodge to avoid change. (2000, 51, 52–53).

Jayapal disagrees with Balakrishnan about the Indian media as a positive force for women, as does Tejaswini Niranjana, who points out that the media may have become more sophisticated, but it has not changed: "The perils of feminism or feminist politics . . . [are that] they are frequently ridiculed [in films, MTV and cable television programs] . . . and sometimes vilified, as imitative of Western aberrations" (quoted in Jayapal 2000, 145). Similarly conceptualized are "the evil Western rituals of homosexuality, dating and sexual behavior" (DasGupta and Das Dasgupta 1998, 124). The irony here is that when those very "Hindu fundamentalists" who conceptualize themselves as "Authentic Upholders of their Culture" vilify feminism—Western or Indian—as "Western aberrations," they nevertheless use the media with great skill, "unconcerned about whether the entry of television into Indian homes affects our 'traditional way of life'! . . . [exposing] few personal qualms . . . about using 'Western' technology or buying 'Western' consumer goods. Nor do they have political qualms about their Third-World nations spending their scarce monetary resources on the purchase of Western armaments" (Narayan 1997, 22, 23).

Jayapal contrasts affirmative action policies of American universities to the common practice in India where men could be accepted who scored "60 percent whereas women had to score 80 percent" (2000, 49). In Indian schools in which "social hierarchies" are inherited, individual ideas depend on "others' perceptions of appropriate rights and roles." In American schools and universities students are expected to question, to be skeptics, to be doubtful, to hold very little as written in stone (2000, 178–179). In my experience, however, Western feminists struggle against enormous obstacles to the full, free expression of their views wherever in their surrounding environment they attempt to do so, extending from their own homes, into the academy (as students, faculty, and administrators), the workplace, and the media. What feminists in the United States to this day can freely and publicly express opposition to the patriarchal institutions of religion, marriage, and the nuclear family without experiencing condemnation, ostracism, scapegoating, or even loss of their jobs?

Like Mahasweta Devi and other Indian women writers and critics, Jayapal also complains about the giant multinational conglomerates that invade the lands where medicinal herbs can be found, remove them, package and sell them, entirely ignoring and bypassing the *adivasis* (indigenous tribal group in Kerala) who were healers since time immemorial. The government does set aside monies for housing for the *adivasis;* however, in order to receive the grant the *adivasis* would have to kick back two thirds of the funds to the governmental representative (2000, 37, 38). In musing about women's situation globally, she concludes that we feel burdened according to what is burdensome in our environment. Sadly, despite the great population growth coming from developing countries,[6] an American baby's impact on the environment is ten times more than that of an Indian baby's (2000, 118; see also Spivak 1999, 384).

To Western feminists, rural Indian women's lives may seem unimaginably difficult, forever carrying heavy water pitchers on their heads, burdened with full-time childcare, endless cooking and housework chores, and field work in the excruciating heat. Western feminists (and Jayapal includes herself by using the pronoun "we") have a working day of twelve hours, can only spend a brief time in that day with our children, and substitute relationships with other people with technological tools that alienate us from them. We rush around, often on giant highways, preoccupied by so many errands, by the need to multitask, "that our hearts rattle from nervousness." As a result, we would-be "supermen and superwomen" (2000, 124) forget the simple, basic pleasures Indians enjoy—such as being with the earth, holding children, the pleasure of rain. Would rural Indian women really want to change places with us? Jayapal wonders. When it came to her difficult pregnancy, however, she suddenly found American "alienating technology" superior to Indian "heart." The most advanced medical developments and the latest drugs are not found in India because their expense is beyond what most Indians can afford.

Like Mukherjee, Jayapal became an American citizen after living in the United States for many years. But she justifies this significant move by claiming somewhat unconvincingly that she had at last become comfortable with her Indian self; that in replacing her Indian passport for an American one she was not removing her "Indianness." Rather she was reaffirming her "trust" in her Indian self by no longer having to convince herself or others that she was Indian (2000, 263).

Jhumpa Lahiri

Jhumpa Lahiri (1967–) compares and contrasts life for Indian men and women in India and in the West from their viewpoint, and as with Bedi, the West loses. "Mrs. Sen's," in *Interpreter of Maladies* (1999), is a story that depicts the trauma and suffering caused by homesickness and culture shock for an immigrant who came to the United States when she married another Indian, a professor. This story is a tour de force because it is narrated by the little boy for whom Mrs. Sen babysits. The contrast between what Eliot sees and feels and what the reader realizes—the enormous extent of Mrs. Sen's suffering, isolation, and stupefying loneliness in this cold and unfeeling country—is extraordinarily powerful. She eventually has a breakdown. Through the person of Eliot's mother, a divorced, righteous feminist professor, Lahiri represents the hypocrisy of this country in miserable contrast to its vaunted democratic theory. Additionally, she also reflects how many Indian/Third World feminists view Western feminists and their culture. Self-absorbed, unfeeling, imperceptive, thick-skinned, inhumane, uncaring, lacking in compassion, and racist. Eliot's mother does not even notice Mrs. Sen as an individual, nor even make the slightest attempt to give her sisterhood, the human companionship she so desperately needs and is completely without.

Each afternoon Mrs. Sen chops and hacks vegetables with a blade that she had brought from India, exactly as she had done in India:

> "Whenever there is a wedding in the family . . . or a large celebration of any kind, my mother sends out word in the evening for all the neighborhood women to bring blades just like this one, and then they sit in an enormous circle on the roof of our building, laughing and gossiping and slicing fifty kilos of vegetables through the night." Her profile hovered protectively over her work, a confetti of cucumber, eggplant, and onion skins heaped around her. "It is impossible to fall asleep those nights, listening to their chatter." She paused to look at a pine tree framed by the living room window. "Here, in this place where Mr. Sen has brought me, I cannot sometimes sleep in so much silence. . . . Eliot, if I begin to scream right now at the top of my lungs, would someone come?"

"Mrs. Sen, what's wrong?"

"Nothing. I am only asking if someone would come."

Eliot shrugged. "Maybe."

"At home that is all you have to do. Not everybody has a telephone. But just raise yoiur voice a bit, or express grief or joy of any kind, and one whole neighborhood and half of another has come to share the news, to help with arrangements. . . ."

"They might call you," Eliot said eventually to Mrs. Sen. "But they might complain that you were making too much noise." (1999, 115–117)

These feminist Indian authors, whether at home or abroad, show that immigration makes it impossible to ever return to the original home again in the sense of things remaining the same upon returning to India, or of the viability of transporting home to America in the form of one's dearest relatives and friends.

Outsiders Silenced

On Domestic Violence and Suppression and Denial of Female Sexuality

*Indian women living in South Asia are embedded in a woman's community, religion,
age hierarchy, class, and place within the family. These roles work in conjunction
with one another, and any given identity is accentuated, depending on the context.
Women experience an extended sense of self rather than an individualistic one.*

NAHEED ISLAM

*The (overt or covert) group ownership of any given woman's sexuality is still the most
pressing subject for a large number of Indian women, including in the diaspora . . .
Individual expressions of sexuality are still considered one of the worst betrayals to
one's parents and elders. . . . What matters is that I am sexual . . . Being sexual has
reshaped my knowledge, my feelings, my very breath.*

GINU KAMANI

Lalithambika Antherjanam

Lalithambika Antherjanam (1909–1987?)[1] was born into a small community of
hyper-orthodox Kerala Brahmins, the Namboodiri. Generally wealthy,
they were powerful owners of large tracts of land, even into the twentieth
century. Not surprisingly, they were unwilling to change and resisted reform.

Protesting the harshness of Namboodiri customs toward its women, called *anterja-nams* (those who live inside) was one of Antherjanam's primary purposes. The Namboodiri lived by strict rules of purity, especially in relation to their women, a few of which do make sense. *Anterjanams* lived in total seclusion, could only wear white, and never went into the sun unless covered entirely and in the company of female chaperones, their faces protected by umbrellas made of palm leaves. Their earlobes were elongated so that they could wear heavy hanging ear ornaments, they were forbidden to look at men unless they were married to them, and they had to bare their upper bodies at home. They could not pierce their noses, nor when they became widows commit *sati* or shave their heads. To ensure that property was kept within the family, only the eldest sons married within the community and inherited property. Younger sons married women from outside, to *nair* (warrior caste) women from their maternal community. For this reason and because dowries were exhorbitant, many fathers married their daughters off to eldest sons already married. Thus, girls of twelve or thirteen could be married to old men, resulting in young girls and women being confined for the rest of their lives to the kitchen and the prayer room. Often older, more senior wives would abuse them.

Antherjanam loved learning from the beginning and was encouraged in that love. She records how her father, a poet and social reformer, deeply resentful of the discrimination against women, threatened to leave, convert to Christianity, and "marry an Englishwoman" because then he could raise his daughter "like a human being" (1998, 134), be free to give her an education, allow her to blossom, and to marry her to a decent man. Note that he still retained the right to marry his daughter to his choice of husband. Nevertheless, given his situation, he did do all that he could for his daughter. Both parents also allowed Antherjanam to wear skirts and blouses, which no other girl of her community had ever done before. They did not have her earlobes elongated and they permitted her to cover her breasts at home. But they were forced to follow certain societal restrictions such as confining their daughter in their home from the time of her first menstruation until her marriage. Paradoxically, Antherjanam considered this two-year period the time when she was educated because she was free to read as much as she wished, as well as to write. During this time, she also became alert to the reforms going on in the outside world that focused on the suffering of the *anterjanams* and that advocated more widespread education for women and widow remarriage. In *Cast Me Out If You Will* (1997) she wrote that "she often thought that the souls of these unfortunate women inhabited her. What if I had been one of them, she would ask herself" (1997, 139). Antherjanam's first publication in 1923 was an article about Gandhi, whom she worshiped, and the Congress Party, which was at that time working to end untouchability.

In 1927, Antherjanam married a man who admired her and who was ever supportive, thus freeing her to join the reform groups. She wrote a play for one of these groups about the remarriage of a young widow, and she and her husband returned from the theater bursting with pride at being part of a group that struggled against *purdah,* that agitated for the abolition of the "laws of pollution," and that worked toward modernizing customs. Just before her death, she wrote that it appeared to her as if these were no longer considered significant issues, but that forty years earlier "they were events of major significance" (1997, 148). One wonders whether she would revise her opinion if she were still alive today. At any rate, Antherjanam and her husband returned from the theater that exciting night in 1934 of the performance of her play without her umbrella or shawl, to be condemned by her family, including her mother, "cast out" for having violated caste law. "Amma wept, beat her head, and lamented, 'I wish I had never had a daughter. If only she had died as soon as she was born. I do not want a daughter like you'" (1997, 148).

Antherjanam's relatives, supposedly progressive, as well as her husband's family, ostracized the couple. Only her father supported Antherjanam. He built the couple a small home in a place where they could welcome all castes. Her husband farmed, and both of them wove garments on their own loom. When "Gandhiji" visited the area, the couple were thrilled to have the opportunity to present him with some of them. Here the couple raised their seven children in the happiest time of Antherjanam's life until her father's death. Then they were forced for financial reasons to move to Antherjanam's husband's family home. There the harsh treatment of widows and single women that forced them to live confined, restricted lives provided Antherjanam with the material for her stories in which she linked India's rebellion against the British with women who fought to attain independence, and especially for the freedom to express their sexuality. If women in Antherjanam's community did so, their shawl and umbrella were removed, they were given funeral rites, and cast out from their own homes and families and from their community to live however they could. Most could not.

In "Admission of Guilt," Antherjanam, writing on behalf of widow remarriage, as well as recognition of female sexuality, depicts a young widow who unsuccessfully defends herself to the (all-male) court. While in the course of her prayers in the temple tank, the temple's handsome reader assaults her, and her frustrated female sexuality is aroused and fulfilled:

> "Human beings have an incurable weakness—on certain occasions, and in certain surroundings, the human mind cannot contain itself. Indeed, I am sure that even experts like you can be vulnerable like this. How then can you find fault with a woman like me? And yet, even in the half-conscious state that I was in, I was truly terrified when two hot arms encircled me. Who was this? Could it be Bhagavan himself? Lord, you have appeared thus so many times before your devotees." (1997, 41–42)

But then the widow realizes that it was not possible for a human being to directly experience God. "A cry arose from the depths of my being, but it was smothered by a gentle kiss. A futile writhing, and I had perforce to yield to a strong embrace. In the surge of sensations my resistance ebbed away. Feelings of pleasure that I had never known or experienced before came alive" (1997, 41–42). The one positive element in all this is that the men who were guilty of adultery with women were also punished. In "Goddess of Revenge," based on a celebrated, true story, a rejected wife became a prostitute and listed sixty-four men who had had sex with her. As a result, they, too, were cast out of the community:

> "The affair provoked a *smartavicharam* [trial] that rocked Kerala to its very foundations. From great prince to highborn brahmin, men trembled, terrifed because they did not know whose names this harlot was going to betray. . . . Tell me, Sister! Who is more culpable, the man who seduces a woman in order to satisfy his lust, or the woman who transgresses the dictates of society in an attempt to oppose him? Whom would you hate more? Whom would you cast out"? (1997, 28)[2]

After independence, Antherjanam became disillusioned with the nationalists because of their sexist insistence on "male-female solidarity" in relation to issues that they alone determined were priorities and that "restricted women's emancipation" (A. Basu 1992, 110). Antherjanam felt that the male leaders had reneged on their promises to all the women who had supported them. The Congress Party government would not permit women in the government and stated that they should be in the kitchen. Because women did not seize the opportunity during these struggles to incorporate their concerns into the various demands prioritized by the male leadership, they did not succeed in freeing themselves from the burden of traditional oppressive forms of sexism. Although they had played so active a part in every aspect of the "Free India" movement from its beginning to its conclusion, these women activists found themselves still excluded from all the processes leading to the party's decisions; they were confined to participating only in ways that the male leadership accepted such as reformist opposition to child-marriage and widow remarriage, education for women, and their increased involvement in the national movement. While involving themselves in all these demands, however, the women failed to disavow the ideals of self-denial and self-sacrifice for women (Talwar [1998] 1999, 230). They permitted their agenda to be coopted by the rationale that women's issues would be included in the party's platform only according to the male leadership's perceived priorities at any given time and perceived vote-getting needs. Men ignored and suppressed women's concerns and assigned insignificant, liminal roles to women members, and still do (Jayawardena 1986, 99; V. Kannabiran and K. Lalitha [1989] 1999; I. Sen 1999, 373). The women activists themselves internalized their male colleagues' perspectives that women's issues were not a priority and focused entirely on what the men considered more important issues. Furthermore, this situation will continue into the future unless the male leaders replace their narrow, ghettoized interpretation of women's issues as special interest issues with "a revolutionary redefinition of public and private [that] has yet to enter the agenda alongside class struggle" (Sangari and Vaid 1999b, 23–24).

Still today, there are fewer women insiders privy to such processes in all the various parties than there are in Parliament (Sangari and Vaid 1999b, 130; S. Ray 2000, 3).[3] Evelyne Accad, a Lebanese, has queried why men even have to construct a binary between women's sexuality and other oppressions; why women have to be situated oppositionally to what the male leaders (and some "female Marxist third world women who claim to speak for all third world women") consider more important issues:

> Marxism versus feminism, economic equality versus sexual equality, national revolution versus women's rights—as if these concepts must be opposed, as if the life of one meant the death of the other. . . . sex is one of the basic needs—like food and sleep—in any culture. . . . No mention was made of the spiritual and/or psychological needs for love, affection, and tenderness, intimately connected with sexuality, which are felt by people in all cultures. To claim that some women live without these needs because of more pressing economic factors seems not only very unfair but an exercise which only some intellectuals can afford. (1991, 238)

Nevertheless, in contrast to the traditional ideal of womanhood, which even today is propagated in various ways, activist Indian women such as Antherjanam have another tradition of militancy and courageous activity and have played a significant role in protest movements over a long period of time (Jayawardena 1986, 108). In *Small Remedies* (2000), Deshpande's heroine refers to this historic situation in the fictional character of Leela, an activist during this period who was "sidelined after years of working for the [Congress party]":

> "She never reached the top of the hierarchy, while men who'd worked under her got there, she never complained. Only once, when a woman was selected as a candidate for a by-election, this woman the widow of the sitting member who'd been killed, only then I remember Leela saying, 'It seems you've got to become a widow for them to remember that you exist.' Only that once, only that one comment about the chauvinism that ruled the party." (2000, 224)[4]

Antherjanam always focused on women, on ways in which they were mistreated, even on outrages by the Communists to women of her own class when they began to break up the landowners' huge estates. This is reflected in the character Govindankutty, "Chief of the Party," who was mothered in his childhood by a saintly *zamindar's* wife, now a beggar. She has come to his office for assistance for her grandson. Members of the upper caste have lost their rights to education and employment, but if the boy could be allowed to attend school he can at least get a lunch. Horrified, the Chief of the Party begs the old woman to forgive him for sinning against her, for his cruelty and ingratitude, for destroying her *illam* (a namboodiri landlord's household), and expropriating the proceeds from the farm. "We fought for the cause of the starving, but forgot the hands that had once served us food. And yet, you do not find fault with us. You envelop us in a blessing more powerful than a curse" (1997, 104). In a fairy-tale ending—because it is too incredible to be believed—Govindankutty requests Kunathol to be his mother and tells his secretary to escort his "mother" to his car, then to telephone his colleagues and inform them that he would not be present at the meeting to be held that day because he has "duties that I cannot shirk" both as "a human being" and as "the son of a woman!" (1997, 105).

In the face of monumental difficulties and opposition, Antherjanam continued her activist feminism until the very end of her life, until a few days before her death when she spoke at a youth festival. She told the audience that the two major aims of her life had been to effect social transformation and to make artists understand that they had the responsibility to work toward that end. As she had written some years before: "I believe that even as the artist, man or woman, pulls down the girders of a narrow, decayed society, he or she must also forge the tools to build a cultured and wholesome new structure in its place. All artistic creation—novels, short stories, and poems—are materials to be used for this purpose" (1997, 156). As I have pointed out earlier, Mahasweta Devi, more than any other activist, follows Antherjanam's socialist vision of an artist's theory and praxis. Antherjanam has been neglected until recently, until after feminists began to reappraise her work from a feminist perspective. Hitherto, traditionalists appraised her dismissively, as they do the work of other feminist writers, as too much politics and too little aesthetics, although they fail to perceive political situatedness in themselves.

Maitreyi Devi

Maitreyi Devi (1914–1989) was more than worthy of her father's enormous pride in her talents and his endless fostering of them. From the time she was thirteen, her father, a renowned, erudite scholar in Calcutta, took her regularly to Rabindranath Tagore (1861–1941). He hoped in this way to inspire his daughter to write poetry. A Nobel Prize laureate in 1913 and the supreme poet and guru of his time, as well as an Indian patriot,[5] Tagore was a reformer who "placed great emphasis on the conditions necessary for the release of creative potential in women" (Jayawardena 1986, 86, 85). When he accepted Devi as his disciple, he began to treat her as his own daughter and ignored her father to the latter's intense disappointment and humiliation. Until his death Devi enjoyed a close and enduring relationship with Tagore and wrote eight books about him, while Tagore wrote the introduction to her first book of poetry when she was sixteen (which her father was instrumental in having published). Tagore predicted about Devi that she would forge her own future, even though he was aware that in India it was almost impossible for females to be strong and independent because they are treated unfairly by the external world and discouraged from expanding their minds. Despite these conditions, Tagore requested her to believe in her abilities, to permit her "glory" to withstand and overcome the future mapped out for her. Even if others subjected her to pettiness or oppressed her, he urged her never to succumb to external pressure. Doubtless he was obliquely referring to Devi's autocratic father and his plans for her, as well as to Bengal Brahmin culture. Tagore thus guaranteed Devi's success, although her father did everything in his power to ensure it, as well. As the excited young girl wrote in *It Does Not Die* ([1974] 1995): "All the littérateurs, artists and poets of Calcutta will be invited. Father is preparing a grand show. Just as in England, when a girl comes of age she is presented to the court with great pomp, so will father introduce the new poet to the society of scholars" ([1974] 1995, 107).

Devi was no child prodigy whose flame burned briefly before sputtering out. She went on to write three more books of poetry, as well as other books on philosophy and social reform. She founded the Council for the Promotion for Communal Harmony in 1965, established boarding schools for destitute children, was closely associated with the Gandhi Peace Foundation and the Quaker Society of Friends, and became vice president of the All-India Women's Coordinating Council. And she finally wrote and published her version of her relationship with Mircea Eliade, an important book in the history of Indian feminism because it exposed the stereotypical constraints against young Indian women that prevented them from expressing their real feelings and desires and, as a result, caused them much suffering.

According to his daughter, Devi's father was an egomaniac, convinced that the world revolved around him. His students adored him, supported him, and would go to great lengths for him, but he did not love them so much as he loved that they loved him. He felt the same way about his own daughter who was also his student. She was his "jewel," not because she spoke fluent English, or was an outstanding poet, but only because as his daughter she reflected his glory. If his students or disciples, or Devi, or anyone else for that matter, ever dared to disagree with him even slightly he would "crush" them "ruthlessly." Intent on preparing his daughter to handle herself in the modern, Western world, he hired celebrated teachers to give Devi private lessons in music, painting, and the violin. But Devi, lacking the necessary self-discipline and persistence, responded to his enormous fuss and bother only as an unwelcome burden on her. She preferred, instead, to read at the window seat, her mind far off and away from her daily reality. One amazing incident that illustrates the lengths to which her father went to prepare his daughter for the modern world occurred when one of his learned colleagues, a Russian, found himself briefly alone with the child in the library. He put his arm over Devi's shoulders and drew her to him and kept repeating this move, although Devi pushed his arm away each time. This in a world and time when it was a sin to touch a female![6] He only stopped his unwelcome advances when Devi put her sandal on his knee and told him she would beat him with it. When informed of this incident, Devi's mother demanded of her husband why "these nasty Europeans" ([1974] 1995, 29) were permitted in their home. But her father's response—to show amusement—was practical by his lights. Familiar with the Western world, he argued that their daughter, in contrast to his wife, would not live a private life in seclusion and therefore would be coming into contact with all kinds of men. Devi must learn how to handle herself. Accordingly, in what Devi defines as an act of rebellion for both her father and herself at that time, he took his gifted daughter to all-male colleges where she would recite her poetry to the boys there.

Nevertheless, this Brahmin insisted on having it both ways. Evidently, he was already dissatisfied with Devi's mother, his first wife, seeing her as narrow, provincial, old-fashioned: not good enough or brilliant enough or learned enough for him. A worshiper of Western modernity such as the men Satthianadhan had satirized, he had no respect for his first wife's, or even his own parents', traditional Hindu virtues. In contrast, he wanted his daughter to become a "New Woman," like his second wife, who held a Ph.D. and was strong and successful in the Western, modern sense. In admonishing his European disciple Mircea Eliade for daring to express the wish to take part in a street demonstration against the English in 1930, her father vaunted the changes he himself had been responsible for in his own home. He defined these changes as being revolutionary in their way because, before he made them, Eliade could not even have attempted to live with his professor's family. It certainly would have been impossible in his parents' time, when his wife would have been veiled.

If Eliade had been invited to their home, he would have had to use separate plates. If by some misfortune he happened to touch the food, it would be considered polluted and he would be treated as if he were an untouchable. Devi at sixteen would long since have been married already and in deep seclusion at her in-laws' home. She would be doing housework while continually being watched over and criticized by her mother-in-law. Yet, at the same time, this Brahmin was modern only when it benefited himself. He expected to be and was treated in his home like an omnipotent potentate whom no one would ever dream of questioning. Jhabvala, a mistress of irony, loves to satirize this type of male Brahmin, so much like Devi's father. "There was something lordly, almost tyrannical in his attitude . . . When he lounged at his ease . . . he became what, as a Brahmin, he perhaps was by nature: an aristocrat for whom the goods and riches of this world were created and whose right it was to be served by others" (1986, 97).

On the whole, Devi was influenced as much by her mother as by her father, which was perhaps instrumental in her ambivalence, in her ability to write the truth about inner female feelings while always remaining outwardly modest and passive. She rarely spoke to boys or men, although she did feel comfortable with older men. Being around young men inhibited her to the point of freezing up, un-less they were related to her. When her father's students would walk him to his car, she would walk behind them, silent, with eyes lowered to the ground.[7] Admitting that in reality she would want to speak to a boy and that he would want to speak to her also, Devi analyzes the source for what really prevented her from conversation, why she was always voiceless. She concluded that it was the after-effect of her be-loved mother's background in *purdah,* especially when it came to matters to do with sex and sexuality, although Devi wore no veil. Before moving to Calcutta, Devi's mother would listen silently to her husband's conversations on literature with his colleagues from behind a curtain in the library room and send them re-freshments while still remaining invisible to them. Once the family moved to the city, she did modify her traditional habits and customs. She no longer wore the veil and began to wear leather shoes. Still, like Satthianadhan's mother, Devi's mother continued to act in accordance with all the traditional Hindu decrees related to husband worship and obedience to the marriage vows, rather than specifying indi-vidual feelings for an individual person.

These observations of Devi's about *purdah* reveal that the custom was easing but far from gone in her childhood and youth. *Purdah* affected her psyche perma-nently for the rest of her life. The taboos around sex and sexuality still remained, still held, still had a hold on Devi's psyche, without her even comprehending what it was all about and why taboos had been and still were imposed. In fact, in the middle and upper classes in her time, and even up to the present day, no expression of sexuality was and is permitted—even kissing or holding hands publicly. Only members of the same sex can do this (Islam 1996, 91). Sex was completely con-cealed, never discussed, and books about sex were prohibited. Parents chose all reading matter (Devi [1974] 1995, 26). It is doubtful that Devi's mother even dis-cussed sex with her:

> In Indian families sexuality in adolescents is not only suppressed and repressed but even feared as potentially dangerous. Rarely does a mother discuss the mystery and serious-ness of sexual awakening with her daughter. Sex education is a taboo which has been handed down for generations. It appears that, in India, artistic expression—including mythology, literature, and mass media—has compensated for such repressions. Sexual-ity is approached indirectly through symbolic and metaphoric language rather than as a human behavior needing open discussion, understanding, and acceptance. These re-pressions are justified with the unspoken agreement that such a potentially dangerous awakening of body and psyche must be controlled and deferred until after marriage. (M. Roy 1998, 102)

Devi describes her mother as also personally kind and loving and (overly) eager to please everyone, especially her husband and his every whim. For ten long years, in the face of continual gossip, Devi's mother resolutely insisted on giving a posi-tive interpretation publicly and privately to the relationship between her husband

and his mistress, his future second wife. But to no avail. Devi's father left her and their six children for this woman. He then signed everything over to his second wife, thus depriving his first family of all economic support. He even cast them out of their former home. As a result of his shocking conduct, Devi's father's personal reputation, career, and life trajectory took a tragic, downward turn from that point onward. It is not surprising then that Devi determined early on to become an entirely different kind of woman than her totally unselfish, self-sacrificing, traditional mother who had always loved and served her husband faithfully. Devi certainly did accomplish far more in her life than her gentle, passive, basically traditional mother who was victimized and whose life became a hell. Devi, instead, became a strong, powerful woman of exceptional intellect. It must be pointed out, however, that as with Satthianadhan, Hossain, and Antherjanam, but unlike her mother, Devi enjoyed the support and respect of powerful men—her father, Tagore, and, later on, her adoring husband. There were other reasons, however, for Devi's ability to surpass not only her own mother and foremothers, but also her feminist predecessors in fulfilling her talents in terms of her public career. More favorable external circumstances prevailed at her birth and throughout her life. Because Devi's lifetime spanned most of the twentieth century, she benefited more than her foremothers did from the far broader opportunities and experiences available to her that combined to assist her talents in flowering.

Still, despite all the benefits she enjoyed and all the opportunities open to her, despite her personal strength, power, courage, and intellect, it is not what Devi did accomplish, but the tragedy inherent in what she did *not* accomplish, that marks her of especial interest. In one crucial area Devi lacked courage, and that lack links her life to her predecessors. She failed in her own life to battle the cultural gender constraints against women that prevented them from fully expressing themselves. She neither asserted the right to choose her own fully self-actualized destiny, nor acted on that assertion. As modern and Western as Devi was, she still internalized in her own conduct her mother's and foremothers' values in relation to gender constraints and inequities: the many customs and codes prevailing for appropriate female conduct. She was unable personally to break free from these codes, from all the mind games about appropriate female conduct that she knowingly and consciously permitted to trap her in the conventional round that led to her personal suffering, her lifelong tragedy. Devi rebukes herself endlessly for not having freely interacted with the man she loved, for never expressing her personal feelings and wishes, for not having risen up and gone away with the man whom *she* wanted wherever their lives might lead them. But Devi failed to do that, no matter how she bemoans her mistake, her lack of courage in following up on her convictions. "No, it is one thing to do something determinedly to help others, be it a buffalo or a human being, but quite another to speak out regarding my own matters—shame, hesitancy and a sense of guilt would seal my mouth—particularly in this matter it was impossible to speak out—it would be immodest" ([1974] 1995, 93), Devi laments. For Devi, her "personal shame [was] "tantamount to shaming one's family." What she considered "personal shame," however, were "rules of the game" for women internalized into Devi by her family according to community "authorized" authorities with whom her family were "complicit" (Feldman 2001, 1109).

Even as late as Devi's final years of life, when Alexander was a teenager in the mid-to-late 1960s, the much younger author testifies to being manipulated through the same sense of shame inculcated into her specifically connected with her sexuality. She was desperately aware of being female. This made her feel ashamed, that she had an intense "power" that had to be suppressed because otherwise it would be threatening "to the order that governed my young life." She therefore was prevented from ever accepting her body and her "desires and what those desires might lead me to" (1993, 111, 141). Kishwar analyzes the source of this feeling of shame as the powerful weapon of "sexual slander" used to threaten and torture women, to create in them an ever-present fear that they might lose their "*izzat* (honour)" (1999, 154) and, thereby, cause them to lose their families, jobs, become social pariahs, and even jeopardize their lives. Sexual slander is so powerful a weapon that it can even badly harm a strong woman like Devi. And it is used not only on women who would speak out about their sexuality and its realities but also on victims of sexual harassment and rape because the women who are subjected to and dare to speak on these matters are socially ostracized as shameless for having the courage to do so (1999, 167).

Although it took Devi a lifetime, she finally did overcome her training in regard to expressing her sexuality honestly. Sadly, too late to fulfill "her unfulfilled desire" with Eliade, the man she wanted, as Alexander did succeed in doing with the man of *her* desire—by the age of eighteeen. Even so, this was achieved at a tremendous price. For Alexander was unable to reconcile her striving for the life of abstract intellectuality that she was leading as a student in England with her "obsessive passion" (1993, 141) for a man. She saw, as all women globally are trained to see, that her passionate sexuality was extremely dangerous to unleash, and as a result of the stress between her mind and body, had a nervous breakdown. She was incapable, given her training, given her value system, to accept the biological drives of her body and where those drives might lead.

Devi herself admits that she could have left her family and India with Eliade, but personally lacked the courage and initiative to do this. She also lacked trust in the stranger, the European whom she loved. For these reasons, she chose to remain with her parents in her own safe, known, little world when it came time to dispose of her in marriage. This, despite her complaints that her suffering and Eliade's were not considered nearly as much in India as were social prescriptions, "customs, and rituals." Her use of emphasis in the following passage shows that she wants her readers to understand that in 1974 the customs that she permitted to constrain her in 1930 are not ancient history in India, but that "[t]his not only *was* our country, it still is" ([1974] 1995, 138, emphasis the author's). Devi's incapacity, combined with an unwillingness to overcome tradition in terms of appropriate sexual conduct for women, places her alongside Satthianadhan and Hossain who also struggled unsuccessfully in their own lives against social, economic, and educational constraints against women. Feminists everywhere still struggle for the right to full free self-expression and self-fulfillment as sexual entities, for women's right to choose their own partners (or not), their own paths in life. "India, like America, is one of the world's most populous democracies. Yet as a woman growing up, so much of what came to me was through the requirements of femininity, the culture and ceremony that sanctified, the strict cast desire was forced to take (Alexander 1996a, 142).

Mircea Eliade, the European disciple of Devi's father, while boarding in his guru's home, had fallen in love with his daughter and Devi had fallen in love with him, although she concealed this from Eliade. Verbally, she never responded to his declarations with any expression of her own feelings, thus preventing Eliade from ever gauging their depths. She always attempted to act with propriety, and when she could not, she prevented his advances or did not respond to them, always remaining passive. Entirely ignorant of Hindu culture, but in good faith by Western standards, Eliade asked Devi to marry him and assured her that his mother and sister would welcome her into his home. He did not have the slightest idea that an unbridgeable chasm existed between his plans and Indian reality. Eliade imagined that if he converted to Hinduism Devi's father would welcome him with open arms as his son-in-law. Even so, Devi explains, he would not be accepted. For one thing, he was not an Indian, nor a Brahmin of the same caste, although as a European, he was not from the same clan. Clan names must be different. Otherwise, it would be incest. But Eliade was both ignorant and arrogant. He refused to understand, to acknowledge these complications, continually questioning Hindu "customs and social injunctions." Even more disastrous, Eliade had no idea about the extent to which Devi's family was "bound by those irrational rules." To her father, happiness did not matter, only caste and clan. As for Devi, she confides to her readers that she had never entered "the prison house of prejudice." Whether or not they married, she determined to show Eliade that she had no use for "these silly customs," that she cared nothing for "Hindu society," for "idolatry or icon worship the way Hindus do it" ([1974] 1995, 88–89).

When her father discovered the youthful romance, he responded with brutal insensitivity. He immediately threw his disciple out into a strange city in a strange country to fend entirely for himself. He sent police to warn Eliade that he would be dispatched back to Europe immediately if he ever attempted to contact his daughter. Moreover, he wrote an extremely harsh letter to Eliade, informing his former disciple that he had tarnished his home. He likened the young man to a snake in the grass, explaining that when a snake appears with his head raised, it must then be struck down, and this is what he had done to Eliade. The rejected suitor fled deep into the Himalayas where he became a beggar and converted to Hinduism.[8] For about a year he attempted to communicate with Devi through an intermediary, a relative of Devi's, who, however, betrayed him by never passing on any of Eliade's letters to Devi, nor indicating to Devi that he knew all along where Eliade was, or how much the European was suffering. He only informed Devi about all this many years later when he handed over some of Eliade's letters to her after she demanded that he do so. Eventually Eliade, who had no idea that Devi fully reciprocated his feelings and was suffering as much as he was, went to France where he married, became famous as a philosopher and scholar—always afterward identified with India—and became infamous for collaborating with the Nazis during World War II.

Eliade wrote two popular novels loosely based on his unrequited passion for Devi in which he used her name, Amrita. One part of her was deeply humiliated, publicly shamed, and angered at being the public object of Eliade's "fantasies" about her and about his use of her name. This enabled readers to identify her as the book's subject, and whenever they did so, she objected strenuously to its "defamatory" material. But there was another part of Devi that ran much deeper than anger or shame, a part of her that had never been sexually satisfied or fulfilled and would never be. In 1970, after being married for thirty-eight years to an extraordinarily supportive and gentle husband who lived only for her happiness, the force of Devi's adolescent love for Eliade suddenly resurfaced in her aging body. After much mental and physical torture, she finally traveled to Paris—with her husband's blessing and approval—to see Eliade again, at least once on this earth before they both died. Because he had heard of her arrival, Devi's visit did not come altogether as a surprise for Eliade. However, he resolutely kept his back turned to her from the moment she barged into his office, while Devi kept repeatedly begging her "dear, dear Mircea" to turn around. Before he finally did turn around and raise his face to her, he said to her in Sanskrit, "*No hanyate hanymané sharire*—it does not die, when the body dies" ([1974] 1995, 256), the statement from which the title of her book, *It Does Not Die,* is taken.

Devi's purpose in writing the book was not just to tell a tragic tale of unrequited young love between a sixteen year-old Indian girl and her father's twenty-three-year-old European disciple. Devi wanted to set the record straight, to tell her side of the story honestly, to reveal the truth of the situation for her, the reality for her, how she felt. She wanted to describe all the manifold constraints imposed on her that she had suffered as a young Indian girl that had prevented her from expressing her true feelings to Eliade, from responding to him, from leaving her father's house and going off with him into a joint future, and especially what it was that had made it completely impossible for Eliade's fantasies to be fulfilled, as he

pretended in his book. Devi explains in great detail to Western readers the varieties
of insurmountable barriers that existed to make lurid Mircea's claims of sexual in-
timacy. She takes great pains to describe the public nature of the Indian home at
that time and especially the constraining conditions in such a home for an adolescent Indian girl, which Westerners cannot understand. Bedi makes the same point
years later when she contrasts the Indian home to the New York home: "The world
of the home was not really separate from the life outside it as it was in New York"
([1989] 1993, 134). And Nanda Kaul of Desai's *Fire on the Mountain,* a character
who comes from the same background as Devi and has led a similar life during the
same time period, also comments on the public nature of the Indian home:

> There had been too many guests coming and going, tongas and rickshaws piled up
> under the eucalyptus trees and the bougainvilleas, their drivers asleep on the seats with
> their feet hanging over the bars. The many rooms of the house had always been full,
> extra beds would have had to be made up, often in not very private corners of the hall or
> veranda, so that there was a shortage of privacy that vexed her. ([1977] 1982a, 29)

Sanjit Baruah also confirms Devi's, Desai's, and Bedi's depiction of Indian
homes as public spaces when he contrasts the Western bourgeois concept of home
with the Indian middle-class home, which he claims is more like the Western
home of the Middle Ages—public, not private, a "part of the social space" (1997,
511) where the activities of daily life are conducted, where people meet to do business and to be entertained. To prove this, Devi emphasized all the untiring familial
vigilance both in her home and in her community, the monolithic cultural constraints on her sexuality that successfully prevented her all her life from achieving
full self-realization until she flew to Paris.

No matter how great her accomplishments were in serving her society, no
matter how pleasant and useful her life was as a loving mother and faithful wife,
despite her superficial adherence to her acculturation throughout the text, from
beginning to end, Devi's damaged psyche mourns an incompletion in her being
that never dies, caused by her inability to escape the webs of her private and public culture that trapped her both in private and in public. At the end, she only has
the possibility of finally achieving wholeness of self and inner peace to look forward to in the afterlife when Eliade promises her he will come to her again on the
shores of the Ganga and at last show her his real self. In writing *It Never Dies,*
Devi wanted to show that she could not be constrained into the Indian cultural
straitjacket for women or defined only in those terms. Devi also wanted to show
readers that she had suddenly become bigger and more of her true self than she
had ever been in the past and to publish to the world what she had finally done in
keeping with the needs and desires of that self. Perhaps the single most important
message that Devi sends to us is about a woman's search for peace in her own self,
for wholeness, and centeredness: to be true to what she really wanted sexually and

not just live a convincing act in conformity with how her life should look to her family, to her neighbors, to Indian society.

Although she fully reciprocated Eliade's feelings, she could not respond to him or even reveal them. She could never do what she really wanted in her life because her public and private constraints prevented her from doing so. It is these constraints that she reveals to us in order to provide us with the keys to understand the nature of her inaction or passivity which resulted from her having internalized these constraints. She enables readers to understand the precise nature of the constraints on Indian females that prevented her from fully acting out on and living her desires. She informs us of what we need to know: all the factors that led her to live a tragic, lifelong limbo, to live like a zombie. Devi, forever suffering physically and psychologically, always went through motions, did what she did not really want to do after Eliade was expelled from her father's home. Her material presence was always elsewhere than where she desired to be and with whom. By providing her readers with this important and valuable historical information about the precise source and nature of the constraints that led her to live such a life, Devi continues the exploration that began with Antherjanam about sexual constraints on Indian women that are still present and still powerful for them and for us. These constraints still control and damage Indian and many other women's lives, preventing women everywhere from full and free self-expression because "in a patriarchal context, all representations of female sexuality are likely to be reactionary" (Gopal 1999, 294).

What Antherjanam began, Maitreyi Devi continued. For the first time, Indian women writers openly and honestly revealed to readers the truth about female sexuality; that females are not passive, naturally "pure," "good," and "virgin," but are as strongly sexual as males. Traditionally, and to this day, women are considered to be the embodiments of *shakti,* which is both positive and destructive as represented by the goddesses Devi/Durga/Kali (M. Roy 1998, 106). The Devi without her *shakti,* the traditional ideal of Indian womanhood, deprives Indian women of sexual autonomy (DasGupta and Das Dasgupta 1998, 125). Ironically, although Indian women are believed to be linked with goddesses because of the gender they share, they do not seem to have reaped any benefits, except to perpetuate the system (Hiltebeitel 2000, 11):

> This triumph of the divine feminine does not seem to have had an uplifting effect on the secular or religious lives of Hindu women. It seems that a society giving rise to *sati,* a culture in which women do not receive the rite of religious initiation (*upanayana*), and in which a woman's primary mode of religiosity has traditionally been the worship of her husband as her spiritual lord (*pati*) cannot be expected to pass the acid test of feminist analysis. (DasGupta Sherma 2000, 24)[9]

If the woman gathers together her female "creative energy" or "inherent generative power" and uses it entirely for her husband in *pativratadharma* through praying, frequently fasting, and serving him, she can gain "dharmic perfection" (Courtright 1995, 187; Hancock 1995, 82). Unfortunately, the sexual aspect of female power is so frightening, such a source of danger to society, so "uncontrollable and irresponsible" that women would tend to favor gratifying themselves sexually over serving their families (Pintchman 2000, 193). Therefore, female sexuality has to be constrained, policed, controlled, reined in, and entirely orchestrated by males. In relation to Indian women's specific predicament is that the good manifestation, like the goddess Sita, is tamed, married, fertile, asexual, and nurturing. The other aspect, like Kali, is wild, unpaired (or adulterous), infertile, sexual, and dangerous (Gold 1995, 120; Rajan 2000, 272).[10] Therefore, to avoid the negative aspects of the female life force, females had to be subordinated to their menfolk, constrained in every way by the taboos of their culture, as is the case in most cultures worldwide. Females, however, are kept far more frustrated sexually than men because the demands of respectability in all cultures permit males far more leeway.

The family structure in India and almost everywhere else that prevails globally is entirely in conformity with the patriarchal concept, discourse, and formation of family units and the limitations on women that entail the success and continuity of the family. The source of these artificially binary images for women can be traced in macho myths that Chinese, Japanese, Hebrew, Greek, Roman, Christian, Indian, and other male scribes wrote and perpetuated, as so many Indian/Third World and Western feminists have noted (Chakravarti [1989] 1999, 57; Gold 1995, 133, 120). Clearly, patriarchal notions of women are remarkably similar historically to those of contemporary times because the patriarchal value system prevails throughout the globe (Dobia 2000, 210).

Many Western and Indian/Third World feminists also deplore men's enjoyment of a sexual, gutsy, rebellious woman's defeat and generally make it a predictable conclusion. Although she is writing only about "a male bard of the Nath caste in a small village in Rajasthan," Ann Grodzhin Gold claims without using any qualifying adjectives that "men" "zestfully describe amoral, independent, saucy, 'bad' women whose rebellion is enjoyable [to men] because it inevitably ends in [the women's] defeat" (1995, 122). This narrative becomes embedded in women's consciousness globally as an unexamined assumption that the same fate will await them if they violate the cultural narrative boundaries set for them.

Kishwar takes a more positive view about Indian men's response to the tradition of *shakti*—that they both revere and are repelled by it; that it has always empowered individual, extraordinary women to embody *shakti* and to take a path different from other women outside their stereotyped conventional roles. For this reason, she claims that Indian society is "far more receptive" than Western society to strong, assertive women, although she admits that Indian society does impose "offensive forms of discrimination against women" (1999, 276). In India, as elsewhere, women's sexuality is heavily controlled and they are also kept economically dependent. The ideals for women are based on the goddess, the "perfect" subordinate to Vishnu, her spouse. Moreover, according to "the reactionary Brahamanic code of Manu" (Sylvia Pankhurst, quoted in Grewal 1996, 76), "a woman must never be autonomous" (DasGupta Sherma 2000, 25; R.Menon and Bhasin 1998, 252; Wadley 1995, 95, 94). If a wife obeys her husband in all things she will be uplifted to heaven. Needless to say, she must be perfectly chaste as a wife and completely desexed as a mother. Furthermore, "imagery of tying and binding abounds" (Hancock 1995, 82):

> The control of female sexuality is the linchpin of the patriarchal institutions of caste and kinship. . . . In practice women's sexuality is controlled by subtle and not-so-subtle arrangements of power that are formed and reformed through marriage and subordination to masculine authority, as well as through the complex set of relational obligations to kin that are articulated through life-cycle and calendrical rituals. (82–83)

Females are considered inherently inferior and unrefined in the way they are constructed internally and their limitations in regard to "self-control." As a female, an Indian woman can never hope to achieve the ten stages toward "perfectibility" (Nicholas 1995, 155), only the two stages of daughter and wife, and she always has to be controlled by a male. In India and everywhere else, females lose their reputation, the reputation of their family, their pride and "honor" if they permit themselves to express their desires before or after marriage to other men than their husbands. They would be shunned, ostracized, prostituted, no longer be marriageable, or accepted within their families and communities.

Although Devi settled, although she fully conformed to these conventions in her world and time, she nevertheless made one significant and memorable contribution in destabilizing time-honored patriarchal conventions. On the surface, Devi wrote her book to redeem her reputation, to refute Eliade's claims about a full-blown, physical affair between them, to expose him as a braggart and a liar, ignorant of all the Indian social customs and constraints that made such an affair impossible. Her book became a bestseller, but was it only because Devi's Indian readers were rooting for her because they enjoyed reading about an Indian woman finally refuting an arrogant European who had made his reputation as an expert on Indian religion and philosophy? By Indian standards, Devi had done no wrong physically or literally. She had ultimately remained obedient to Indian sexual standards of appropriate female conduct and she became famous in her own right. But Eliade, by using her real name in his book and making it appear to readers as if his exaggerated fantasies were reality, had violated and shattered the privacy of a respectable and honored woman. And he had done this for money, for notoriety, whereas in writing her side of the story, Devi sought to expose far more than Eliade's grossness in distorting their private relationship and making it public, which was at the very least opportunistic. Perhaps she did this unwittingly in her need to tell it "like it was." But Devi, in fact, exposed the lie that "good" women were forced to live and the truth of their actual biological, physical reality.

In 1986, the Indecent Representation of Women (Prohibition) Act was passed in India, based on the enduring belief that respect for women is founded on their innate sexlessness. All that Devi attempted to show went for naught. Instead, this bill led to increased segregation of women, curtailing their movements and how they dress, strengthening the notion of women's inherent "chastity and purity" and continuing the division of women along "good" and "bad" binaries. "Wives are good because they have little choice. The nuns in nunneries are good. Little children in their cradles are good. The Hindu wife is a Hindu wife and can be nothing else. And it is not until we can take the goodness of women less for granted that we shall learn to value it" (Sahgal [1986] 1988b, 128–129). In any event, the Prohibition Act conforms to and reinforces "patriarchal, reactionary and fundamentalist notions regarding women and their sexuality" (F. Agnes, 1997, 553): notions that come at a prohibitive cost to women, penalizing them by curtailing their female sexuality and its expression (Alexander 1996a, 192; Oza 2001, 1073). Policing women's sexuality through laws regulates, manages, prescribes, describes and embeds women's sexuality within state, patriarchal, and economic structures, thereby maintaining and reproducing gender asymmetry and normalizing patriarchy. Men's sexuality is naturalized as incapable of being controlled, whereas woman's sexuality is prescribed by cultural mandate and if she transgresses in any way she is conceptualized as a threat to the Indian way and to Indian "sovereignty" (Feldman 2001, 1119; Oza 2001, 1085, 1081; Sangari and Vaid [1989] 1999b, 5).

Because of his character, Devi eventually did come to love her brilliant, gentle, kind, but unattractive husband as her best friend. But she never wanted him sexually. She only wanted Eliade. As a result, Devi lived a lie until she finally went to Paris, barged into Eliade's office, and forced him to talk to her. In conforming to appearances throughout her life, in living through all her passages of womanhood as a lie, in making everyone else happy except herself and her husband, Devi conveyed to the world in her book the enormous suffering endured by women such as herself under a sexually repressive regime, even in the best of circumstances. If Devi could return to life, she would not be surprised, for the situation has not changed: "Instances of censorship in popular culture signaled systematic measures to curtail women's sexuality and sexual expression" (Oza 2001, 1073). This is the kind of oppression to which women throughout the world can relate, for they themselves still experience it.

Devi differed from and went beyond her feminist predecessors in covering new ground. Satthianadhan and Hossain, for example, were careful not to disturb the prescribed female mold for fear of jeopardizing the social, political, and educational goals for women for which they struggled. In revealing through her writing that young women were sexual human beings despite being imprisoned in a mass of rules and regulations that make it virtually impossible for them to express themselves as such, Devi, like Antherjanam before her—but better known—made one further move forward in the cause of women's human rights: the freedom to acknowledge that we are sexual entities.

Kamala Das

It remained for Kamala Das (1934–) to move beyond Maitreyi Devi in the attempt by Indian women earlier in the twentieth century to have their society include and integrate sexuality into women's identity. Das was born in Punnayurkulam in South Malabar, Kerala, in 1934, middle class on her father's side, and royal on her mother's side. In *My Story* ([1988] 1996), Das writes that her childhood paralleled Maitreyi Devi's in almost every way, except that both her parents ignored and "neglected" their children and never treated them as if they were individuals ([1988] 1996, 2, 74). Around 1928, her parents and other members of her family came under Gandhi's spell and began to live according to the Gandhian ideals of simplicity and antimaterialism. At Nalapat House, her ancestral home on her mother's side where Das spent much time, pictures of Gandhi hung on all the walls. Because her beloved grandmother and other female relatives had given all their jewelry away to their leader, Das thought of him as a thief whose devilish purpose was to strip women of all their ornamentation in order for them to lose their attractiveness and thus no longer offer him temptations of the flesh. Her family's decision to live an austere life under Gandhi's spell struck Das as "a cruel practical joke" ([1988] 1996, 14) because she longed for wealth and all its trappings, a glamorous life, romance, and white skin. She traces the source of the self-hatred she internalized as a child to the fair-skinned British colonizers who deemed themselves so superior to Indians that they had inscribed into their subjects what she now perceives were erroneous ideas of what was beautiful and refined. Or, as Mukherjee has expressed it, only more succinctly, "self-hate was a colonial construct" ([1977] 1995, 221).

Every author discussed in this text makes this point: that lightness of skin is an Indian ideal, one of the key factors in marriage choices. Sidhwa's character Feroza in *An American Brat* (1993) comes to the United States to study and eventually decides to remain here. She finds that her American classmates either ignored her or acted in an exaggeratedly friendly manner, but were in reality uncomfortable in her presence, which made her aware that they did not really accept her as a member of their group. "Dismayed by her own brown skin, the emblem of her foreignness, she felt it was inferior to the gleaming white skin in the washrooms and the roseate faces in the classrooms" (1993, 153).

Suneeta Peres da Costa born in 1974 in Sydney, Australia, records a solution for combating such a construct—to be given an alternative education—in her case by her anti-Indian Goan father who, possessed of "countercolonial peccadilloes" (2001, 171), teaches his daughters that school is "an ideological apparatus of the state—*don't submit!*" (2001, 152, emphasis the author's). Peres da Costa's sarcasm is even more devastating in the following passage:

> Where we would learn in school of the plight of the poor convicts, taken in chains to the barren continent of Australia, he would fill that history with tales about the unpublicised murder of people, dark like us. On the day at school that Shanti and I had recently to dress ourselves as famous Australians, he insisted we go as Trugininni twins, naked and with spears he'd spent an entire weekend carving by hand in the garage. . . . He explained in no uncertain terms that the history of the very land on which we were living was founded in blood and that it was not because the people that lived here were either weaker or more stupid than the dough-faced conquerors who came, but simply that they were poorer; and their poverty was due to no lack of enterprise or laziness or godlessness at all, but because these people didn't have the meanness of spirit to go to the continent of Africa and turn the bodies of many Africans into fast money, selling them to the sweet free cause of Sugar, Cotton, and Cocoa. And with this money to make guns with which to empty the world of its people; and when that endeavour itself became futile, imposing upon them a loveless God, writing books in the metropolitan academies about a strangeness that to their own depraved souls, had seemed devoid of beauty. And when, because they had enslaved and permanently exiled the native inhabitants of those places they had conquered, they found themselves without enough cheap labour to build railways and bridges, when they discovered that among their own dough-faced kin they felt homesick and all alone, they dragged people of coffee-colour from India, from China, to build these things, to populate and indenture. . . . We would look contemptuously at the tourists who marvelled at how beautiful and young the city was; and then we would stop at Bennelong, where lie the shops containing the artefacts of those whose ancestors had been slaughtered in order to make room for the shops containing the artefacts of those whose ancestors had been slaughtered. (2001, 163)

Unlike Peres da Costa, Das had no such parental armor to shield her from projecting the occupier's perspective onto herself. When she began to write at a very early age, Das often wished she could have had parents who were white who would have been proud of her poetry, an odd statement from the daughter of a famous female poet. At any rate, Das's earliest ambition was not to become a writer, but to become a lawyer because lawyers enjoyed great wealth, owned several cars, and employed many servants. She longed to find a rich husband, "a *zamindar,*" to live in a mansion in Calcutta filled with art objects, precious metals, and beautiful furnishings. Above all else she desired to become "a snob" ([1988] 1996, 55).

The anonymous advertisement for *My Story* makes the claim that Das has "blazed a new trail of emancipation for Indian women," that she "combines her love for truth with candour and poignancy," that her autobiography "has been read by millions of Indians and has evoked violent reactions—of admiration and criticism: the symptoms of a great work." On the book's cover, she is described as "the most controversial Indian writer." Why is Das read by millions and in what way has she caused so much controversy? More than anything else, feminist readers might wonder what she could possibly have written that would be described as having "blazed a new trail of emancipation for Indian women." What Das has done is dare to express in her own life, as well as make the claim in writing, that not only do women have sexuality, but that we deserve the right to proactively, freely, express that sexuality. When Alexander writes that women's bodies were burdened with having to repress their desire, with "the pain of withdrawn sexuality" (1996a, 182), she courageously and accurately expresses the major constraint on Indian women. As Chatterjee contends, the home was the primary site for women's struggles, not least in relation to their attempts to express themselves as sexual beings. The responses of Das's famous family to her publications surprised her most, she claimed, because in their eyes she had "embarrassed" and "disgraced" them by informing her readers that she had committed adultery, and not only with one man, which was sinful enough in their eyes, but with other men. It seems odd to me that she should have expected otherwise, that she should have been surprised and disappointed, not only by her family's response to her revelations, but when she returned to her home state, by her neighbors' failure to receive her warmly.

Das's earliest notions of sex were formed by her female relatives who never discussed it, treating it as if it didn't exist. Das explains that this was because their only experiences with sex were violent and bloody. In contrast, even in adolescence Das's attitude toward sex was marked by boldness. After she had seen a man who was considered "notorious," one of her teachers immediately warned her that this man had been responsible for ruining some "good girls" and therefore bringing disgrace to "some of the best families in India." Instead of feeling aversion and fear, as the teacher expected, Das fantasied about becoming this man's "mistress" when she grew up. When she was thirteen, Das fell in love for the first time with a "student-leader" who had been imprisoned for "revolutionary activities" ([1988] 1996, 62). When he displayed no interest in her, she decided it was because she dressed too simply and wore no jewelry. To make up for this lack, she put flowers in her hair. His only response was to tell Das to begin to study Marx and Engels as soon as possible. Later, Das's relatives were mortified to read about what they considered her unseemly attempts to arouse this young man's interest, or that she should have had such thoughts at that age, and worse, attempted to act on them. During that period in Das's life, a young married woman would visit Das's parents with her husband and would answer Das's questions frankly. This is how Das discovered to her amazed amusement what she visualized as "sexual acrobatics" in order to attain what Mrs. K called "the great orgasm." Was this what marriage was about? Das wondered. Turning into "a clown in bed, a circus-performer?" ([1988] 1996, 70). She concluded that she hated marriage because of her fixed aversion to exposing her body, an aversion that proved lasting, even after her marriage.

Das's second crush was on her art tutor when she was fourteen and he was twenty-nine. Observing that his daughter had suddenly begun to dress as stylishly as she could, Das's father immediately terminated the tutor's employment. When a friend advised Das to go to her tutor and tell him that she loved him, she did so. On her way to him, however, she was caught in a sudden rainstorm, and by the time she arrived at his room she was sobbing uncontrollably. Her tutor removed Das's tunic, wrung it out the window, dried her hair with a hand towel, replaced her tunic, took her home in a taxi, and shook her hand at the gate. Das never saw him again, but periodically she would remember his tender touch in removing her garment and in drying her.

Das also describes her sexual feelings during her adolescence for a female teacher, for some of her female classmates and friends. She fell in love with her English teacher's unusual voice and wrote a poem to her in which she compared her to a rose. But, because Das was a flower as well, she found her interest in another flower "odd" and "tragic" ([1988] 1996, 74). Her teacher did like the poem, but apparently nothing further transpired. After that, Das met an eighteen-year-old college girl whom her mother's friends had warned her against because she differed from other girls. Obviously, this is Das's euphemism for the girl's being a lesbian. Of course, like most of us, whatever Das is warned against is what will then attract her. Already predisposed in the unusual girl's favor because of these warnings, Das found herself attracted to her as soon as she met her. While traveling on a train, they first kissed in a berth. This kiss was the first of its kind for Das in a life that had heretofore been entirely devoid of the giving and receiving of any physical manifestation of affection. If her mother had kissed her when she was an infant, Das could not remember. And after that time, no one, not even her grandmother, to whom she was very close, had ever kissed her. Consequently, she was traumatized by that first kiss and had difficulty in breathing. The girls made love throughout the night. After arriving at their destination the next day and after everyone had left for lunch at a neighbor's, her friend took her to their host's bathroom and talked Das into taking a bath with her, then perfumed her body, and dressed her. Afterward, both girls felt "giddy with joy like honeymooners" ([1988] 1996, 80). On the train ride home, her friend kissed her passionately, but, once arrived at the railway station, Das did not even return her farewell wave. She only wanted to forget about her friend, only wanted to return to the order and safety and comfort and predictability in her life that she had known before meeting her. Nevertheless, Das felt haunted by memories of the girl.

Like Maitreyi Devi, Das married a man whom she did not love. She was younger than Devi at the time of her traditional marriage, only fifteen. Her husband, whom she claims was a cousin[11] whom she had known all her life, worked as a clerk for the Reserve Bank of India at Bombay. Before their marriage, he made sudden, brutal, crude, painful advances to her that hurt and humiliated her and left her with black and blue marks. He would crush her breasts, while demanding of her why she didn't care for his touch, why she was "cold and frigid." He kept begging her to expose "her breasts." Das had expected romantic love, intellectual dialogue, friendship, and companionship to bring an end to her lonely life, not "rough hands riding up my skirts or tearing up my brassiere" ([1988] 1996, 82, 84). After marriage, she was bitterly disappointed by the reality of their relationship, as she claims was the reality for girls in her family. They were all married off when scarcely more than children to older men who brutalized them on their wedding night. Mukherjee echoes Das when she describes the Hindu marriage brilliantly in a series of disarming uses of the word "after" that suddenly end in unanticipated horror. After the priest has finished, after the fire is lit and prayers made to the gods, after the clothes of the couple are knotted to everyone's approval, after all the guests have eaten, the servants taken care of, the children put to bed, "then the groom takes his bride, a total stranger, and rapes her on a brand new, flower-decked bed" (1971, 150). And as recently as *The Better Man* (2001), Anita Nair (1966–) records that the situation has not changed:

> In the middle of the night she woke up to feel him push the nightdress above her thighs. He stuck his tongue into her mouth, squeezed her breasts, and shoved his knees between her legs. When he thrust into her, the rudeness of his pumping hips made her gasp in shock, in pain, in anguish. . . . Wide eyed, she watched this man, her husband, grunt and moan as his hips ground into her. Glassy eyed, she watched his face clench in concentration as he sought release. Wet eyed, his wetness flooding through her at last, she saw him collapse on her as she lay there bruised in spirit and body, unsatiated, and feeling strangely empty. Was this the ecstasy poets and romantic novels promised? (2001, 227–228)

Das's husband was in keeping with this tradition. He failed to satisfy Das's physical or emotional needs, especially her romantic dreams, which included moonlight and flowers. Das surprises readers with the information that within a few months, however, she did fall in love with her husband to the point where she was willing to do anything to please him, but she claims that at fifteen her body was not yet mature enough. She also confides to readers that there was a darker side to her yearnings. She wonders why she could not find fulfillment in her husband's arms and concludes that it was because she wanted her "ego" to die, that she wanted "an executioner whose axe would cleave my head into two" ([1988] 1996, 71). I assume this is her exaggerated hyperbole for a man who would "sweep her off her feet" in the most high-handed, imperious manner possible, as in a bodice ripper. For some time Das endured her husband's neglect and silence, while yearning in vain for kindness from him, for some show of concern until she arrived at a critical juncture, a watershed of interest to all women universally. Somehow she was able to pass beyond all her internalized cultural constraints and take her own individual sexual needs as a woman into consideration. She began to realize that her husband had only married her for status and money and that what she had hoped to find in marrying him might lie only outside marriage, "outside its *legal orbit*" (emphasis mine). She therefore decided "to be unfaithful to him, at least physically" ([1988] 1996, 95).

This was not only a bold decision to make in private. It was a far more daring and dangerous one to make public to the world. Das informs readers of the social conditions at that time and what would have happened to her had she decided to leave her husband. Whenever, as in Maitreyi Devi's case, an individual young woman took an independent action of any kind, her parents and family cared only about what others would think, how others would react. For Das to have divorced her husband was tantamount to her having contracted "leprosy." She would not have been able to marry again because she was not that attractive. She had a small child, which would have been a burden to a man. She also lacked an education sufficient to allow her to succeed in the job market. She also lacked the capacity to become a prostitute because she was "frigid" and loved her husband.

What were the influences that served as Das's models for such a remarkable transformation from dutiful to disobedient daughter, despite having parents with such high principles, and despite Das's relatives continually complaining to her that she had brought dishonor on her family because of her unconventionality? Das claims that her models for change were the authors she read—"[Anton] Chekov [*sic*], [Gustav] Flaubert, [Maurice] Maeterlink [*sic*], [Dorothy] Mansfield and Virginia Woolf" ([1988] 1996, 121)[12]—who gave her "the courage to be myself" ([1988] 1996, 152). She especially singles out "Isabella [Isadora] Duncan because of her advocacy of free love as the "best" kind of love.

Interestingly, Das does not include her husband as the major influence in her life and work in terms of her advocacy of free love. Nevertheless, he is in all probability the original catalyst for her insistence on women's full and free expression of their sexuality, although Das's reading may have reinforced it. Instead, she claims that her husband became a shadowy presence in her life. In the beginning her husband had a close friend with whom he had a sexual relationship, perhaps more mutually satisfying than that with her. The two men conducted themselves "like lovers" in her presence. And once, on her birthday, after throwing her out of the bedroom, they locked the door. Das could not understand what they were doing together that could possibly bring them "physical rapture" ([1988] 1996, 104). Later, when Das suffered a nervous breakdown, her husband took her away for a rest. During their time away alone together, he bathed her, dressed her like a man, seated her on his lap, fondled her, and called her "his little darling boy" ([1988] 1996, 111–112). To Western readers confused by his conduct, Islam's explanation serves as a clarification:

> According to the cultural norms of South Asia, homosexuality does not negate marriage.
> Just because you are homosexual does not mean you can refuse to get married. Especially

the men are frequently asked, So what has that got to do with marriage? One is seen as quite capable of carrying on both roles as a heterosexual husband and maintaining a homosexual lover on the side. (1998, 89)

Das does not consider divorcing her husband for adultery because women were prohibited from doing so in India, where adultery was defined only as an intruder violating a husband's "property rights over his wife," specifically her "sexuality." The wife is not viewed as having such rights. Such an egregious inequity is naturalized so as to justify the gender asymmetry upheld by law. By this means deeply engrained sexist naturalized beliefs about qualities that do not inhere in women but are the results of societal constructions of differences of gender remain unquestioned. Inevitably, these beliefs are sexist and oppress women (R. Kapur and Cossman 1999, 239; Panjabi 1997, 160).

After her marriage, Das began to send her work out for publication. Eventually, all she came to care most about in life was her writing. She discovered that she loved her writing more than she loved her parents, her children, and even her "doting" husband. Das's use of this word in relation to her husband is shocking, given her contradictory description of him. Perhaps that was what he was—contradictory. In 1963, Das won PEN's Asian Poetry Prize. Because of her success, despite being badly and oddly dressed, wearing saris that were always torn, and despite being given to self-admitted extremes of emotion, Das was always surrounded and courted by male admirers. She luxuriated in having "fan mail" and crowds of people always around her—especially men—who hung on her every word. Actually, according to Das, such men responded to Das's publications about free love either by being infatuated with her or by assuming that she was a loose woman or a nymphomaniac and propositioning her. Because she was indifferent to sex and rejected lewd propositions, she was then criticized and harassed and became the object of unsavory, hateful rumors, causing her to become notorious. This would never have happened, she argues, if, instead, she had actually been "promiscuous" and "obliging." Under patriarchy there are many responses designed to figuratively destroy the well-being and reputations of women who attempt to openly express their sexuality and still retain their value as individual human entities—as men do. The invalidating and demeaning responses that so upset Das are neither uncommon nor unusual.

Das continued to take lovers in a long and unsuccessful quest to find transcendental true love, which included sex. Although she yearned to find all this in her own husband, he continued to refuse to show her the slightest affection or ardor, except a mechanical kind of physical lust in the bedroom. Interestingly, he accepted Das's infidelities, even gave her advice about them in an avuncular fashion. At one point, when a letter from a lover fell into her husband's hands, his only comment was to compare the lover's stupidity to Das's intelligence. Another time, after an illness, which necessitated an operation and an extended stay in a nursing home, Das informed her husband that she was in love with her doctor. His only response was that because the doctor was a woman Das would not be exploited by her. She also went out with her husband and another admirer, a colleague of his, and danced with her admirer while her husband sat at their table watching them "sleepily." He did not take this man's interest in Das seriously because of her admirer's advanced age. Das also discounted him, but not for the same reason. She boasts that she was not exactly desperate for male admirers. On another occasion, when Das told her husband about an affair (which she seems to have done routinely), her husband advised her not to fall in love with that man because he was incapable of caring for anyone but himself. Her husband claimed that for him Das was forever childlike. He gave her permission to "play around," but on condition that she choose her "playmates" ([1988] 1996, 151) with care because he never wished her to meet with any harm. Since her husband was the one whom Das blamed for her decision to become unfaithful in the first place, such a response on his part was either unwittingly ironic or unconscionably sadistic. It would explain why Das flaunted her affairs to her husband—in an effort to hurt him as he had hurt her. Later, she enjoyed the company of a younger man, especially when she needed an escort for public functions. Her husband also liked him, to the point where if Das went into depression or expressed boredom, he would suggest that she go out with the young man. It also appears as if this was her husband's characteristic way of avoiding unpleasantness—to use stand-ins for himself—that is, when he did not change the subject or leave the room.

Das paid a price for her courage, for rowing against the social tide. Because she was "emotional" and highly sensitive—the stereotypical characteristics of a creative artist—whenever she heard "unjustified" accounts about herself, usually from her family, she would go into lengthy periods of crying. In order to sleep, she took to drinking with her pills. A point finally came when Das matured through becoming socially conscious politically. She felt it insufficient to do things with the goal of receiving faint and passing approval from other countries because India had a sufficient amount of Indians suffering from hunger and homelessness. But Das only *saw* these unfortunates out in the street, in the rain, "coughing their lungs out" ([1988] 1996, 190) from a convenient distance when she would return home from festivities at the Taj Mahal Hotel. Das often *wonders* why the government doesn't let the homeless into the basements of abandoned public buildings, or why hotels cannot use a percentage of their earnings to feed the poor. She blames the change in Indians who were traditionally charitable on the former British occupiers and on the influence of the media because these two groups display cruelty and callousness toward the poor. If the media would publicize those who give charity, Das is convinced that others would follow suit. She longs to read such a story, instead of stories about crime and politicians' "empty statements" ([1988] 1996, 191).

Das was an observer of public events, and a bored one at that, including the condition of Indian agriculture, the area of her husband's expertise until he experienced difficulties at work after expressing his (correct) conviction that all the foreign aid pouring in to India for agriculture did not assist small farmers, only large farmers. This got him into trouble with his superiors. Not surprisingly, his colleagues then ostracized him, and not one of them sided or sympathized with him when he was given three hours to remove himself from his chair and his room. As a result, his health deteriorated.

Even when he was not away traveling on business and physically present at home, Das's husband's demanding job with its complex internal, often brutal politics caused him to be absent. Ambitious and driven, he hardly spent time with his family, which eventually included three sons. When he was at home, Das and her husband never had any intellectual exchanges such as had impressed her when he had first courted her. If Das ever tried to begin a discussion about her unhappiness with him, he would react by talking about something else or walking away.

Periodically, he and the family would be transferred to various cities, but somehow his career never really flourished. Das's outrage at the injustice to her husband leads her to use a crude double entendre when she informs her readers that "Bureaucracy expected the smooth running of machines," but did not permit "independent thinking" which "was as bad as a blockage in the bowels of a computer" ([1988] 1996, 195). B. P. R. Virthal supports Das's point, but more elegantly, when he describes officers in the Indian Civil Service being treated by their colleagues and superiors as if they had failed a "loyalty test," implying that "if you are not committed, you are omitted" (1997, 223) when they dare to express opposition to some programs.

In the hope of getting her husband to retire there after his work-related problems had emotionally devastated him, Das then returned to her ancestral estate. Here Das began to attempt to farm her land efficiently, but always the entire village whispered about her and her lovers. Old men from the village began to visit her surreptitiously because of the sexually free reputation her writing had given her, and she had to throw them out of her house. Das also became the object of sorcery, to which she responded by making the sorcerers the object of *her* sorcery. Then two of her servants attempted to poison her. Instead of holding them responsible, she claimed that her rich neighbors who were spreading scandalous stories about her had bribed her servants to murder her, but that her servants loved her so much that they had only given her a small dose of poison so that she could survive. As a result of all this stress, Das collapsed with a heart attack and was forced to leave her beloved estate and her experiments in agriculture and return to Bombay.

The builders in Bombay, migrant workers from Andhra Pradesh, lived in mud and brick huts with corrugated iron roofs, and had to work from morning to night carrying cement and climbing scaffolding. Their loud music at night disturbed the neighbors, like herself, wealthy people who only wanted to spend the evening drinking, talking shop, discussing books and poetry and their adulterous affairs. One night she was no longer able to control herself and pulled her husband down to the workers' colony. Das left the scene feeling that the outcasts were more alive than she was, more optimistic. Her life had been spent on trivia, on furnishing her home, and only caring about their own narrow circle of friends and relatives. Until then, she had mistakenly thought of herself as unique, as a separate and distinct individual apart from all around her.

When her Communist friends asked Das what she ever did in her life for the poor and the hungry, why she did not use her talents to write about their plight, Das revealed more than guilt. She revealed that she expected retribution in the future for her lack of activism, at least in her writing. If the poor had not been fatalists, they would have long since rebelled and "devoured" her kind, including herself, whom she describes with unblinking accuracy as the "selfish, self-centred ones, obsessed by our weight problems, our tax problems, and our colour problems" ([1988] 1996, 210–211). Das does *see* the possibility of such an uprising in the future by the poor and outcast, but it does not cause her fear. Rather, it causes her to anticipate destruction with shudders of delight.

Perhaps in reaction to these accusations and her guilty response to them, Das does begin to make certain *action plans* that she *hopes* to send to the government: to collect a small amount of money from every middle-class household for constructing low-cost tenements to house those who live in the slums and to get the hotels to allocate one tenth of their receipts to the poor, to start a residential school where teachers from all around the world will each live with ten students in a cottage. She then complains that no one has helped her to make these *dreams* of hers a reality: that the outside world is corrupt and self-absorbed, caring only about their own wealth.

Ultimately, what has Das accomplished? She claims that maturity causes her to expand her loving feelings to all kinds of people, to shed her "carnal desire as a snake might shed its skin" ([1988] 1996, 191). She mourns that although students admired her because she fought for "a new kind of morality" ([1988] 1996, 199) in her publications, her relatives did not, because they saw her as a threat to their respectable image. Her publications only embarrassed her family. Her life was too much in public view. Only her readers have remained loyal to her throughout her controversy-ridden career, from its beginnings to the present. But on the whole, Das felt that she would still have taken the same path—compromising her reputation with her outspoken writing, forever tweaking "the noses of the puritans" ([1988] 1996, 209–210). Das came to this feisty conclusion in 1988 when *My Story* was first published. Then, in 1999, she rejected her own reputation for being a sexual iconoclast by converting to Islam. She gave as reasons that she could veil and thus enjoy free movement without attracting the male gaze and unwanted male attention. In addition, entering *purdah* assured her complete privacy from strange males in her own space. She had always maintained that she was not promiscuous, only honest about her feelings and experiences. In converting, she proved her point. Nevertheless, what she had revelled in earlier in her life—her sexuality and the interest of males—both of which had caused her so much grief, stress, controversy, and bad publicity—may no longer have been active components in her life by 1999. At any rate, conversion clearly afforded Das a welcome protection from the turmoil that had always surrounded her, from ever having to write anything in relation to sexuality ever again. Lucky for her readers she did not decide to do so until she was sixty-five. I make this comment because I was born in 1933, only one year before Das, so I know from personal experience how difficult her life must have been in attempting to expand the parameters of a culture based on an enduring and underlying "fear of the autonomous sexuality of women" (N. Menon 2000, 95), on the "much-maligned" (Kishwar 1999, 105) Manu's saying that "[s]ince inherently women are attracted to different men, are fickle of heart, and lack affection, even when guarded with effort, they will be unfaithful to their husbands" (quoted in Goldman 2001, 391–392, fn. 10; see also Chakravarti [1989] 1999, 35, 57, and on "the widely shared understanding that women should never be independent":

> Women should not be left to their own devices but should be supervised and protected by men. The main concern behind this notion is not that women will go about indiscriminately killing and maiming like the frenzied Kali but that they might succumb to sexual temptation, which will destroy their purity and the purity of their lineage. Women in society must be protected from such temptations by social strictures . . . or society will disintegrate. For society to prosper, women's power must be channeled toward procreation and the protection of the family. Representations of control and privation are found throughout the world in which women operate. Symbols of binding and confinement show up in many female customs and manners. (Harlan 1995a, 10–11)

I do not make these comments lightly in regard to Das's courageous efforts at honesty in terms of female sexuality that ended in her conversion to Islam. I make them in connection with my interpretation of Das's motives for converting and with my sympathetic response to her recorded problems and issues in relation to her full and free expression of her sexuality. Whereas Das's life was literally in danger in India, Second-Wave feminists in the West who demanded the right to control our bodies were, instead, submitted to endless forms of character assassination. Still, we all suffered because both cultures—as many cultures globally—make "problematic assumptions about female sexuality" (N. Menon 2000, 96). Fear of women's free expression of autonomous sexuality is expressed through the creation of "patriarchal pedestals of 'chastity' and 'virginity,'" but the "pedestals" on which "ladies" are presumably placed do not permit real women "to move." Pedestals in reality allocate to women only a "pseudostatus based on attempts to curtail power rather than recognize it" (Minturn 1993, 326).

Perhaps it was easier for Das as a sixty-five-year-old woman to renounce sexuality when she became a Muslim. I do not intend to convey and thereby succumb to the common stereotype of an ageist essentialism about older women but, rather, that the culture's demands would deprive us either of any claim to attention as women with any desirable material attributes, or any claim to sexuality still inhering in ourselves, or the capacity to attract any one but members of our own generation, at best. We are only accepted as grandmothers/grandmotherly. To my knowledge, of all the sexual stereotypes, of all the constraints against women's free, full expressions of female sexuality that feminist Indian women writers have addressed, none has ever addressed this issue: how to convey what an old woman feels about her sexuality—except Divakaruni in *Mistress of Spices* (1997).

There remains a doubt in my mind as to whether she did take this topic on consciously, or whether it inadvertently revealed itself as an inevitable by-product of the myth she was adapting. However, Divakaruni's contribution in relation to freeing women to express their sexuality or to even describe and discuss it—(even including old women's sexuality)—does not take place until the end of the twentieth century, after older women writers such as Das have struggled to the place where Divakaruni and her generation begin.

As late as 1998, DasGupta and Das Dasgupta in "An Intergenerational Dialogue" both agree that among many of the difficulties that arise for women from the Asian-Indian community is its rejection of female sexuality, particularly young women's sexuality, a rejection that "has created fearsome myths that effectively silence and divide the women in our community" (1998, 111). If there is such total rejection of *young women's sexuality* and so much time and energy spent by feminist Indian writers on confronting its suppression and denial, then what could readers expect or even hope for in relation to these writers undertaking to confront the suppression and denial of *old women's sexuality?*

Anita Desai

As my discussion of the women writers in India up to the last third of the twentieth century reveals, they create characters in their texts who struggle for a long time trapped under a mountain of complex, incredibly burdensome customs, laws, and constraints. Anita Desai (1937–) illustrates the burdens of innumerable constraints on women in a subtle and oblique manner as one aspect of many societal issues; for example, the female artist's predicament. Every woman, no matter how talented, is conceptualized as an outsider.

In Desai's novel *In Custody* (1984), her male protagonist is a miserable, poverty-stricken teacher of Hindi in a college in Misore whose only distraction in life is his passion for Urdu poetry and his adoration of the great Urdu poet Nur.

Deven attempts to make a tape and even dreams of publishing a book on Nur's work, but when he actually gets to meet and know Nur he is disgusted. Nur surrounds himself with crude, dissolute hangers-on who disrespect him, which gives Deven excruciating pain throughout most of the book until he has an illumination. He alone, for better or for worse, is the worthy custodian of this unruly artist who has many other sides to him, who is a total man, not just an abstraction. He is coarse, interested in petty nonsense, wastes time, whines and complains, is preoccupied with petty family matters and his poverty, nags Deven continually for assistance for his every need, and does not write any more. On one occasion, when Deven visits in the hope of hearing Nur recite his poetry, he finds a woman dressed like a prostitute doing a recitation in an egotistic, vainglorious way to the accompaniment of a band, while to his horror and amazement Nur and his hangers-on all listen to her with great respect. This reversal, in which (masculine) merit sits by while (female) ignorance is applauded, repels and outrages Deven so much that he rushes out as soon as Nur rises to go.

The singer of her verses turns out to be Nur's second wife, a celebrated dancer who became his disciple and whom Nur is now jealous of because she has appropriated his "audience," as well as his friends, and is conducting herself as if they were her audience. Before cursing her in the coarsest possible manner, Nur angrily shouts out to Deven that the audience is not hers, but his. Such a mean-spirited response to the woman poet is based on incidents in traveling troupes when male poets loudly leveled distracting insults against their female comrades in the midst of their performances: for bellowing in public, for being without shame, for losing all sense of propriety. Doubtless this hounding of women off the stage—which eventually succeeded—occurred whenever male poets felt that they were being outshone and when the female poets mocked and satirized men in their verses, which may have caused the female members of their audience too obvious pleasure (Banerjee 1999, 140).

Deven is closed off to the possibility that this woman who is never even named is the victim of a sexism so profound and powerful that her voice remains unheard and her talents ignored. Only when she writes him a letter which in the "elegance and floridity of her Urdu enter Deven's ears like a flourish of trumpets and beat at his temples," does he begin to suspect "[t]he essential, unsuspected spirit of the woman." She accuses Deven of believing that she had "inveigled [her] way out of a house of prostitution into the house of a distinguished poet." Such a belief is an insult to her since it would have been impossible for "a common dancing girl to win the heart of a great poet." She insists it was "her mind" that was of interest to Nur: her conversation, her poetry, her wit. Enclosing her poems in the letter for him to read, she requests him to bear in mind that as a woman she has not been educated, but that Deven permit her to prove the existence of her talents. She has had to educate herself, has "seized" it for herself. For, unlike male "poets and scholars," she never had a patron's "encouragement" or "sympathy." Yet Nur was "impressed" by her "early verses" (1984, 195). She challenges Deven to read her works, "to face them and admit to their merit" unless "they fill you with fear and insecurity because they threaten you with danger—danger that your superiority to women may bcome questionable." She accuses Deven of leaving her performance because he feared that if he listened to it, she might "eclipse" Nur and all the "other male poets whom you revere":

> Was it not intolerable to you that a woman should match their gifts and even outstrip them? Are you not guilty of assuming that because you are a male, you have a right to brains, talent, reputation and achievement, while I, because I was born female, am condemned to find what satisfaction I can in being maligned, mocked, ignored and neglected? Is it not you who has made me play the role of the loose woman in gaudy garments by refusing to take my work seriously and giving me just that much regard that you would extend to even a failure in the arts as long as the artist was male? In this unfair world that you have created what else could I have been but what I am? (1984, 196)

She asks this custodian of what is most valuable in Indian literature—the great male writers—to have the "courage" to give her "the time" to read her work, the work of a woman writer, but Deven has neither. To cap all the ironies both implicit and evident in this letter and in Deven's response to its female writer, his wife comes into the room while Deven is tearing up both the letter and the enclosed poetry and screams at him: "You're dropping rubbish all over the floor I have just swept!" (1984, 197).

This letter could be interpreted as written by a delusional hysteric whose only worth to her husband is that she has borne his only male heir. Actually, this letter is written by a despised woman to the male custodian of Urdu tradition and culture in his custody, the gatekeeper of the best of arts and literature. This letter is Desai's own letter to her traditional masculinist Indian colleagues, written in a veiled effort to open their closed minds to the possibility of a woman's talents and abilities equal to those of the canonical male writers whom their male custodians admire so extravagantly, living and dead. As Hélène Cixous puts it: "The moment women open their mouths—women more often than men—they are immediately asked in whose name and from what theoretical standpoint they are speaking, who is their master and where they are coming from: they have in short, to salute . . . and show their identity papers" (quoted in Minh-ha 1989, 44).

Shashi Deshpande

Shashi Deshpande (1938–) also has shown marriage as an entrapment and has devoted much attention to domestic activities in the Indian home: not to deplore them, but as one of the key aspects of her feminism. She focuses on the characters within domestic situations—on those brief moments when irreconcilable chasms open between generations based on insurmountable differences in their perception of reality caused by acculturation and training and by different environmental conditions. Deshpande, an ardent feminist, illustrates the precise nature of twentieth century women's struggles better than any other contemporary Indian woman writer in India. From the beginning of her career Deshpande has dealt with all the various ways in which women are oppressed and subordinated in India. But Deshpande does not only treat women's problems, women's sufferings. She goes on from there. And this is why she begins her books with the ugly source of her characters' problems. Then, after a long period of time, her characters gradually begin to understand, to grow, to gain insight, not only into their situations, but those of other women. After enlightenment, Deshpande's heroines are always aware that their private situations in their own homes and families may be improving as a result of their resistance. However, other women are still embedded within an enormous superstructure, the "network linkages" (Walby 2001, 502) of prevailing patriarchy; all the suffering that R. Menon in her afterword to Deshpande's *A Matter of Time* (1999) lists as the author's topics in her works: "rape, child abuse, single motherhood, son-preference, denial of self-expression, deep inequality and deep-seated prejudice, violence, resourcelessness, low self-esteem, and the binds (and bonds) of domesticity" (1999, 264). Deshpande's heroines ultimately look on other women with anger, sorrow, and compassion because they have become conscious of the source of their suffering only after experiencing injustices themselves as subordinates (Alcoff 2000, 865). These injustices are so naturalized within the patriarchy that they are accepted as the normal course of things, as " 'natural moral facts," including the notion that their "'voluntary' self-subordination" conveys their "power" (Hiltebeitel 2000, 18).

There is another issue in which Deshpande is very interested, one that writers of Deshpande's generation, as I have shown previously, struggle to resolve with such frustration and suffering: the expression of their sexuality. Through Sumi, the protagonist in *A Matter of Time* (1999) who is about to write a play on an idea that excites her, Deshpande illustrates this generation's quintessential problem: how to own their sexuality and to express it:

> She's been thinking . . . of this demon sister of the demon king Ravana, who fell in love with the Aryan prince Rama. An unpleasant story, it's occurred to her, with the two princes Rama and Lakshmana mocking and ridiculing her and finally mutilating her by cutting off her nose. . . . Female sexuality. We're ashamed of owning it, we can't speak of it, not even to our own selves. But Surpanakha was not, she spoke of her desires, she flaunted them. And therefore, were the men, unused to such women, frightened? Did they feel threatened by her? I think so. Surpanakha, neither ugly nor hideous, but a woman charged with sexuality, not frightened of displaying it—it is this Surpanakha I'm going to write about. (1999, 191)

Unfortunately, Sumi never gets to express her position about female sexuality in print, although fortunately for her readers, her creator does.

A Matter of Time deals with the most traumatic event in the life of a family when Gopal suddenly leaves his wife Sumi and three young daughters; with how they cope with that shocking abandonment during the year that follows; with all the complex and intricate shifts in their relationships with one another, and their varying and diverse perspectives during that time.[13] Aru, the oldest daughter, just beginning college, begins to identify with the feminist cause as a byproduct of her suffering caused by her father's abandonment of the family and her obstinate resistance to accepting the situation. She eventually becomes a lawyer, while her mother Sumi gradually transforms into a nascently independent woman. Also ironic is that just before Sumi dies she is happier than she has ever been in her life. She has just been hired to work at her first job teaching with the prospect of true and real independence before her: "'I have a job,' she says . . . as if she's crying out "Hallelujah". . . . This is the first thing in my life I think that I've got for myself. It feels so good, you can't imagine! . . . Now suddenly I want to do so many things'" (1999, 229–231). Ironically, the very next morning on her way to perform the most trivial and ordinary of errands—to the bank, the post office, the market—Sumi's life is snuffed out in a scooter accident.

As of this writing Deshpande, a wonderful writer, is still unknown in the West because she does not publicize herself and does not live in a major city to provide her media coverage. Furthermore, Deshpande does not concede to concerns about whether her work is marketable and refuses to consciously cater to the tastes or prejudices of Western readers. Primarily, however, Deshpande remains unknown in the West because all of her characters are Indian and remain in India and her focus is entirely on them. "My novels don't have any westerners. . . . They are just about Indian people and the complexities of our lives" (quoted in R. Menon 1999, 248). In relation to the charge by male sexist writers that her work and its topics are peripheral Deshpande asserts that wherever she stands is the center. In the West and globally, the charges by traditionalists made in order to discredit feminist perspectives as trivial, insignificant, irrelevant, and liminal are identical. These charges are transparent, nothing more than a "vehicle to circulate established power relations" (Minh-ha 1989, 6).

Deshpande led a totally isolated house-bound life as a wife and mother of two children, a lifestyle that prevented her from having any association with any kindred spirits with whom she could share her work. Even though she is now free from most of the early demands on her time, Deshpande still retains her privacy and does not share her work with anyone before publication. As many Western feminists and Indian/Third World feminists have noted, this lifestyle features continual jolting interruptions in the midst of one's concentration so that it is continually being fractured. In Appachana's lengthy list of acknowledgments at the end of

Listening Now (1998), she places as last the writers' retreat at Hawthornden Castle, Scotland, where she was a Hawthornden Fellow in 1993. She credits this retreat as being one of her favorite memories because she was able to write without interruption for one month "in that exquisite solitude." Tellingly, Appachana was a young married woman with two small children at the time. A married woman's work, apart from our domestic and childrearing duties, is too often not really considered to be work by all those around us. Instead, it is thought of as a hobby that we do "in bits and pieces, in between chores" (R. Menon 1999, 252–53) and only when husband and children are asleep or away.

All of Deshpande's work deals with middle-class Indian women who are continually insulted and humiliated. By this means, Deshpande exposes the culture's oppression of women, as well as how powerful women cope and survive within such constraints despite being inevitably demoralized and psychically damaged. The originary site for these constraints is the home, women's daily activities in the home, which is conceptualized as "the natural domain of women" (R. Menon 1999, 265). An enduring sense of "displacement" and "violence" both in the home and the external environment always constrained by "a ritualized order" are all integral elements of the constricted world in which women live out their lives. Deshpande believes that the family is the most universal grouping in human life and that no relationships are more basic and meaningful than those between family members. The most significant members of the family are women. In the family setting, she is incomparable in depicting interactions, shifting family alliances and estrangements, their random, clumsy attempts to reach out to one another, their ludicrously off-the-mark misinterpretations of one another's thoughts and feelings, their resentment, even hatred of each other, their fears and misgivings about expressing and explaining themselves to one another. Suddenly, and at odd moments in the midst of all these emotions, feelings of deep love for one another descend upon them before differences and misunderstandings close them down once again to each other.

Women's resistance is "framed by silences, a refusal to speak" (R. Menon 1999, 264; Visweswaran 1994, 100), and women's silence is also one of the major elements of Deshpande's works. Within this cocoon of silence and in the face of enormous barriers that society imposes on women to prevent them from action that effects positive change for them in their negative situation, women struggle to find themselves, their own identities, what it is they really want to do and say. As Deshpande puts it about her work: "My writing comes out of my consciousness of the conflict between my idea of myself as a human being and the idea that society has of me as a woman" (quoted in R. Menon 1999, 267). As is characteristic of twentieth-century feminists, Deshpande's feminism came to her little by little and is not theoretical. Instead, she defines her feminism as a creation of a work of art that describes a woman's gradually becoming conscious of the oppression she has endured and gradually beginning to shape her life in accordance with her own desires. In the course of describing this process, Deshpande feels how powerful it is, not only for her female characters, but for herself. As a result, she realized that the Old Boy Network's trivialization and marginalization of women and women writers who write from a woman's perspective about a woman's life cause women to be perceived as failures. Instead, Deshpande asserts, it is the establishment writers who are out "in the margins" (quoted in R. Menon 1999, 267).

In *The Dark Holds No Terrors* ([1980] 1990), Deshpande shows the gradual movement over time of a seemingly successful woman with everything any (straight) woman would want—a love match with her husband Manohar, now a professor, who had been a promising poet when she first met him. They had crossed caste lines in order to marry because he was of lower caste than Sarita's Brahmin family. The couple had defied her mother's rejection of the match, thereby causing a breach that never healed between the proud and rather inflexible Sarita and her mother. The couple now have two children, and Sarita has an important, vital, and economically successful career as a "lady doctor." In the beginning she had felt contempt for her unliberated patients who have internalized all the patriarchal culture's revulsion for woman's material essence:

> Backache, headache, leucorrhea, menorrhagea, dysmenorrhea, loss of appetite, burning feet, an itch "there" . . . all the indignities of a woman's life, borne silently and as long as possible, because "how do you tell anyone about these things?" *Everything kept secret, their very womanhood a source of deep shame to them.* Stupid, silly martyrs, she thought; idiotic heroines. Going on with their tasks, and destroying themselves in the bargain, for nothing but a meaningless modesty. Their unconscious, unmeaning heroism, born out of the myth of the self-sacrificing martyred woman, did not arouse either her pity or her admiration. It made her angry. "Why didn't you do something about it earlier?" she often asked. But they had schooled themselves to silence. ([1980] 1990, 107, emphasis the author's)

Ironically, her own life is a picture and her marriage a façade. Sarita feels that she is at bottom no different from her patients in her unwillingness to break silence to others, to herself even, and certainly to her husband about what goes on in "the dark." She cannot bring herself to tell anyone that "*My husband is a sadist*" ([1980] 1990, 97, emphasis the author's). Nor has she gone to a lawyer to seek a divorce. Sarita's picture-perfect marriage is like the surface of a floating iceberg that by the end finally thaws and disintegrates because under the surface level lies the hidden frozen mass that holds it together—a lie. Her handsome, loving husband rapes her brutally in "the dark" of night and then tortures her again during the light of day by acting as if nothing has happened. She cannot even cry out in her pain for fear of frightening her children: "The same face smiling at me the next morning, saying, 'Morning, Sarita. Slept well?' . . . A sham, a farce, a ghastly pretence? Or, was it I who was dreaming, going through a terrible nightmare that left behind this horrible aftertaste of fear? But what about my bruises then?" ([1980] 1990, 112).

Returning to her parental home after her estranged mother's death, Sarita gradually achieves insights about herself and her relationships. One after the other, various illusions have died for her during the course of her marriage: "Love? Romance? Both, I knew too well, were illusions, and not relevant to my life anyway. And the code word of our age is neither love nor romance, but sex. . . . And for me sex was now a dirty word . . . one more illusion destroyed" ([1980] 1990, 133).

While not excusing it, there is one scene that sheds light on Manohar's strange conduct. He had shown great early promise and was expected to have a glittering and successful career as a creative writer. After their marriage, his rising star wanes as he makes compromises demanded by Sarita, who ends by supporting both of them while he works at a low-paying, dead-end job teaching in a third-rate college. During an encounter with a former friend and colleague, now famous and popular, the playwright thanks Sarita for talking her husband into pulling out of a magazine they had begun together. As a result of Manohar's desertion, the journal had folded and his friend had been forced to go it alone. This had led to his friend's current success. Manohar had not wanted to leave the magazine, had seen it as a golden opportunity. It had regalvanized him into his former sense of purpose and self-worth, but because of Sarita's disapproval and contempt for the project, he had given it up.

It is clear in this situation that Sarita has been insensitive and controlling for years—subordinating her husband's career to hers and to middle class luxuries from the beginning of their marriage and that this has destroyed Manohar. Sarita justifies her manipulation of Manohar and his submission to her on the grounds that he was a self-deluding hypocrite. He had wanted the good life she had been able to provide him—fine clothes, excellent food, all the books and magazines his heart desired, theater and films on a regular basis—more than he had wanted the gamble of struggling against the odds to achieve success as a writer. In contrast, Sarita had lost her nerve when Manohar had been out of work for a time. She could not comprehend what benefit he had achieved from having published a few stories and poems and having won the admiration and friendship of a circle of other creative artists. She finally admits to herself that her middle-class training had caused her to react to her husband's unemployment as nightmarish, as horribly humiliating. She had talked him into taking the teaching job by using her pregnancy, a tremendous influence on his decision, to convince him to leave the magazine and the opportunity to pursue his dream and his talents.

In the light of day, Manohar now presents a picture to their children and to the world of Sarita's domination and control over him. But his hostility and rage against her for his frustrating life, for being subjected to his own and to his circle's disapproval in permitting himself to be supported by a pragmatic, unimaginative wife who has no respect for his needs and desires, who has thwarted his ambition and his great promise, have gradually boiled up in him until it spills over into an expression of physical venting of violence against her under cover of dark. He uses the only means of domination and control he can exert over her—his greater strength—to rape her.

Here what R. Mazumdar remarks about Indian cultural values in terms of South Asian immigrant women is also true of Indian women in India: that in India the culture permits rape within marriage, thus preventing the women who experience it and who have internalized a "notion of obligation" (1998, 130) from confronting their husbands about it or telling anyone else. Husbands who rape find justification for doing so in the work of "Dead Indian Sanskritzing Males" (Hiltebeitel 2000, 116). The most prominent of them all, Manu, listed rape as one of the forms of acceptable marriage, which then makes the woman the man's property. Most influential of all is his statement that women belong to their fathers, husbands, and sons according to the stages in their lives; that the purpose of wives is to produce sons (R. Mazumdar 1998, 134).

In contrast, Deshpande shows that Sarita sees the source of her problems as both her culture's and her husband's refusal to accept her superiority to her husband. In a lecture to students on women becoming doctors, Sarita decides not to disillusion them. But she fantasies being able to tell them that if they intend to have successful marriages they must not be equal to or superior to their husbands in any way: "No partnership can ever be equal. It will always be unequal, but take care that it's unequal in favour of your husband. If the scales tilt in your favour, god help you, both of you" ([1980] 1990, 137). Does Sarita ever realize that the issue is not her being a doctor and supporting her husband in a lifestyle to which he has become accustomed and which he resents? She has blackmailed him through "the weapon" of his ties to his children and his love for her into conformity to her middle-class wishes that he be a professor, a respectable, worthy profession that she is proud to tell people is her husband's. This is what Manohar resents so bitterly: the loss of *his* sense of self worth—the loss of *his* self-respect, the loss of all meaning in *his* life which was *his* writing career. In this regard, Sarita does realize that she, too, would have to change, although not so drastically as Manohar because she has already acknowledged, if only to herself, what behavior she has to modify.

At the end of the book, without consulting her about his action, Manohar is imminently expected to come to retrieve her from her father's house where, without admitting it, she fled for protection after her mother's death. Sarita is suddenly called away to treat a neighbor child who is having convulsions. As she leaves the house, she tells her father to have Manohar wait for her. This statement leaves readers in "the dark" about what will happen next after the ending. Is Sarita going to confront Manohar about what he has done to her in "the dark" and refuse to return to him unless he undergoes treatment and succeeds in modifying his behavior? Can a rapist change? Can Sarita ever return to her original feelings for her husband and get over her fear and loathing of him, as well as endless apprehension that at any time he could return to his Jekyll and Hyde behavior? Can she learn to give him financial and emotional support by encouraging him to return to and fulfill his writing talents? Can she respect his friends? However, above and beyond all these questions about Deshpande's inconclusive conclusion to this book lies the fact that Deshpande has her heroine finally break her silence by confiding her experience of marital rape to her father and that through this creative act the author has herself broken silence on this taboo subject.

Chitra Banerjee Divakaruni

In her perspective about women's sexuality, Chitra Banerjee Divakaruni (1956–) focuses on the same injustices against women as the writers of the previous generation. Then how is she any different, or for that matter, how is the generation after hers different from the older feminists? Throughout this text I have discussed and analyzed the works of feminists who sought equality for women and for the right to freely express their sexuality, despite the legal system having resolutely clung to "culturally prevalent ideologies," to traditional, naturalized notions of "women's nature and of gendered rights" (S. Basu 1999, 265, 266) that perceive women as helpless and at the same time as entitled to far less than men. In their works these writers have attempted to put an end to all kinds of injustices against women. They have fought against every inconceivable injustice to women. They have protested *purdah,* protested dependence of females on their menfolk because of lack of education, protested child molestation, protested rape, protested incest, protested wife beating and child abuse, protested husbands deserting their wives and abandoning families to fend for themselves. These writers have described the sexuality of young girls, how restrained and constrained they were from expression of their sexuality. They have fought against arranged marriages where the husband was far older than the girl, where the girl was invariably raped by her husband. They have fought against girls being sold into prostitution or slavery in factories. They have demanded acceptance of lesbianism. They have demanded the right to have sex outside of marriage if their husbands were indifferent or failed in other ways to perform their marital duties. They also have demanded acceptance of every conceivable aspect of female sexual identity, but only for young women.

Until Divakaruni published *The Mistress of Spices* in 1997, I am unaware of any feminist Indian woman author who has ever depicted old women other than as caretakers of their children's children who acted as cultural gatekeepers and trained and enculturated them into cultural norms. If old women characters were the mothers of female characters, they were depicted as involved in domestic tasks or in emotional conversations with other characters about family matters. Or they are depicted as the mothers-in-law of brides, often difficult and cruel, but sometimes kindly, whose role is not so much to enculturate their daughters-in-law as to make sure that the culture is perpetuated onto their daughters-in-law; that what they had to endure when they were married, their daughters-in-law would in their turn have to endure, so that they could at long last enjoy the privileges of being served and entirely catered to by their sons' wives. Here Grewal Inderpal's and Caren Kaplan's remark about privileges "in the world system" is germane and applicable within the context of mother-in-law privileges in the Indian family system, as well: "One's privileges in the world-system are always linked to another woman's oppression or exploitation" (1994a, 19).

Old women have never been described in their present stage in life as in voluntary, active, mutually satisfying sexual relationships with men. There is the custom of levirate marriages, in which older widows could marry their husbands' younger brothers. And Vanita does mention a miraculous accomplishment by "Avvaiyyar in medieval Tamil Nadu" who turned herself "into an old woman so that her prospective husband would stop pursuing her" (1999, 535). Nevertheless, it does not seem to occur to her in her emphasis on women to include old women who have conducted themselves as active agents rather than "victims," as it seems to have occurred to Divakaruni. At any rate, no feminist Indian woman writer until Divakaruni has described for public consumption and from the woman's own perspective an old woman who has sexual feelings, as still a female in that sense, as fully endowed with what are traditionally considered desires and responses that have always been described as inhering only in young and middle-aged females.

Whether Divakaruni consciously intended to add this hitherto overlooked aspect of female sexuality—the possibility of old women's having sexuality, as well as the right to express that sexuality—to the lengthy list of feminist demands that they have been making for nearly a century, is unclear. However, Divakaruni has succeeded in fleshing out a myth about a young sorceress who in order to become a mistress of spices and serve humanity must be embedded forever in the shell of a decrepit old woman. She is sent to Oakland, California, to perform her healing duties through the spices in an Indian spice store. The author goes into great detail about the responses of this mistress of spices to all her diverse customers and of the continual disapproval and warnings her responses provoke from the spices whenever she breaks her vows and goes beyond the parameters of her detached healing role. In doing so, she takes a spectacular step forward in relation to a deeply engrained cultural taboo about old women.

The narrator of this myth, originally Nayan Tara, has been gifted with remarkable abilities of prophecy from an early age. Unfortunately her parents did not love her for herself. They abused and neglected her, although all she wanted was for them to love her. After she begins to bring wealth to her family from her talents as a sorceress, her parents only treated her well because they were afraid of her powers. None of this ever made the girl happy or fulfilled. She believed in and practiced the "calling thought" that could draw anyone she desired to her. If this power were not used properly and without the proper safeguards, however, it could bring about unimaginable devastation. One day, pirates invade her village, burn it, murder its inhabitants, including her entire family, and kidnap the young woman. She believes that she is the cause of all this because she would issue the "calling thought" to bring the pirates to her: to bring romance and glamor into her life.

Renamed Bhagyavati—Bringer of Luck—by the pirate chief, she overthrows him and becomes the queen of the pirates. Longing for death, she unleashes a typhoon, but is saved by sea serpents who tell her of the island, The Old One, and the spices. They want her to stay with them and to give her a new name: "Sarpa-kanya, snake maiden" (1997, 24). They predict that if she does not remain with them, everything she possesses—the ability to see, to speak, her name, even her identity will be lost. Still, the young woman longs to go to the Island, and eventually the oldest sea serpent tells her how to do so because he is able to see "the spice-glow under her skin" (1997, 25), the emblem of her fate.

After an apprenticeship with other maidens, after going through fire and emerging in a new shell in the form of the body of a bent and decrepit old woman (in order to be removed from desire or lust, or from provoking desire or lust in others), she becomes a Mistress of Spices. She herself names herself "Tilo short for Tilottama . . . I will be Tilottama, the essence of *til,* life-giver, restorer of health and hope" (1997, 44). The Old One who rules the island and trains the future mistresses of spices accepts her heresy and justifiably calls her a rule-breaker. Foreshadowing what will happen to Tilo in relation to the spices, The Old One reminds her of the Hindu myth of Tilottama, the most beautiful dancer at the Rain-God Indra's court, who was warned by Brahma when he made her Indra's chief dancer never to fall in love with a man, only with dancing. But Tilottama did so, and for her disobedience was thrown down to earth for "seven mortal lives of illness and age, of people turning in disgust from her twisted, leprous limbs" (1997, 45). I wonder whether a woman of any age could have written this myth that Divakaruni uses as a skeletal outline for her own version. Needless to say, her ending is much more humane.

At any rate, The Old One then assigns Tilo to Oakland, California, to do her magical work through the spices: to heal those humans to whom she gives the spices appropriate to them with the bent and crippled fingers of an old woman. The conditions are that she must never look at herself in a mirror, never leave the store, the shell of her shell, never get personally involved with human beings, or she will lose her powers to heal, or worse. Above all, she must treat all who come to her with equal detachment. Tilo joyously accepts these conditions. She is not that pretty anyway, she thinks, so what did she have to lose in being turned into an ugly old hag? (1997, 43). But Tilo turns out to be incapable of disinterest in her customers' problems. For example, there is Haroun from the Punjab whose family was slain by rebels, who kisses her hands to thank her for reading his palm. "His mouth was a circle of fire, burning my skin, and his pleasure flaring along my veins, burning them too. . . . I should have not allowed it. But how could I pull away" (1997, 29)?

In contrast, there are the Bougainvillea girls who never bother to look at Tilo, the hag in the old, stained, torn sari who runs the store where they shop. Their self-centeredness, their obsession with their beauty move her to competitiveness, to the forbidden thought that she had the power to make herself more beautiful than they. That is her problem, as The Old One had told her before Tilo left. Her highly emotional reactions might cause her to forget why her power was bestowed on her. Almost, but not quite deprived of envy of their beauty, she supplies the beautiful young women with bay leaves to make them "irresistible" to men and blesses their purchases as she rings them up.

There is also Daksha the nurse, with all her additional obligations to her mother-in-law, cooking special food for her because she is a widow and having to cook food fresh every night after she comes home from working at the hospital. Her mother-in-law insists that "old food from the fridge is good only for servants or dogs." Daksha does all the chores "because after all isn't the kitchen the woman's place?" She has forgotten how to express herself because nobody has ever listened to her. "No, that word so hard for Indian women. *No* and *Hear me now*" (1997, 83, emphasis the author's).

Then there are Geeta's conservative grandfather and Geeta. When Geeta leaves home by mutual agreement because she has outraged her parents by matching herself with a Chicano, Tilo intercedes and brings happiness back to the family. Perhaps, Tilo admits to herself, not only out of altruism but also because Geeta's "forbidden love" (1997, 136) reminds her of her own. Also, Tilo admits that she likes to dominate, and to help others is in some ways to dominate them, even though The Old One has cautioned Tilo and the other mistresses that "Power is weakness" (1997, 184).

And then there is Ahuja's wife who believes that she is to blame for being beaten by her husband and that she must sleep with him, whether she wants to or not, which is standard Indian belief. But Tilo tells her that "No man, husband or not, has the right to beat you, to force you to a bed that sickens you. . . . You deserve happiness. You deserve dignity" (1997, 110–111). After being beaten very severely, Ahuja's wife summons the courage to leave her husband and move to a women's shelter to begin a new existence. There Ahuja's wife will begin to grow to become her own person with her own name—to become Lalita.[14]

And then there is Raven, who turns out to be half white, half Native American. From the beginning, he looks at Tilo not as though she were wrinkled and old but as if he were actually able to see her. Somehow he "likes what he sees" (1997, 71). Tilo naturally cannot understand how this is possible. Right here, the remarkable thing about Divakaruni's characterization of Tilo's responses in this relationship first reveals itself as a comprehension of how it feels to be an old woman relating as a woman to a young man. Divakaruni goes into great detail about Tilo's complex feelings from the beginning of the courtship, as if Tilo were a young girl. Is she thereby intimating that such responses never change, never go away, but that when the stimuli no longer appear, the responses remain inert and are mistakenly believed to have left in age?

When Raven first gazes into her eyes and continues to do so, something lurches in Tilo, "like something stitched up tearing loose." She marvels at the length of time that has gone by since anyone so much as gave her a look. She begins to feel extremely lonely, something aches dully in her weighing her down as if she were "drowning." Then she returns Raven's gaze, thinking that she had thought her looking with desire at men had ended once she had committed herself to working for humanity through the spices. That is, until she set eyes on Raven. And therein lies the suspense. Can Raven be attracted to her and desire Tilo as she is attracted to and desires him—sexually? How is this possible? What terrible fate will descend on Tilo if she breaks the rules and shows partiality to him?

This, however, was a problem for Tilo even before Raven enters the store. It remains a problem—her sense of caring, her going out of her way personally to interfere in the lives of her customers in the hope of making their lives better—as opposed to the spices' and her own conscience's continual reminders that such responses are forbidden to her. If Tilo permits herself to to lose her impartiality, to love one human being beyond all others, to use her powers for her own private ends, the inalterable rule is that she will then rip "the delicate fabric of the balanced world," and "chaos" (1997, 96–97) will ensue.

She imagines Raven undressing, even though in her whole previous life and through all her adventures she has never before either wanted to see a naked man or even seen one, which seems odd. For surely as the queen of the pirates on a pirate ship for some years she must have, even inadvertently, seen her men naked. But now she masturbates just imagining Raven naked, although she tries to stop herself: "Not now, hands, not now. Give me just a moment more. But they are immovable, adamantine. Mine and not mine. Fisted around something hard and grainy, a pulsing lump whose acrid smell cuts through my vision" (1997, 75–76).

Tilo begins to long to use spices to get rid of her wrinkles, to turn her hair black, and to make her flesh firm. At one point, Raven's entry into the store surprises her and she cuts her finger, which he sucks, and causes her to fantasy that they were having sex. Even after this gesture, which should have made Raven's feelings more than obvious to her, Tilo seems still not to realize that he is attracted to her. He keeps returning to the store, causing Tilo mingled torment and pleasure. She begs forgiveness from The Old One who responds that Tilo is only using words; that she cannot be forgiven because she is not really willing to abjure what caused her "to stumble" (1997, 122) in the first place.

Once when she returns from an errand, she finds a note on the shop door from Raven, inviting her to take a drive with him and spend the day. "Like any woman in love" (1997, 197) she presses her cheek to the paper he had written on and begins to worry about what to wear for the date. Her head then fills with fantasies of how Raven will react if she relents and uses her powers to make herself young and beautiful for him, imagining their bodies in the act of lovemaking. With enormous difficulty Tilo resists, even the temptations sung to her from the spices, who sometimes conduct themselves like sirens. Instead, she lowers her old woman's body, aching and stiff, down on the floor where she sleeps at night. Only this night she tosses, frustrated, wondering why she cannot love both—the man and the spices—why she has to choose between them. But the spices do not respond because they are sure that she will soon break.

The next morning Raven brings her a present, a beautiful dress that she realizes is suitable for a young woman, but he responds that it is a dress for a beautiful woman and that she is that woman, as he traces a finger over her cheekbone. She begs him to see her as she is—an old and ugly woman. For her to wear the dress would be inappropriate, as well as the two of them going out in public together. He embraces her, caresses her, and tells her that he knows that her body is not really her; that each one is able to see the other better than they are able to see themselves, and she yields. Near a beach Raven prepares a picnic and gives her wine to drink, another rule she is breaking. He then drinks from where Tilo's lips have pressed the glass and gazes at her eyes. He begins to talk to her about himself, of his mother who passed as white, of how he got his name, and of the heaven on earth which he dreams of constantly: mountains, pine and eucalyptus, the smell of the redwoods, a stream that tastes better than any other water. They then descend to the beach where Tilo secretly hopes she will see the snakes return to her again. Raven continues his story about himself, primarily about his troubled relationship with his mother, and in compassion Tilo kisses his cheek. He returns the kiss, but on her lips, and it is not in mutual compassion that they kiss, but as lovers, and she wishes that it would never end.

At this point, Divarkaruni inserts a humorous scene, one of two such scenes in the book. By coincidence, the lovers have picked a spot beneath a trendy restaurant with a view of the ocean, which the Bougainvillea girls are about to enter with their escorts. One of them sees Raven and Tilo embracing and cracks a joke about "the view" while her white escort whispers something in her ear:

> The woman is not so discreet. "Some people—" she says. "I guess there's no accounting for taste." Her glance sweeps Raven now. . . . A heat begins to pulse behind my eyes, little explosions of red. The other woman laughs again, leaning into her man, his arm around her slim lamé waist. I see with rage the lovely line of her neck, her breasts. "You know how it is, people get turned on by all kinds of kinky things."
>
> "And that dress," says her friend. "Did you see that dress?"

"It's pathetic, isn't it," says the other one, "what some women will do to look young."
The man's eyes slide over us, bored, as though he's seen worse. As though it isn't
worth the waste of his time. (1997, 235)

Raven urges Tilo not to pay attention to these people, that they have no idea
who she really is and don't understand about the two of them: not to let the incident spoil their evening. But it does, and she rejects his attempts to see her again.
He takes her hand, kisses her palm, and laughs and jokes in a vain attempt to
lighten her mood.

Given signs that she will be destroyed because of her final perpertration, Tilo
prepares for her imminent immolation. Raven returns to the store and continues
his story, telling her that in his recent dreams she is now with him in the place he
dreams of, except that in his dreams she looks different, in a way that he is sure she
really is. When some attractive girls enter the store and Tilo sees Raven looking at
them, she becomes jealous, but he is critical of their high heels, wondering how
they balance on them when they are like "pencil points." When she belittles herself, he squeezes her hand and reassures her that she has powers those girls do not
have, can never have; the girls could never hope to be as authentic as Tilo. But, tor-
mented by her jealousy, Tilo proceeds to transform herself so that she can have one
night with Raven before her death. By the next morning she has reversed to middle
age. She begins to sell off or give away the contents of the store in order to close
down the shop, while claiming that she is doing it for her aunt who has already left.
When Raven comes to the shop that night after she has reversed to youth, she asks
him if he can see her underneath her beauty, and he claims he can still see her in
her eyes, although he also claims that he doesn't dare to dream of or to touch such
beauty.

After a night together, Tilo leaves him a farewell note. When she returns to the
store, she mourns about no longer being "a goddess," but only a woman. She admits to herself that she never wanted to face this fact. Where once she felt she
"could save the world, now she realizes that she has only made a few people
happy—briefly" (1997, 318–319). Tilo goes to sleep in the store for the last time and
when she awakens, she is in Raven's car fleeing an earthquake. He has returned,
found her in the rubble, rescued her, and is escaping with her to the world of his
dreams. She finds that she is neither old any longer, nor young and beautiful. She
is, as she has described herself, now only an ordinary woman because of her love for
a mortal, and apparently the spices have heard. They have put her in her own body
as it was, neither young nor old, but in middle age. And, underneath it all her eyes
are the same, still filled with bright curiosity, still "rebellious," still "ready to question, to fight" (1997, 327). Tilo has been consigned to her fate. When she accepted
her punishment, when she expected retribution, The Old One thought mortality
approaching middle age was sufficient. Tilo did not have to experience bodily suffering as well.

And what is Raven's response to Tilo's latest and final manifestation? It provides the second humorous moment in the book. As far as he is concerned, she is now more the way he always imagined her: that when she became young and beautiful for their night of lovemaking he had actually found her flawless beauty "a bit intimidating. I felt like I had to stand tall all the time, stick in my stomach. Things like that" (1997, 326).

At the tollbooth on the road to his paradise, they discover that the quake centered in Oakland where Tilo's store stood, although there is no fault line there. Readers are aware that the quake is related to Tilo, that the fault line is in her. The fire that has ensued has done more damage than the quake, however, and Tilo and Raven can see the city on fire. They then quarrel because Tilo insists she must return to attempt to help out, that she cannot leave such suffering. Raven, however, feels that she has done nothing but help people for as long as she has lived and that she deserves to have her own life with him. Tilo is adamant and tells him to go to his heaven on earth without her; that she will get a ride back to Oakland. The only earthly paradise they could have together would be "what we can make back there, in the soot in the rubble in the crisped-away flesh. In the guns and needles, the white drug-dust, the young men and women lying down to dreams of wealth and power and waking in cells. Yes, in the hate in the fear" (1997, 336). Raven yields then and agrees to go back with her. They kiss, and he jokes that their relationship is his heaven on earth. They begin to work on a new name for Tilo because that name is no longer suitable. Raven comes up with Maya, which means, among other things, "Illusion, spell, enchantment, the power that keeps this imperfect world going day after day" (1997, 338).

In highly poetic language within the context of a feminist myth based on the myth of Tilottama, Divakaruni conveys the feelings of all the characters, their problems in their everyday existence. Tilo's and Raven's feelings, their dialogues throughout the courtship, the varied and complex emotions before, during, and after each meeting are handled realistically, as any reader who has ever fallen in love can testify. Perhaps intense sexual desire connected with romantic illusion about love that we have seen as such a prevalent problematic in so many of the texts, especially in Deshpande's *The Dark Holds No Terrors,* is yet another preoccupation with feminists born in the earlier part of the century. It is exactly what Maitreyi Devi's title *It Never Dies* states, revealing that Devi's feelings of passionate love for Eliade when she was sixteen are the same as those when she is in her sixties. And apparently it is the same for him, for this title comes from Eliade's statement and promise to her: that they will meet after their deaths. Certainly with Divarkuni, the same mingling of romance with a passionate sexuality in her heroine seems to be continuing into the very end of the century. Only Divakaruni ends where the relationship between the lovers begins, presumably to live "happily ever after" working side by side for the good of humanity. In Deshpande's book, however, the lovers marry and live together for many years and all romance and sexuality dies.

Except in some small degree for lower- and upper-class women, the expression of autonomous female sexuality was not permitted until after marriage in the privacy of the bedroom. As we have seen, the earliest feminists did not dare to write about such things. Even today, in many quarters, the topic of sexuality is considered to be a marker of Western degeneracy and something alien and foreign to Indian culture (DasGupta and Das Dasgupta 1998, 117; Oza 2001, 1080). Das Dasgupta states that, if not for the Kama Sutra and Kokashastra, books and articles about sexuality were minimal. Women, because of having been more repressed, "suffer more" from this repression than men (quoted in R. Mazumdar 1998, 137).

When the later feminists, born in the first third of the twentieth century, began to advocate for the freedom to express our sexuality, it is always mingled inextricably with romantic illusion. We appear to require illusions, fantasies about our "Other(s)," the object(s) of our desire, in order to provoke our sexuality, as we see in Das's and many other writers' complaints about Indian husbands who do not take this romanticism into account. Romance and sexuality, intertwined, can only be felt when the Other is a stranger or remains distant and unknown because after marriage or a daily relationship such conditions no longer exist.

Feminists of this generation have not resolved this problem. Divakaruni, a generation younger than these feminists, is clearly still situated where her predecessors are emotionally and does not resolve the problem, either; rather, she evades it because her couple is just beginning their relationship after going through many trials and tribulations before moving on into the future together after the book is closed. The author has reversed the Beauty and the Beast myth, with the Beast becoming an ordinary woman who wants a husband, a home, children, and to serve her community.

"Exclusions shape inclusions, as we know, and both are products of the belief systems" (Moglen 1993, 20). The feminist authors are devoted to unpacking such "exclusions," including those of female sexual realities. Are they built on solid foundations or on nonsense? Divakaruni's great contribution to the feminist struggle is to move the mountain of falsehood that the culture has erected about what it is to be a female in that she (un?)consciously takes on the issue of an older woman's sexuality. Is Divakaruni's contribution to the ongoing effort to protest the suppression and denial of female sexuality an accident—in the course of following the thread of her myth of the mistress of the spices? Or is it by design—an example of the extraordinary capacity of a gifted author to project into, understand, and treat a female character realistically who is much older than she is? In terms of the ongoing feminist project I have described in this text, Divakaruni in *The Mistress of Spices* has tunneled beneath the most heavily inscribed cultural proscriptions in relation to women and succeeded in realistically representing, under the umbrella of the adaptation of a myth, an old woman as a sexual and romantic subject who desires and then loves the "Other," a young man, and amazingly, is also the object of the "Other's" sexual desire and love.

Anjana Appachana

Appachana spent approximately ten years writing her first novel *Listening Now* (1998). All the writers I have discussed in this text have contributed each in her own unique way to the ongoing feminist project. Divakaruni's contribution resonated personally for me as an old woman myself, and so did Appachana's, exposing how Indian husbands conduct discordant, highly stressful dialogues with their wives. I actually found that she had replicated my deceased ex-husband's strategies, as well as those of most Western men to whom I had been exposed in my lifetime in many venues—personal and professional. To read Appachana's "Bahu" and *Listening Now* was an acutely uncomfortable experience for me because at each turn I saw yet another technique employed by men that successfully suppressed and silenced the heroine: techniques that I myself had experienced for too many years without having the slightest clue as to how it was done, like many other women around the world. For example, in recent South Asian women's focus groups, it was found that although participants were able to recognize and identify "various types of abuse and violence" they felt that verbal, psychological, and emotional abuse were more "pervasive" and of more crucial significance in their lives than "sexual abuse which they were loathe to discuss" because those abuses *were more difficult to "document and explain"* (Krishnan and Baig-Amin 1998, 150, emphasis mine):

> They were socialized to be "obedient daughters," "faithful wives," and "caring mothers," and these social norms required conformity to certain behavioral standards: subservience, propriety, and putting others' needs ahead of their own. These expectations ruled out any discussion regarding sex, pleasure, and personal enjoyment. The fact that they had moved into the public arena with their stories of domestic violence was already a great departure from tradition, and to discuss sexual abuse, another taboo issue, would have further taxed their coping skills. (1998, 151)

What was true for the focus group was true for me, as well as for most of the world's women. Like these Indian women, I had no support system in my world and time, only the same sense of vague outrage beautifully expressed by Alexander as "a black space in my ear, a savagery I could not yet decipher" whenever she recalled her mother's injunction to her that "'The first thing a girl should learn is when to keep her silence'" (1993, 191). The reader's suffering—at least this reader's—comes from reading Appachana's dialogues between husbands and wives and seeing exactly how and in what ways the wives are being manipulated and dominated.

Here I disagree with those who see a great difference between Indian men's positive attitude and Western men's extremely hostile attitude toward feminism (Burton 1994, 222; Ramusack 1999, 62). In my opinion, what Jawaharlal Nehru said in a speech at Allahabad on March 31, 1928, still rings true: "The women of India will not attain their full rights by the mere generosity of the men of India. They will have to fight for them and force their will on the menfolk before they can succeed" (quoted in Jayawardena 1986, 73).

Furthermore, I would expand his statement to include Western women and, indeed, all women globally. What took our generation of feminists most of our lives to learn and to see through and understand, young contemporary feminists now describe very clearly so that the next generation can have the tools and the clarity to perceive and describe exactly what is going on, what is being done to us. It took us many years to penetrate patriarchal discursive strategies, gain comprehension and understanding of them, and then to name them into existence—all the patterns in the discursive techniques and skills that husbands, male colleagues, friends, relatives, and most men in general deploy(ed) routinely when "dealing" with us to maintain the status quo, to get their way, to put off, disarm, to silence complaints or troubling perceptions.

In all probability, Appachana does not mean her work to be a specific educational tool, but in the course of "Bahu" and *Listening Now,* she exposes and illustrates "the discourse of male dominance and physical violence" (Goldman 2001, 230). Through these dialogues Appachana details dialogues between men and women in marriage as they actually take place. The situations—the contents—may change in Appachana's works, but not the message, not the context.

The title of Appachana's *Listening Now* is an admonition to men to listen to the women they supposedly love and care for, which the heroine's lover finally does. Indeed, he is listening now, only it is too late. The title seems to say to Indian men: "You have not listened ever before. It is time that you listen now. All that I will show in this book will go to prove this." Needless to say, the women in it are continually begging the men to listen to them, continually complaining that their men don't listen to them. The content of this lengthy novel may be different from the later "Bahu," but the context is the same. Of great value to all women—Indian as well as Western—is that Appachana pinpoints the same techniques for controlling, silencing, and dominating women as she will later condense in "Bahu," only in *Listening Now* she includes more, some of which I have listed below:

Subsuming the personhood of the woman by embedding her entirely "in family structures" (Humes 2000, 143)—in roles of daughter, wife, sister, and mother as full-time jobs
When Madhu, who did not finish her B.A. because she married a year before graduation tells her wealthy husband that she would like to return to school in order to

finish, his response is to catalogue his current wealth and what she will be left as a widow. So why under such circumstances, would there be any need or justification for Madhu or any woman to get an education? But women, thereby subsumed, then have no life or meaning of their own, except in relation to others. Madhu gets her degree secretly, anyway.

Making laws entirely in men's favor

Whether or not a man commits adultery—not once but many times—it is not considered sufficient reason for a woman to leave her husband because "'men are like that'—men's sexuality is naturalized as uncontrollable" (Oza 2001, 1081), and if "every woman does that then there will be no marriage left" (Appachana 1998, 73). Mrs. Moitra ran away from her husband to England with her son and "Another Man" whom she could not marry because her husband would not give her a divorce. When she returned to India because her mother was dying, her husband then had her hauled into court, divorced her, and took custody of their son because of Mrs. Moitra's bad moral character. She was denied all visitation rights because her husband proved to the court's satisfaction that she was immoral because she smoked, drank, and had an affair. Ironically, Moitra had been having many affairs during their marriage, which was the actual reason that Mrs. Moitra had left him. Nevertheless, he was given custody of their child because he was not deemed to have a bad moral character. This situation is a composite of many real-life court decisions in India. With the skepticism and rebelliousness that is more characteristic of Guddo's daughters and of the succeeding generation of Indian women writers than of Guddo, and doubtless of the ambivalent Bedi, Lakshmi Persaud records this major cultural prescription for married women:

> I could not help thinking that such tales had little effect on men. This may have been because adultery committed by men had a lot going for it, since it was seen as "the way of men," one of the crosses wives had to bear with stoic calmness. That, I felt, was unfair and unjust. And I saw women's acceptance of this not as a result of their having a greater capacity to absorb pain or to forgive, as older women believed, but because of their helpless dependence upon their husbands. I was overcome by a deep sorrow for my sex in bondage, and for the real and terrifying predicament biology and custom had placed them in. I was not aware of how strongly I carried this sense of injustice until one day . . . I was startled to hear myself say: "Men who commit adultery should be shot." (1990, 99–100)

Name-calling

"Selfish," inconsiderate, "mistaken," "Are you going mad or something? . . . Not only are you going mad, you're going deaf" (1998, 82, 181). "No need to get hysterical" (1998, 209). "Hysterical" is one of the most common adjectives used to describe women under stress, never men.

Posing as meta-rational and calm in contrast to the "hysterical" woman

"Imagining all sorts of things," "Stop talking in this nonsensical manner," "You have such a wild imagination, Shanta" (1998, 80, 282), another husband tells his wife. Translation: "You are out of your mind. You have lost your grip on reality." This combines the demand for the woman's silence with the argument that she is void of sense.

"Don't shout." This is used to get the woman to shout more: to lose control, to lose her temper: "The words came out all wrong . . . she found herself accusing; instead of sounding measured and logical, she sounded emotional and high pitched" (1998, 168). The husbands, like the *bahu's* husband, by calmly proceeding to do some task that has nothing to do with the argument, thereby imply that the issue that the woman is bringing up is trivial, insignificant, and that she is overreacting.

It does not matter which female character Appachana is describing. All of them respond to this verbal abuse the same way. Shanta recognizes that the real problem is that "Fury made her speechless" (1998, 181). But she does not realize that getting the woman furious is a technique used by her husband to silence her. Sadly, at the time of the argument she either could not "find the words," or by the time she finally did, they were not only "wrong," but came out wrong in shouts. Then her husband had justification for not wanting to listen to her at all. She also realizes how futile her "shrill responses and emotional arguments" are in attempting to communicate with her husband, but not how to handle the situation. During their quarrels the woman is aware that she can never really tell the truth: that this "was what made her rage virtually sing in her ears, his complacency when he knew nothing, his dismissal of her words as rantings. She was reduced to ranting because she couldn't tell him the truth" (1998, 200).

"I don't know what you are talking about." The husband, always with a blank look, pretends never to understand or believe or accept a woman's perspective. He maddens the woman by refusing to comprehend what she is saying; that is, she is raving, incomprehensible. He is thus refusing, in yet another strategic ploy—to understand the woman's "babble"—to take the woman seriously, to listen to a woman's point. Anuradha, like many women around the world, holds "imaginary conversations" with her husband because in real life she somehow cannot ever express herself to him, what it is she wants and needs to say. She can never "find the words for all that agitated amorphous mass inside her." In her imagination he understands her, believes her, and feels "consternation and remorse." He loses "his habitual calm" (1998, 101). In reality, his only response is to express incredulity and to question whether she can even understand. When the woman, always on the defensive, tries to explain herself, to defend her position, to control herself, she always fails, as those on the defensive generally do.

"Stick to the subject"

When Madhu is pawed on a bus (known in India as "Eve Baiting")[15] her husband suggests that she buy a scooter. When, instead of telling him to stick to the subject, she goes defensive, informing him that she has no money for a scooter, that she has never asked for money for herself. Her husband then intimates that Madhu is incapable of adhering to a logical argument, whereas it is he who has strayed from the topic at hand. But even if Madhu's complaints or arguments were illogical, there is no abstract logic separate or independent from personal situated feelings, from any mortal human being's perspective or position, even a male's. Or as Shanta perceives as through an obscure fog: "Perhaps it was her dim realization that just because she wasn't logical in the way Narayana [her husband] wanted her to be, it needn't mean that she was wrong, as she was often told and believed" (1998, 203).

Giving their wives the same allowance no matter what and requiring that they manage that allowance under any and all circumstances

What it amounts to in many cases is that the wife learns to starve herself, to go without, while everyone else eats (and of course her husband never notices), something with which Madhu is familiar from her childhood, having to let her brothers eat first according to their wishes while serving them "the best, the biggest, the hottest" (1998, 84) portions of food.

Never listening

Amma attempts to defend herself from her husband's criticism of her reading romance books after he tells her that if she had "something up there" she would not be reading such rubbish. She tells him that she has read the classics, read more than he has, including the newspapers "when the children and the servants aren't sitting on my head," but "he wasn't listening, he wasn't there, he had gone to the bedroom" (1998, 163). Shanta begs Narayana to "listen properly." His response is to sigh [mock patience tried to its limit] and tell her that he is "'listening,' and she couldn't go on" (1998, 205).

But women—sisters, friends, some mothers and mothers-in-law—do listen. Her female students say of Padma who becomes a professor that she opened their eyes, that their lives were transformed as a result of having taken her course (1998, 241–242). Yet, whenever she attempted to dialogue seriously with him, her lover Karan would claim that he was listening to her. His face would take on an amused expression, although he would protest that he was listening to her, but then she would begin to "see the laughter creep into his eyes and that was the end of that" (1998, 243). Karan refused ever to listen to Padma, ever to tell her something she had said was "interesting," or even disagree with her, no matter how "she longed for him to listen to her" (248–249). As soon as he noticed "the look of frustration on her face he would begin needling her and predictably she would rise to the bait" (1998, 249).

Narayana's mother-in-law meditates on Karan's never listening to her daughter, never hearing her, or if he does, he disregards what he hears, and dismisses it: "Men did not want to hear about their wives' unhappiness. It was not because they had no knowledge of unhappiness. Far from it. It was because their knowledge of unhappiness grew out of contexts external to the contexts their wives knew; their wives' unhappiness sprang out of a territory so near and so foreign that to acknowledge it would destroy the men" (1998, 340).

Solutions

Susham Bedi

S usham Bedi (1942?–) may be torn and ambivalent as evidenced by the different attitudes of Guddo, the widowed heroine and her two daughters in *The Fire Sacrifice* ([1989] 1993). However, she anticipates the perspective of younger writers on gender issues. For example, in Appachana's "Bahu" and *Listen, Now,* which take place in India, the perspective is identical to that of Guddo, a recent immigrant in New York, when she states in *The Fire Sacrifice:* "I feel that to hold myself together, to keep strong and complete, I simply have to avoid any physical contact with a man. . . . I just feel that being close to a man makes me weak, dependent. And alone" ([1989] 1993, 93). Simultaneously and paradoxically, Guddo is conventional about marriage in relation to *her* own daughters, firmly convinced that nothing good in life can happen without a man; that society simply has no room in it for a single woman. She concurs with her Indian acculturation that once a woman marries she has to make the best of it, "no matter what. Whether it makes you cry or suffer . . . whatever the situation" ([1989] 1993, 152). She teaches her daughters that if women do not have their own homes and families they have no anchor and that women have a fundamental relationship to their families and to all things domestic, although while denying her daughters the freedom she herself never had in India she is never meanly obstinate (Feldman 2001, 1108; M. Kapur 1998, 102; Kishwar and Vanita 1984, 226). Ironically, her daughters do not internalize her traditional messages because the courageous manner in which Guddo has dealt with her single life after widowhood has provided them with a different, more inspiring model for a woman. Guddo has immigrated to this country on her own and is attempting to make it on her own despite poverty, exploitation as an Indian woman, and at the end of the book the very real and imminent tragedy of losing her adolescent son to drugs and to gang warfare.

Contemplating divorce, Guddo's daughter Anima asks herself defiantly: "What difference does it make anyway if you're married or not? People can be happy living alone too. Why is a woman compelled to spend her life with a man?" Then, despite her mother's misgivings and advice, the maze of warnings and prohibitions, the negative, constraining voices of tradition that predict a terrible price to be paid by her for her decision—the name-calling, ostracism, and being cast out by her society—Anima leaves a marriage that is filled with "fighting . . . stinging sarcasm and insults [and] beatings" ([1989] 1993, 153). She is going to live with her best friend temporarily until she finds a job. Anima's friend, in fact, serves as the catalyst for her decision, arguing that if Anima were truly independent, she would not put up with anyone tyrannizing over her; that women who do not really want to free themselves from "the marriage trap" ([1989] 1993, 153) are the ones who are responsible for their misery. At this point, Anima finally realizes that only she can put herself in control of her own life. She will no longer obey her mother's wishes, nor her family's. They did not necessarily know what was right for her. Their fears and worries were all based on Indian society, on Indian customs—that she would not be able to find another husband if she divorced and that she would be too old to compete in the marriage market. At twenty-eight!

Anjana Appachana

In Appachana's "Bahu" (Daughter-in-law) in *Incantations and Other Stories* ([1991] 2000), all the events take place in India and illustrate the gap between the generations, specifically between the Westernized and modernized daughter-in-law and traditional Indian mother-in-law. The *Ammaji* (mother-in-law) displays an underlying resentment, actually sadism, toward her *bahu,* keeping the *bahu* on the defensive while her mother-in-law peppers her with continual criticisms. The latter's agenda is always to annihilate the *bahu*'s individual identity through using traditional customs as models for constraint "in order to cause immense psychological tension and lead to a cruel annihilation of [the *bahu*'s] identity" (Talwar 1999, 228). A large part of the mother-in-law's motivation stems from accepting and believing in the denial of her own identity. Having given over her life to obeying the traditional controls over women, she begrudges the *bahu*'s modernity and Westernization, her economic independence as a professional who daily comes and goes in a world which the mother-in-law has never seen (Kishwar and Vanita 1984, 226).

She argues that because the daughter-in-law has a job she is therefore not home enough. The *bahu* responds that she does all the work when she comes home from work, but her mother-in-law reminds her that "that is your duty" ([1991] 2000, 12) because traditionally it was. In fact, she should consider herself lucky to have come into a liberal family that did not take a dowry—recently more "a form of plunder" (Dietrich 1999, 91) than dowry—a family that allows her to call their son by his name, to go out to work, to spend her earnings as she pleases. In contrast, other *bahus* give their earnings to their in-laws.

Still the *bahu* does not care about her in-laws' feelings. She wears trousers in front of them instead of keeping her head covered. Some background to this generational conflict is in order here:

> The common practice in a typical Hindu family was that as soon as the daughter-in-law stepped into the house, the mother-in-law and sister-in-law retired, as it were, and the newcomer was burdened with all kinds of responsibilities. The girl was often scolded for any minor fault by her husband, mother-in-law and any other elder member of the family. Most mothers-in-law had little sympathy with the young daughter-in-law and often ill-treated her so that she felt miserable in her new home and was forced to live in a state of tension and fear. . . . Women were expected to wear veils and were not permitted to speak to the elders, a practice considered a mark of respect. They had to talk to the younger family members in a low voice. They had to obey the mother-in-law and other elders of the family alike. Allowed to have meals only after the elders had been fed, they had to wait for them to retire before they could go to sleep. The elder members of the family were always free to take them to task for the most trivial matters. The young housewives, as a rule, could never meet their husbands during the daytime, the couple were allowed to meet only at midnight. They were thus expected to go to bed late at night and get up early in the morning. (M. Basu 2001, 5)

There are no matching gifts to the *bahu*'s family from her husband's family, even though the *bahu*'s parents had to spend 10,000 rupees on the mother-in-law's relatives when the couple married. In contrast, in the past, "[g]ifts or money from the bride's family were never used as a pretext to harass the bride by her in-laws. In other words, the dowry system had not taken its roots in the naked and ugly form it is today" (M. Basu 2001, 30).[1] The *bahu* is forced to spend all her free time with her husband's family, relatives, and friends, cooking and serving them. She never gets to have time for her family, relatives, and friends. When her friends try to visit, she is kept so busy serving her mother-in-law and her family that her friends cannot really be with her and stop trying. She serves everyone, including her sister-in-law when she visits, sometimes for months at a time.[2] Still, the mother-in-law complains incessantly:

> There is no variety in the fruits and vegetables we eat, she said, when I managed the house we had something different for breakfast, lunch and dinner. I don't know what is happening these days. There was variety. She said, so much food is wasted in this house, no one seems to do any budgeting here. Her daughter comes to stay for two months at

a stretch. She said, there is no one to indulge my poor child, no one to cook her favourite dishes, she cannot eat from a servant's hands. ([1991] 2000, 16)

She asks her daughter-in-law after she has arrived home from a day's work to get fruit for her daughter, although the shop is behind the house. She tells her to let her grandson sleep in her room because he likes to and not to shut the door on him. She should learn "to share."[3] Once when the *bahu* came home from a recital, her mother-in-law said that in her time a *bahu* acted with a greater sense of responsibility and remained at home far more. This became "her constant refrain" ([1991] 2000, 17). The couple had to stop going out because they found her so displeased when they came home. If the *bahu* responds to her mother-in-law, her unfeeling, insensitive husband gets angry with her, never at his mother, who takes care never to criticize her daughter-in-law in his presence, or else he uses trivializing, condescending, invalidating language to get her to accept the situation. He tells her not to be "silly" and justifies her mistreatment on the grounds of tradition that no one can "break." On his behalf, it must be pointed out that it is forbidden for Indian men to disrespect their mothers, or, to put it more positively, motherhood is glorified and Indian men are taught to revere their mothers.

Kishwar finds some positive things to write about in terms of this training for women who are mothers and who can be perceived by Indian men as mothers. They will then be respectful and not sexually harass women because they do not consider mother-women as having to make themselves "sexually attractive." In great contrast to Western society, Indian society often accepts it when a man abuses his wife, whereas a man who abuses his mother is condemned. Even after marriage, as with the *bahu's* husband, "bowing before a mother's commands and obeying her wishes is considered the appropriate behaviour for sons. . . . A dutiful son is held up as a social ideal" (1999, 188). Such an acculturation of unwavering respect, even in the face of patent injustice toward their wives prevents sons from challenging their mothers (Narayan 1997, 11).

Indian men are also taught to similarly respect older female relatives so that they become softened and act sentimentally toward these females, accepting their nagging and being ordered around by them. For these reasons, the majority of Indian women begin when quite young to emulate matriarchal conduct which, Kishwar claims, frequently undermines "their role as attractive sex partners" (1999, 188). The problem here with her conservative solution to sexual objectification and harassment is that it does not address the problem directly by focusing on change in men's conduct to other women than their mothers and certain female relatives through additional training. If they can be acculturated to respect these female relatives, they can be acculturated by their parents to respect all women.

Kishwar condemns Western feminists' individualist perspective, their insistence on the necessity of enjoying "personal freedom" and "individual rights"

(1999, 232). In contrast, both Indian men and women place "the interests of the family" over any individual "interests" (1999, 211). She accuses Western feminists of valorizing the nuclear family and the marriage ties to the point of excluding other relationships, but this is not so. One of the major struggles for Western feminists is to modify or transform the nuclear family within patriarchal marriage. We view these systems historically as privatized, heterosexist, naturalized systems constructed by men, imposed on women and children, and used to oppress them. Similarly, Kishwar critiques the male-dominated family as being the foundation for undue control over women, for denying women their rights. Furthermore, we also tend to remain publicly silent (or silenced) on these issues because we are subject to suffering from the same policing mechanisms of constraint as are Indian/Third World women: fear of familial and societal name-calling, rebuke, and disapproval, ostracism, scapegoating, and loss of jobs.

Not only Indian/Third World women, but also Western women are enculturated, heavily indoctrinated into having far more interest in everyone than themselves, into internalizing that everyone's needs come before their own. Men are acculturated to include their needs, rights, and interests as well as those of others, at best. At worst, they prioritize their agendas over those of others, or subsume their family's needs, interests, and rights into theirs—as theirs. Women globally are trained to continually strive to yield themselves up to their family needs and to feel guilty if they want anything for themselves. Women globally are enculturated to feel different and separated from the rest of the family. They are the subject givers with the family as objects to whom they give of themselves, with men included first and foremost. All records show this, especially in poverty. Men first, in food and education and every other requisite, with women and female children last (Umrigar 2001, 87).

Kishwar then waxes enthusiastic about the glories of motherhood for Indian women—of nurturing and dominating while being completely worshiped, the recipients of obedience and love from their children, of being served by their children, mainly sons, in "dependable, enduring, and fulfilling" relationships. In contrast to maternal glorification, marriage means that Indian women have "to serve and surrender." Their relationship with their children is superior to their sexual relationship with their husbands because it lasts longer. They receive more "emotional sustenance" from their children than from their husbands, and merely to be in "a sexual relationship with a man is to enter into a power relation" (1999, 225). However, Kishwar's description of Indian mothers with their children is equally weighted with power relations as is her description of Indian wives and husbands.

She also firmly, if naively, believes—and provides anecotal evidence to prove her point—that if a husband is unfaithful, the wife should remain with him and refrain from infidelity or disrespect. Her superior conduct will shame him into fidelity and respect. Additionally, the errant husband's family and the couple's children can effect change in the man through disapproval of his " irresponsible sexual behaviour." Their disapproval will cause the man to restrain himself somewhat and additionally can create a gradual "but definite shift in the power balance somewhat in a woman's direction" (1999, 233).

Kishwar admits that this is a "costly" solution, far from what she would see as an ideal of "full freedom and equality for women," but we do not live "in an ideal world." For this reason alone, we should begin our attempts for improvement and transformation with current situations as they are. In differing from Western feminists openly through her advocacy of women's attempting to work within a situation that already exists for gradual transformation rather than through confrontation and demands, Kishwar speaks from much personal experience as the co-founder with Vanita of the journal *Manushi* and famous in India in the late 1970s for having been "in the forefront of organizing against the spate of bride burnings that were taking place" (Alexander 1993, 209)

Appachana's *bahu* has no knowledge of or interest in perpetuating the kind of relationship with her husband that Kishwar commends. She wants a Westernized, private, sexually fulfilling marriage with him. The couple has no privacy, however, as is the case in most Indian homes. His nephew insists on sleeping in their room, and her husband accepts this. He acts surprised when she complains that they never spend time with one another, never talk to one another privately. Laurie Leach points out that there are "fundamental differences" between the Westernized *bahu* and her husband and his family, and these differences mark crucial "differences between American and Indian concepts of privacy [that are] likely to continue to cause tensions even if the most favorable resolution is reached. . . . When Western ways and those of the homeland are incompatible, as over concepts of privacy, conflict is inevitable" (1997, 209). The *bahu's* husband's response—that she should "stop exaggerating" because if his mother criticizes her, she probably has justification for doing so—indicates that a favorable resolution will not be reached in this area.

Although Leach calls for "compromise" as "essential" as a solution to such cultural conflicts, Appachana goes on to detail other fundamental differences between the *bahu,* her husband, and mother-in-law that culminate in the *bahu's* coming to a different resolution to conflict than Leach does. Whereas Leach views women's unwillingness to compromise in such a marriage as leading to tragedy—their ending up alone and isolated—Appachana seems to envision such a dire ending as not a dire ending at all, but a beginning—to a new, improved life shaped more in keeping with the woman's identity.

The *bahu* is not permitted to go home to her parents because her mother-in-law does not approve, although her own daughter comes home for long stretches at a time. When the young woman expresses the desire to visit her parents, her mother-in-law taunts the *bahu* by claiming that it feels to her as if it appears that there is no *bahu* in the house the way the *bahu* runs it; that she is obligated to this family as well as her own. Meanwhile, her husband is not obligated at all to his wife's parents. When she becomes pregnant, she discovers that she is expected to stop working, take care of the baby and everyone else, causing her to feel imprisoned. When she would try to return to work after the child started school she would have been away from the job market for so long a time that she would not be able to reenter it. Of even greater concern to her is that because of her pregnancy her parents are expected to come up with gifts once again for her husband's family that would total approximately 12,000 rupees. She then asks what *her* family gets in return. Her mother-in-law responds that on occasion her complaints are senseless. When the *bahu* tells her husband that she refuses to allow his family "to fleece" hers, his response is that she sounds as if she were "going crazy."

He speaks only to defend custom. He claims speciously that because his mother is "old-fashioned" it would not be remiss if his wife followed the traditions. He takes this position because according to traditional Hindu ideology his family could not specifically require gifts, but in reality, "insofar as household goods and other gifts were concerned, the bride's mother-in-law was supposed to have the highest authority to decide how these items should be distributed. It was largely women, especially elderly women, who controlled the flow and pace of gift-giving both within the household and outside" (M. Basu 2001, 85). These mothers-in-law, either obedient and submissive to tradition without thinking, or afflicted with tunnel vision, do not comprehend the price to be paid.

> When a woman maltreats another woman she does not enhance her own power as a woman, she enhances the total power of men as a group within the patriarchal family. Women can get power only as agents of domination and oppression within the male-dominated family structure. The woman who comes to gain the upper hand is usually one who has the backing and the approval of the powerful men. This tussle among women plays a crucial role in most families. . . . Very often, women play the role of tyrants or agents of tyrants [toward] other women. Even when women perform this role, however, they do not strengthen the power of women as a group but rather the power of the male dominated family. Keeping women thus divided against each other is an important way in which they are kept oppressed. (Kishwar and Vanita 1984, 16, 230)

When the *bahu* miscarries, her mother-in-law comes to her room where she is resting and tells her that she is broken-hearted about *her* daughter having to work in the kitchen because she doesn't want her mother to do the work. So the daughter-in-law has to get up and return to her housework. Her husband then blames the miscarriage on her, claiming that she had worked herself into a state. When she admits that she did not want a baby, Appachana then begins to show the husband deploying his full artillery of discursive attack weapons. He tells his wife that he supposes she will blame that on his mother as well. He is disgusted with the situation. If the *bahu* is incapable of adjusting, she should not vent to him. He also calls her "neurotic" and describes her as "imagining things as usual." Any problem that the bahu repeats to him elicits his impatience with hearing the repetition, not in addressing it: "Oh God, there you go again" ([1991] 2000, 24). He ignores her physically as well, by moving into another room, reading a newspaper, watching TV with his family, and allowing members of his family entrance into their room when he and his wife are there together so that she is prevented from continuing to talk to him about what is distressing her. These techniques convey that the husband is a superior, objective and impartial God or judge or jury who has decided after reasoned observation that the *bahu* is not to be taken seriously, nor to be listened to, or respected because she is hysterical.

First, the husband always situates the *bahu*'s perspective and language as wrong, no matter what. The husband always puts the *bahu* on the defensive. He never uses the word "I," only the word "You." Second, the husband always uses abusive discouse like "irrational," "crazy," "nag," "neurotic" to describe the *bahu*'s complaints or requests. The term "nag" is used for the *bahu* because it was what her father had called her mother and what her father-in-law called her mother-in-law, and so on, *ad infinitum*. This term is used by men in situations where women have requested them repeatedly for some change. After each repeated request, the husbands remain stolidly resistant. Instead of listening to the women's requests and taking them seriously, the men put the problem down to women's nagging. In reality, when women "nag," it is because they are powerless in the situation—victims without agency, reactive and dependent on their menfolk. Or they see themselves as victims because this has been the case for so long that they cannot see beyond the parameters of seeking assistance from their menfolk.

Appachana clearly explains the background first—the mistreatment, the abuse, the scapegoating—to which the *bahu* has been subjected for the past two years since her marriage. The *bahu*'s husband plays a critical role in failing to support her and colluding with his family, instead. His mystification of his family as an enclave of harmonious love in unyielding opposition to his wife's persistent attempts to expose it as a source of gender oppression represents Indian feminist attempts for at least thirty years to identify the family differently as "based on inequality and injustice which are gender based." It is perhaps the most oppressive site of all for Indian women. When conceptualizing alternatives to this family setup, many Indian feminists are opposed to Western feminists' preference for private, individual solutions which they perceive as "self-defeating" (N. Menon 1999a, 269).

Once Appachana has laid this groundwork for the *bahu*'s predicament, she then shows her movement mentally and physically to resolve it. The *bahu* has to become fully aware of the negative situations and to understand exactly what was unjust about them. To do this, the *bahu* has to interpret all the cultural customs imposed on her, then translate them into the reality. Her husband's family is out to get everything they can materially from her family by invoking unfair customs and is making her into a free household slave at her expense, again by invoking tradition. Appachana thereby exposes the difference between a former generation of feminists and the *bahu* and her generation. Her suffering has gone on for two years. All the *bahu's* responses to what she is put through are identical to the responses of the previous generation of feminists, but we took a very long time, if ever, to rise up and respond to ill treatment in a self-nurturing, proactive manner. Previous generations of feminists have written on our struggles of various kinds lasting many years, and still to this day feel defensive, filled with a sense of insecurity, self-doubt, or self-blame in unfair situations where we are subjected to discrimination. The previous generation of feminists made demands for equity and justice and perceived the necessity of action when our demands were not met, but it was a very stressful and long-drawn-out process with many failures and few successes. We attempted and still attempt to penetrate the cultural morass in which the insistence upon unquestioned but unfair, irrational customs causes us infinite pain. We have struggled and still struggle in the face of monumental opposition to attempt to attain clear insights as to the exact sources of injustice to us, as to what exactly is making us suffer. We may finally have reached clarity about what they are, despite continuing obstructions to equality and freedom, as illustrated by the *bahu*.

Her problems are no different; however, she goes through the process from suffering to clarity in the course of a week or two at the end of a two-year period, whereas situations like this took prior generations of feminists many years—over the course of our lifetimes. After many compromises, many yieldings, the *bahu* realizes that:

> Each time you give in you persuade yourself that the adjustment is necessary to marriage. . . . You give in again, and again, and again. There comes a time when it isn't such a small matter any more. But, still overwhelmed with guilt, still determined to please, you succumb again. Imperceptibly, but irrevocably, you slide into the kind of life that is completely and terribly contrary to everything you believe in. The kind of life you discussed in those pre-marital days (blissfully principled) saying, *I* would never accept such a thing. *I* would walk out. ([1991] 2000, 13, emphasis the author's)

From this point on, the *bahu* begins to move inexorably to certain conclusions. Like all previous recorded generations of women she has fantasized "a knight in shining armour" ([1991] 2000, 22), or as Appachana puts it in another story, "The Prophecy," "He would never tire of me, nor I of him. Marriage would be that wondrous path of rapid heartbeats and unending, intimate discoveries" ([1991] 2000, 57). In yet another story, "Incantations," Appachana's heroine also has romantic dreams and fantasies, illusions of her youth, as she waits for "my Rochester, my Rhett Butler, my Darcy" while actually confronting an "uncomprehending, angry husband." Nevertheless, she still continues to hope in dreams that her "resisting husband" will give her "empathy, tenderness and companionship" ([1991] 2000, 107).

Like this young woman, the *bahu* realizes after two years of marriage that her husband has chosen to collude with her oppression. He has not stopped her mother-in-law from treating his wife unfairly. He has not protected the *bahu*. He has not sided with her in objecting to unfair financial burdens on her parents. He has knowingly allowed the situation to remain as it was before his marriage, a situation in which he is still treated like a king, while she is treated like a servant who should be grateful to have been brought into his family. The husband, in maintaining the *status quo* and then claiming that things cannot be changed, is acceding to the continuity of oppressive customs for women. As Padma's mother in Appachana's *Listening, Now* (1998) tells her daughter's lover Karan, who married another woman to please his mother because he believed she was dying: "Listen to me. Hear me. You had a choice. Even if you chose what your heart did not want, it still remains what you chose. It does not mean you had no choice. . . . You did what you did because you did not have the strength to do otherwise" (1998, 395).

Unlike her mother and generations of her foremothers who were trained to then accept whatever their fate brought them in marriage, she feels that if she accepts the situation it would mean that she would be willing to live forever as she is living now. She cannot leave and return to her parents because they would argue the importance of preserving a marriage at any cost. It is the woman in the marriage who must "give in more." Their daughter must accept that "marriage means sublimating your desires" ([1991] 2000, 83). A wife must remain silent: "Nothing could thrive without her silence—not her husband, not her children, not her marriage. Mouth closed gently over a captive tongue, that was all" ([1991] 2000, 340).

> I remember minding particularly that the injunction to be silent came from my mother, who told me so early, because she had no one else to tell, about her sufferings in her conjugal home. I remember my mother's anger and grief at my father's resort to a silencing "neutrality" that refused to "interfere" in the domestic tyrannies that his mother inflicted on my mother. The same mother who complained about her silencing enjoined me to silence, doing what she had to do, since my failures to conform would translate as her failures to rear me well. (Narayan 1997, 7)

In addition, the *bahu* must consider the enormous difficulty a divorced woman has in India. Many Indians consider marriages for love as well as divorce "the result of corruption and Westernization" (Harlan 1995b, 207) and "symbolic of uncontrolled sexuality" (Oza 2001, 1089). The *bahu* also realizes that it would be hard for her to find a job because she had only a brief experience in the workforce. If she lives on her own, it would be pleasant, but her male colleagues at work would then think her "easy game" and there would be gossip about her, that she wasn't as nice as they thought her. Nice women don't divorce men.

Still, she leaves. When she informs her husband that she has made up her mind to do so, he repeats that nothing can be done about the way things are, that she must accept it. For him, the answer does not lie in the abdication of her duties. She leaves, anyway, and in the taxi she takes a deep breath and smells the "wet earth" ([1991] 2000, 26), an indication that her life is going to improve.

In *Listening Now,* because Padma has had a child by Karan without being married, she and her family have lied about her marital status for many years—maintaining that Padma's husband had been killed in a car accident. When Karan returns and wants to marry Padma and be a father to their daughter, Padma rejects him. She has enjoyed a large support system of friends—her sister and female neighbors—and has come to realize that all these women, like herself, are constrained in Indian culture. They "seem to lead lives opposed to their dreams and desires" (1998, 460), especially those who are married, a statement identical to Deshpande's. Because of this support system, Padma has survived being jilted by her lover and having become a single mother. She has gone on to earn her Ph.D. and to become a professor. She lives in a home with her daughter that is filled with books, furnished to her taste, and is surrounded by supportive and caring neighbors. Although she believes Karan dead, she communes with him in her imagination and secretly waits for him for thirteen years to come to her door some day, to knock on it, to enter, and to apologize, as he finally docs.

Through her various characters, except Padma and the *bahu,* Appachana shows that women have to give up everything once they marry because of the constraining demands of Indian culture and customs. One of Padma's friends, an expert singer of Indian classical music had to give it up after marriage, another gave up her B.A., another, who won a gold medal, the top student in her university, now does nothing but housework. Padma realizes that if she agrees to marry Karan she will join the generations of Indian women past and present and will lose her home, her friends, her sister, and her mother because she will rarely, if ever, be able to see them, as Appachana described in *"Bahu."*

Instead of following her son Karan's wishes and allowing him to marry the only woman he ever loved, Padma's cruel and now mentally disturbed mother-in-law (who called her a prostitute because Padma became pregnant) would come to live with them. Karan's sisters would come on extended visits, and Padma would be expected to serve them all. She would lose her job because Karan is a civil servant and is frequently transferred. She would lose all she has constructed over the years of waiting for him to return. In refusing marriage, she accepts, instead, the joys of the free and independent life she now lives, surrounded by loving family and friends—but stigmatized by the surrounding community for being an unwed mother—as doubtless her daughter will be stigmatized for being a bastard.

Padma's decision echoes Bedi's conviction about the negative impact of marriage and motherhood on women, due to the overwhelming demands and burdens of a patriarchal system. Appachana feels that only a support system of other women can ease these demands and burdens—somewhat—because she does not conceptualize or believe that husbands or male lovers will ever modify their behavior, or (perhaps betraying Western cultural and feminist influences) that children will ever pull their own weight in sharing home duties according to their ages and capacities. To this day, many Western feminists do not practice communal work in the home. They conceptualize their children, at best, as passive, one-dimensional recipient-objects of their care and concern. At worst, judging by recent Western commercials, Western children are depicted as monsters—impish, self-absorbed devils who delight in destroying objects in the home or making messes that their parents (usually mothers) always smilingly clean up with doting pleasure. One of the reasons that parents traditionally had large families was to allocate and distribute chores, and all Indian texts show daughters as a matter of routine assisting their mothers. Nevertheless, I cannot think of one instance where the sons do, except for Hari in Desai's *The Village by the Sea*. Bedi's heroine Guddo in *The Fire Sacrifice* begs both her accomplished daughters to get their husbands to help them at home, to work together with their wives, to get them to enjoy doing so. She tries to show them that they are "absolutely equal" to their husbands in education and competence in their professions. Yet her daughters allow their husbands to lie around at home while they cook and clean. She feels that if her daughters continue to indulge their husbands in this way they will end up wearing themselves out "slaving" for them while their husbands will continue to "just take it for granted" (1993, 105). And they will do so as long as mothers "continue to indulge" their sons in this way from the beginning of their lives.

Vanita perhaps best expresses the perspectives of contemporary Indian feminists such as Appachana when she calls for the development of alternatives that "most feminists and non-feminists, rightists and leftists, Hindus, Muslims and Christians in India share" about the notions of gender and sexuality within an institutionalized heterosexual monogamous family. Rather than work to repair "the structure of heterosexual marriage and family" to make it "somewhat more equitable," "any women's movement" should instead emphasize, "validate" and "encourage" the reconceptualization of "gender and sexuality" in order to develop alternatives (1999, 531). Vanita faults "women's movements in India" (although I would expand her critique to include Western women's movements, as well) for focusing "on people as victims rather than agents" and especially "their reluctance to question gender and sexuality categories," which she feels stresses only demands "for equity rather than liberation" (1999, 534).

Unlike the heroines of the older generation of feminists, in the majority of these younger writers' works—like Appachana's—most of the major female characters do resolve their problems by developing alternative ways of dealing with patriarchy in all its institutions, including "in the economy, household organization,

[and] family relations" (Feldman 2001, 1101). Still, Vanita sees these writers as "end-lessly" repeating a "victim narrative" when their characters leave "a bad marriage" because so much of "the body of the text is taken up with the struggle to get out and the text ends as soon as the heroine does get out, because there is logically no-where for her to go except another marriage, suicide or lonely depression" (1999, 535). I disagree. At the end of their texts the younger writers' discourse offers the possibility of hope rather than failure because the trajectories of their female char-acters are movements forward and away into their own self-created future after leaving their families and/or menfolk.[4] These (re)solutions, however, are individual ones, privately formulated, although in all probability, with the tacit support of many feminists globally.

Appachana and other contemporary Indian feminist writers feel that the only viable moves for Indian women are to opt out altogether rather than to put up with hopeless marriages. Neither putting up with the marriage, nor murdering the hus-band, but opting out of it altogether, seems to be the favored solution for the gen-eration of Indian feminist writers born after 1950. Whichever way the Indian woman turns, she is always on the outside looking in. For a woman to separate from her husband or divorce him is a move so wrought in Indian culture as to draw down upon her enormous suffering and ostracism. Not only do major female char-acters do this, but they also make plans as to how to do this and how to live after-wards so that their lives are better. Such plans fly in the face of all presuppositions about the fate of a woman without a man. In describing these moves and these plans, younger feminist Indian writers not only provide blueprints for such specific situations but also provide the means to topple traditional foundations that seemed to be written in stone, to unglue the fixed assumptions based on religious and social sanctions for women. Neither the Indian/Third World feminist move-ment nor the Western feminist movement has expressed support in a public plat-form for these writers' alternatives.

Indira Ganesan

The Journey (1990) by Indira Ganesan (1960–) details a flight—not from a hus-band—but from the self by a sixteen-year-old girl, preoccupied with her past and with herself throughout the novel. Ganesan's Renu—although much younger than Deshpande's Sarita, Bedi's Anima, Appachana's *bahu* and Padma—also begins the same journey outward into the present, into the world:

> Imagine that with each step, she was walking away from her superstitions and fears, away from her self-wrought sickness, her desire to live in the past. Imagine her step-ping away from her inherited weights, demanding flight. This is our secret dream, our need to break free from the ground on which we half the time drag our feet resentfully,

because we have been told that it is important and correct to feel the earth beneath, even while flight is in our hearts. Weightless travel, metaphorical soul soaring, a shedding of swallowed stones, a mobility that can hold the keys of the universe. . . . Our heroes are those who defy gravity, the gods who live in the clouds, beings who walk on water, those with magic boots and capes. *There are some of us forever at our windows, waiting for rescue from the world outside. But even the sages walked on the earth; they gathered staffs and bowls, placed foot after foot further into life, eyes open, palms open.* . . . Renu Krishnan stood on the beach on the island of Pi, ready for her journey. (1990, 173–174, emphasis mine)

Sunetra Gupta

In *Memories of Rain* (1992), Sunetra Gupta (1965–) again subscribes to the courageous solution of leave taking, of flight into the frightening vacuum of a new life. Her heroine Moni emigrated to London with her English husband Anthony many years ago against the wishes of her family. After some years and many passing affairs, he falls in love with a young Englishwoman, Anna. Throughout the text Moni is forced to share her husband with Anna, even the humiliation of their exhibiting their passion for each other in her presence. What has kept her fixed in this humiliating and tortured predicament is her lingering passionate love for her husband and her dread of returning to India to be mocked and pitied and outcast as a failure.

Anna even openly attempts to steal the heart and mind of Moni's and Anthony's daughter, involving herself in the family's life as if she belongs there. She coopts Moni's role as a mother in her extensive, even extravagant preparations for the child's sixth birthday party, which takes up a large part of the book (to readers' bewilderment), until the denouement. Moni is relegated to picking up the birthday cake from the bakery, and neither Anthony nor Anna shows the slightest concern for Moni's feelings in this regard or any other. In fact, Anthony believes that his gentle, silent, obedient, yielding Indian wife will forgive him anything and everything always, according to the well-known verse: "This is the only dharma, only vow and only course of action / to serve with body, speech, and heart, your husband's feet lovingly" (Tulsida's *Ramcaritmanas,* quoted in Nilsson 2001, 379, fn. 1). Anthony even imagines (and the thought comforts him greatly) how at the inevitable end of his affair with Anna, his devoted and loyal Indian wife will remain with him forever.

Instead, Moni, much like Appachana's *bahu* and Bedi's Anima, comes to the end of her rope, seemingly suddenly, but actually after much soul-searching and inner turbulence. She begins to undertake complex and secret moves: somehow forcing herself to get her passport in order and book a one-way flight to India, and just hours before the birthday party, kidnapping her daughter from her school and flying back with the child to India. Her intention is to hide out somewhere in that vast country where Anthony, who adores his daughter, can never find them. The book ends as Moni pictures to herself with great satisfaction the shocking moment when the celebration runs aground without ever having begun. A large, expectant company of children and grown-ups will serve as public witnesses to Anthony's humiliation and subsequent endless suffering when it will suddenly dawn upon him what his mousy, taken-for-granted wife, has done to him and Anna.

In all preceding generations, including the feminist generation, the major quality of life was *waiting for*. In these texts by the younger generation of Indian women writers, the quality of women's lives has clearly changed forever. Enough already. At a certain point no more waiting.

Conclusion

Contemporary younger feminist Indian women writers born after 1950 tend to focus on daily activities revolving around private, domestic life—to foods and food preparation, to activities of all kinds in the home, to personal and economic conditions within the family, with relationships in the family between children, parents, and relatives both in India and abroad. This domestic focus becomes endlessly, microscopically detailed and omnipresent, suffocatingly so, although it has a feminist agenda. The authors focus on these excruciating domestic details for the purpose of illustrating with ever-increasing sophistication the private nature of the causes of women's suffering, the overwhelming difficulties of their existence.

Indian patriarchy—its religions, its educational system, its customs, its social life as illustrated in the home is the source of the injustice of the cultural expectations, demands, and burdens placed on women according to gender roles. Indian patriarchy, a complex of "hegemony-seeking masculinist ideology" (Alcoff 2000, 852) is also part of a global system that controls "women's labour, fertility and sexuality" (N. Gandhi and N. Shah 1999, 339). As Oza points out: "The All-India Democratic Women's Association (AIDWA), in objecting to "the commodification of women and their bodies that in turn reinforce their subordinate status," also rejected "the notion of any one definition of culture, womanhood, and tradition being imposed on women" and seeks "to expose to public scrutiny the [patriarchal] state's priorities and its alliance with global and domestic capital" (2001, 1082, 1080). Men "control the resources" and use "evaluative standards" projected from their own values. Hidden behind the veil of the "important," the "interesting," and the "rigorous" are:

Systematic selection patterns that reflect the [male] evaluators' stakes within the existing
network of prestige and their own experiences of social life and their own class-, race-,
and gender-based intests in how social life is organized. . . . Gender is part of their own
basis of privilege. They do not have to be intentionally trying to legitimate gender hierarchy—they are simply not in a position for gender domination to be salient in their
own experience and primary in their political interests. (Sprague 2001, 532)

Throughout the twentieth century there was an ever-increasing focus, sourced
in the home and family, on women's achieving independence. These feminists en-
visioned a time to come when through the efforts of the feminist movement,
through the achievement of an education and ensuing economic independence,
women's relationships with their menfolk within their families would improve.
"Then Indian women . . . educated, and supported by their families will assume
rights already guaranteed by their legal system. Until then, laws contrary to custom
and belief will continue to be ignored, for . . . equality, for any group, is ultimately
won by the efforts of group members" (N. Gandhi and N. Shah 1999, 321).

Surprisingly, the younger generation of feminist Indian women writers describes a younger generation of men within the families who do not modify, with
whom it is not possible to live compatibly. These writers now advocate women
going on into free and independent, self-fulfilled lives regardless of lack of support
for doing so from their menfolk and their families. The earlier generation had attempted to show that the personal plight of women (and other oppressed groups,
as well) is directly related to the culture's political, economic, religious, and educational practice. Mahasweta Devi's broad canvas, her overwhelming concern for and
emphasis on the poor and the outcast in India, while containing women's issues
specifically as a subtext in her work, was not representative of her generation, a
generation that focused on women's becoming liberated from former and present
constraints and that made other related political, social, economic, and cultural
concerns secondary.

This younger generation of feminist writers born after 1950, however, continues to show the indelible influence of constraining cultural traditions and institutional customs perpetuating earlier discriminations against women, earlier codes of
male honor, prerogatives, and duties on both males and females, and the cultures'
political, economic, social, and religious impact in terms of the daily personal
home life of their characters in which gender roles are constructed. Sadly, despite
the awareness of this younger generation of women of the possibilities of choice in
terms of education, of going on into the workforce, of fully and freely expressing
their sexuality, very few if any of the men in the texts who are influential in their
major female characters' lives are shown as having modified their conceptions of
masculinity and of appropriate male (and female) behavior. Therefore, these
younger Indian women writers show their major female characters up against the
same problems, the same issues, the same obstacles to free and full self-expression

in their lives at home and abroad as the earlier generations of heroines. But now the issues are primarily drawn in terms of how they play themselves out in the home as the primary battlefield, the primary source of conflict between the generations and between the sexes. And this is true whether they remain in India or immigrate abroad.

Mukherjee's powerful tragic novel, *Wife* (1975) sought to bring attention and sympathy to women suffocating in domestic cages of cultural prescriptions, as has Chitra Banerjee Divakaruni's much later *Arranged Marriage* (1995). Even earlier, the feminist Deshpande had begun by 1980 to focus with that intensity characteristic of younger feminists on the same issues. But she did so consciously from the firm conviction that her microscopic focus on the domestic duties in the home, in the world of women, was truly a feminist service to women and to her culture because she believed that therein lies the strength, the power of women. Concerns about money matters and how to survive from day to day are now the focus within the context of individual worries by members of the family or close friends and within and beyond that family context. Religion and religious ritual still play a role in the texts, but are used like the domestic emphasis—to show one more cultural difference among the many differences between the generations and between immigrants and those who remain in India. The expression of political opinions, both on a national and international basis, which I was able to cite frequently from a variety of texts, has now dwindled almost to nonexistence, except in the texts of critics, where it is the primary focus. A woman's relationship politically to the nation is metonymized as her relationship socially to her husband in marriage (S. Ray 2000, 136).[1] The authors use women's oppression in marriage and the family as reflections of the political, social, religious, economic, and educational institutions in India and the West that situate Indian women as outsiders. Under patriarchy and its complex system of hierarchies, these provide an "excess of markers of identity" . . . that lead in turn to the diminution of [women's] political value as citizens equal before the law" (A. Rao 1999, 232).

The majority of younger Indian feminist writers and critics "with over a century of one of the most powerful and complex women's movements in the world behind [them] of gender injustice" (Gopal 1999, 298) do not view Indian women's oppressions and perspective as analogous or similar to Western women's. But like Namjoshi, I view gender injustice, not as a local issue, but as a global issue in terms of one common oppressor—"male rulers" everywhere. I believe it is imperative for Western feminists to work to bridge this divide between women, as Namjoshi has. In her memoir *Goja* (2000), Namjoshi contends, as Second-Wave feminists in the West a generation before her, including myself, have contended for many years—despite recent strong critiques from many younger feminists globally that such a contention was and is narrow and essentialist—that being gendered female in a patriarchal world is the one issue that outweighs all other issues such as rank and caste and race and class and ethnicity. Despite being vastly "unequal in rank," Namjoshi contends that her untouchable servant Goja and herself, a royal princess, are, nevertheless, as bodies that are gendered female, ultimately "equal at bottom, because men rule" (2000, 17). Patriarchal oppression is a worldwide phenomenon undergirding any fragile privileges any women anywhere might seem to enjoy. All women of the world are oppressed in common because men, who rule everywhere, are in Namjoshi's definition "fiendish." This is because they first "exploit human beings" and afterward condition them in such a way as "to persuade them that in that very exploitation lies their self-respect, their place in society, indeed, their duty. And that's what they do to women and to servants. That's what they do when they set up a stable hierarchy, and then . . . the glory of the masters is the glory of the servants" (2000, 110). It took the loss of Namjoshi's seeming "power" after moving to the West for her to have this illumination. "Now when I have very little power I have at last understood something about power. I think some sort of conditioning went on—for humanists and 'civilized' people and especially for women—which prohibited any serious thinking about power. It would not have been comfortable" (2000, 66).

The issue of women's sexuality is now becoming only one element within a domestic focus, limited to the sexuality of young and middle-aged females and males. It is in the context of patriarchal control over female sexuality that younger feminist Indian women writers describe institutional constraints as reflected in Indian home life in India and in the diaspora. Their solution is to leave this home and the men who control it, or to run a home without them. This is a difficult solution, certainly, at first: lonely and hard and isolated. In addition, the consideration arises as to how women can leave an intolerably oppressive home situation unless they have some place to go, unless they also have employment. Then in order to actually be in the workforce, don't they have to go out into a world run by men who really also run the home by extension?

Asha, in the short story "Burning Turtles" by Hema Nair (?-) is an educated career woman in the United States who has risen to become a vice president in a large company. She illustrates the thinking of every writer and critic I have discussed in this text about the necessity for women to achieve economic and sexual independence as a priority. She also illustrates the need to act with dignity, even when frustrated, to refuse herself sexual fulfillment when a partner is abusive, or when the relationship is conducted by the man in terms humiliating to the woman: "A woman who has an independent source of income, assets and resources is less likely to experience or need to succumb to sexual manipulation than if she lives a life of dependence" (Kishwar 1999, 169).

Contrary to Leach's grief over proud and independent and unyielding wives who refuse to be humiliated by their husbands and end up isolated and alone in the marriage bed, Kishwar tells it the way it is: "Those who do not know when to reject sex end up far more messed up than those who can do without sex when it is available only as part of an unsatisfactory relationship" (Kishwar 1999, 221). Before the story opens, Asha had summoned the courage to divorce the husband who abused and beat her and to establish a new life of and on her own. This is still very rare. In the focus groups that I discussed previously, Satya P. Krishnan, Malahat Baig-Amin, and others found that those women who had done what Asha has— left "violent relationships"—finally admitted that it had been "excruciatingly difficult and painful to start living on their own" (1998, 155). Nair brilliantly illustrates the lonely aftermath of this brave act for most women through the use of symbolism in a typical drive home by Asha after work:

> Asha, who was rarely home before seven, when all the lights in her three-bedroomed townhouse were blazing [was driving] home from work. The car was a home, she reasoned, waiting for a gap in the traffic to merge into the smooth-running river of red lights, a caravan of leather and chrome with windows that revealed the world as it carried them *between destinations*. Some nights, driving in the dark with *nothing visible except the length of road* illuminated by the headlights, Asha was grateful for the silent companionship of others moving alongside. She was not just a pair of hands *steering towards an invisible future*. The flicker of signals as cars switched lanes were cheerful winks of recognition. (1996, 333, emphasis mine)

The story continues to show Asha even more courageous after she meets a man who seems to offer her all she needs, whom she hopes will bring a permanent end to her loneliness: handsome, successful, sympathetic, charming to her young daughter. Asha is thrilled and delighted at the possibility of a new and wonderful relationship with an apparently totally desirable man, until he burns some turtles on the beach for his pleasure and that of a group of boys. Additionally, Asha begins to suspect that he has also beaten her dog while she was elsewhere in her house. He too, like her former husband, is abusive. Uncompromising in her courageous decision to live with self-respect and dignity, despite having to live by herself, Asha, ignoring pressure from others, then cuts him out of her life immediately. She is determined to enjoy her life as she has shaped it—successful in her chosen career and a lovely home, with an adorable little girl and their dog.

In *Listening Now* and in *Memories of Rain*, Appachana and Gupta proposed that the solution would be for men to listen to what women are complaining about. They must then change, modify, and transform, which Karan does, only too late, and which Anthony never does. Taking Karan's hard-learned lesson and Anthony's endless suffering to heart, men should listen before it is too late, before they have estranged and lost women who would love them, before women build new lives that would exclude them. In this regard, Parvati Athavale warned women over one hundred years ago that "[i]f freedom from servitude is meant freedom from men and a life of independence from them, then that freedom is unnatural, impossible, disastrous, and opposed to the laws of right living" (quoted in Grewal 1996, 228). Despite her warning, as far back as the beginning and as late as the end of the twentieth century, Rokeya Sakhawat Hossein and Suniti Namjoshi had both attempted in *Sultana's Dream, The Mothers of Maya Diip,* and *Babel* to reverse reality—by envisioning a woman-run society in which men are constrained. But neither author was able to sustain a separatist world. They only reversed the current system of injustice and oppression against women by treating men like women, as women's inferiors.

I am impressed by Mohanty's dismissive arguments against reversal—what she calls "inversion"—because women are then viewed "as a coherent group across contexts, regardless of class or ethnicity." This structures "the world in ultimately binary, dichotomous terms":

> Women are always seen in opposition to men, patriarchy is always necessarily male dominance, and the religious, legal, economic, and familial systems are constructed by men. Thus, both men and women are always apparently constituted whole populations and relations of dominance and exploitation are also posited in terms of whole peoples—wholes coming into exploitative relations. . . . If the struggle for a just society is seen in terms of the move from powerless to powerful for women as a *group,* and this is the implication in feminist discourse which structures sexual difference in terms of the division between the sexes, then the new society would be structurally identical to the existing organization of power relations, constituting itself as a simple *inversion* of what exists. If relations of domination and exploitation are defined in terms of binary divisions—groups which dominate and groups which are dominated—surely the implication is that the accession to power as a group is sufficient to dismantle the existing organization of relations? But women as a group are not in some sense essentially inferior or infallible. (1991b, 70–71)

I am also impressed by Spivak's pronouncement that "[o]ur work cannot succeed if we always have a scapegoat" (1999, 309). This pronouncement, however, necessitates a philosophical detachment from the inexplicable, irrational, and gratuitous injustices of patriarchal gender oppression, not the least of which has been the repression of our sexuality, to which we have all been subject.

Women have rarely, if ever, tried reversal in reality. Perhaps if we did try to see how this solution would turn out, we might find that it might work better than what has been in effect since time immemorial. Judging from the apocalyptic results of men's running the world wherever one turns at the beginning of the twenty-first century—"[w]hat hasn't he contaminated? Can you name it?" (Minhha 1989, 52)—perhaps Hossain and Namjoshi are correct in dreaming of reversing "deeply sedimented relations of inequality" (Walby 2001, 499), but not, in my opinion, in viewing one sex, the male sex, as inferior to the female sex and therefore constraining *them.* What I find myself intrigued by is Hossain's and Namjoshi's dream of women assuming primary responsibility for running the world. Could women possibly do any worse than men have done so far?

Notes

Preface

1. I use the terms "Indian/Third World feminists" and "Third World" throughout this text because the majority of Indian writers and critics use them.
2. Mira Nair's recent film *Mississippi Marsala* is one example.

Introduction: Background and Overview of Major Topics

1. Earlier, the American white women's suffrage movement spun off from the Abolitionist movement when they began to realize that they were battling against the enslavement of Africans and African Americans when they themselves were not free.
2. According to Rupal Oza, one of the qualities most deeply embedded into Indian women to this day as an ideal and publicized to the rest of the world by the Indian government as a premier quality of female Indians is the compassion of women, especially for children. Such an attribute "serves to contain their sexuality within respectable boundaries" (2001, 1076).
3. Anannya Bhattacharjee sees this nationalist view as "predictably similar" in both Indian communities in the West and in India (1998, 169). She also calls the fantasy of the Indian immigrant communities about India as it was "a cannibalization of a mummified heritage" (1998, 200).
4. It happens in Pakistan, as well. Fundamentalists complain about children in "tight American Jeans, destroying their morals by watching obscene films on the VCR and by listening to that American singer with a woman's face [Michael Jackson]" (T. Naqvi 1997, 62).
5. Partha Chatterjee writes that "[t]he period of 'social reform' had two 'distinct' phases. In the first phase, the reformers sought for social reforms through the 'colonial authorities.' In the second phase, the nationalist phase, they resisted British intervention in any matters

affecting 'national culture'" (1993, 6). British intervention in India led to underdevelopment in the first place; postcolonial emigration to the West further deepened India's relative poverty (S. Shah 1998, 310).

6. Perhaps best known as the screenwriter for the renowned moviemaking team of Merchant-Ivory, Jhabvala is also a novelist. Born Jewish in Germany, she fled the Holocaust and moved to India permanently after her marriage to an Indian.

7. Sanjit Baruah contrasts the Western bourgeois concept of home with the Indian middle-class home, which is more like the Western home of the middle ages—public, not private, a "part of the social space" (1997, 511), where the activities of daily life are conducted and where people meet to do business and to be entertained. This seemingly "value-neutral description" (Grewal 1996, 107), however, provokes many questions: What are Indian women's roles or activities in these "public homes"? For whom are Indian homes "public"? How and in what ways are Indian homes public for women? For men? How and in what ways does their being public impact on the women who are responsible for running them? Like Baruah, the Indian feminist Anannya Bhattacharjee is suspicious of or feels superior to Western feminists in that she feels it necessary to warn us not to be "seduced or hindered" by arguing with each other as to whether spaces are public or private. But she does not altogether dismiss us, as Baruah does. In her discussion of the "multiple homes" of abused Indian immigrant women, Bhattacharjee asks Western feminists to examine our theories about "public, private, and state . . . in new ways," to "be vigilant against their miragelike quality." For only by "understanding" how they are constructed "can we hope to change them" (1997, 309, 327, 329). By the use of the pronoun "we," Bhattacharjee expands the ranks of the Western feminists to include all feminists, Western, and Indian/Third World feminists, as does Grewal when she states that the concept of "'home' is a category that, especially for women, is extremely problematic" because "given a patriarchal nationalism, a country cannot be home for a woman. Nor can an immigrant call a country of adoption home, especially if the immigrant is a woman of color in a white, patriarchal society" (1994, 235, 250). Many Indian critics claim that the kind of vigilant theorizing on crucial distinctions between public and private space is best provided not so much by Western feminists as by other feminists who are from postcolonial cultures (Chatterjee 1997; R. Kapur and Cossman 1999; R. Menon and Bhasin 1998, 108; Sangari and Vaid 1999b). See also Dipesh Chakrabarty on the difference between Indian and Western notions of public and private space (1997, 374–375). Grewal devotes an entire book to this from a feminist perspective. She views "home as a place mediated in the colonial discursive space through notions of the harem . . . not only as the original site of nationalism but also of feminism, since it is here that women can resist nationalist formations by rearticulating them as a site of struggle rather than of resolution" (1996, 7). Carol Pateman sees one of the major aspects of feminism as the distinction between public and private. In fact, she sees this distinction as "what the feminist movement is about" (quoted in S. Ray 2000, 177).

8. In 1917, Annie Besant (1847–1933), an English feminist and Fabian Socialist, became its first female president.

9. This concept of Earth as Mother who provides shelter (although eternal) for Sita is reminiscent of the Demeter-Persephone relationship in Greek myth, only here the daughter is sheltered by her mother Earth half the year; the other half she spends in Hades. Either way, these are cruel, undeserved fates for young women that I doubt flowed from the imaginations of female mythmakers.

10. I wholeheartedly agree with Spivak, and query of her and my readers rhetorically: Can any of us think of any prescription for woman's conduct within any rite, in any part of the social fabric or structure that is not the result of male domination?

11. Phule was a celebrated caste leader against caste and women's oppression who opposed polygamy and child marriage and advocated the education of women and widow remarriage.

12. Even though in 1961 the Dowry Prohibition Act limited dowry to 500 rupees, the dowry demands ever increase through loopholes in the act such as the one that permits "gifts" (Minturn 1993, 321).

13. For the same point made less persuasively, see Paula Richman (2001a, 319). Many books have been written on the topic of "dowry death," some of which are listed by A. Basu (1992, 242). M. Basu, in *Hindu Women and Marriage Law* (2001), has an entire chapter ("Dowry," 85–88) in which she focuses on "dowry deaths," especially murder of brides by in-laws.

14. She then proceeds to give some typical gruesome examples from newspaper accounts (2001, 96–97).

15. This applies in Pakistan, too. Additionally, homosexuality is viewed in South Asia as "a Western phenomenon," despite homosexual images in temple carvings in Khajuraho and Konarak in India (Surina Khan 1998, 65). See also Naheed Islam (1998, 78) on the reasons for the suppression of homosexuality in India.

16. Lubna Chaudhry (and others) inform Western readers that "in East Indian and Pakistani films and in most of the Sufi renditions of heterosexual love, passion between men and women is a subversive force capable of undermining the dominant order, for which the segregation of the sexes served as a mechanism of control. Such love was untainted by earthly considerations, and its consummation involved a union at the spiritual level. The physical realm was secondary or completely insignificant" (1998, 53).

Chapter 1: Outsiders Within I

1. Sarojini Naidu (1879–1943), Satthianadhan's contemporary, was a feminist poet who wrote about "private, pained women suffering emotional deprivation, even psychic imprisonment . . . trapped in an unredeemed sexuality" (Alexander 1996a, 174). She was elected president of the Indian National Congress in 1925 and was a close associate of Gandhi's. She led Gandhi's famous Salt March in 1930 and was imprisoned by the English with Gandhi and his wife Kasturba as a result of the Quit India Movement. In contrast to Satthianadhan, Naidu claimed with Nationalist fervor that the English colonizers had robbed Indian women of their "immemorial birthright." She also claimed that when India was liberated from the English, Indian women's "ancient" rights would be restored (quoted in Alexander 1996a, 178).

2. Perhaps wearing light saris did not help. Certainly it exposed her to racism. She reported that when in London she went out to a National Indian Association gathering in a sari, someone shouted out: "Hallo . . . what is this freak?" (quoted in Burton 1994, 197). Sorabji ended up attending Lady Somerville College, Oxford, and became the first Indian woman to graduate from Oxford in law. Jayawardena places the date as 1882 (1989, 89), but Burton places it as 1892 (1994, 197). In any event, women could not practice law until 1923. Returning to India after her graduation, Sorabji then became a barrister of the High Court, Calcutta, working as a legal adviser to women landholders under the Court of Wards. This court supervised landholders, primarily women, deemed "incapable of managing" their affairs (R. Kapur and Cossman 1999, 229). Sorabji also served as consulting counsel to the government of Bengal. Although ignored today because of her antifeminist, antinationalist, Anglophile perspective, she was well known in her time for her legal work on behalf of women in *purdah* (Burton 1994, 197).

3. This is not a new idea. Bankimchandra Chaddopadhyay (1833–1894) wrote a letter in response

to his own earlier essay in a journal, pretending that the letter was written by a woman who offers to change places with men: "Come indoors and take charge of the house. Let us go out to work. Slaves for seven hundred years (under the Muslims), and still you pride yourselves on your masculinity! Aren't you ashamed?" (quoted in Chatterjee 1993, 136).

4. A. Basu writes that the major source of construction work "in the lean season" are government roads "through the Food for Work and Rural Works Programs" (1992, 265). Kishwar and Vanita report that despite the passge of the Rural Labor Enquiry Report of 1974–1975, the differences in pay between men and women increased. Defining certain work as skilled means that men work at those jobs, that women's jobs are "low value jobs." Never considered is the "amount of work done, nor its tediousness, nor the time consumed, nor its productive value" (1984, 17). According to the United Nations, women around the world who work at home, in "family businesses, and in child care," all "unpaid and undervalued in economic statistics" are worth $16 trillion. They perform "two-thirds of the world's labor," get "one-tenth of the world's income," and "own less than one-hundredth of the world's property" (S. Shah 1998, 215).

5. See also Bhattacharjee (1998, 173) on "the binary" between women and men. Women are kept private—in the home—where through maintaining the home they represent "Indianness" and true "Indian Womanhood," whereas men are free to function in the outside world. This is still applicable today in both India and the West.

6. In 2002, a girls' school in Saudi Arabia burned. Most of the children perished because when their fathers rushed to the scene and attempted to enter the school, they were denied entry by the police on the grounds that the girls were not wearing their veils.

7. Sadly, sixty-five years later, Flavia Agnes, "one of the founder members of the Women's Centre, Bombay" (N. Gandhi and N. Shah 1999, 317), observes that the situation has not changed for women: that the majority of Indian women are entirely unaware "of their legal rights" (Agnes 1997, 535). She writes that from 1850 to 1930, the English-run Privy Council ruled in case after case against women's having property rights. "Gradually, the Hindu widow lost her right to deal with her property and, on the least pretext, the property would revert to the husband's heirs" (Agnes 2000, 122), although as early as 1904 the Indian National Congress had worked on the issues of education, *purdah,* child-marriage, and polygamy. The Hindu Marriage Act of 1955 also permitted Hindu women to divorce. Muslim women had been given this right in 1939. The Hindu succession Act of 1956 finally gave equal rights to inherit to male and female heirs, except in the case of coparcenary groups where male heirs always prevail, and abolished property rights only for life for widows. And, although the Indian Supreme Court had granted women divorced by their husbands the receipt of maintenance payments for themselves and their children, in order to gain votes from fundamentalist Muslims when he was prime minister, Rajiv Gandhi had a law passed that Muslim women would not be included in such laws. Instead, they "would be subject to medieval interpretations of the shariat, Islamic religious law on marriage and divorce" (G. Mehta 1997, 187). In other words, back to square one.

Chapter 2: Outsiders Within II

1. These *zamindars* were for the most part descendants of those Indians who did not revolt against the English. As "loyalists," they were consequently rewarded with land confiscated from the rebels who were hanged.

2. Vandana Shiva in "Colonialism and the Evolution of Masculinist Forestry," 1999, agrees

and expands on Devi's points to emphasize the hardships this "programme" imposed on female tribals especially.

3. Vandana Shiva also deplores the World Bank's domination and its "indifference to the needs of nature and vulnerable social groups" (1999, 60). Sucheta Mazumdar reminds us of the network of rich and powerful nationalist patriarchs who control their immigrant communities and influence Indian affairs at every turn. For one example, when the World Bank abandoned its plans to build the Narmada Dam in Gujarat under pressure from "environmental and humanitarian groups," Gujarati immigrant leaders "raised bonds" in order to finish the project because their Gujarati relatives who were wealthy farmers "stood to benefit" (1996, 467) from the completion of the project. M. Jacqui Alexander and Chandra Talpade Mohanty, adding the IMF and the GATT to their critique of the World Bank, propose a solution, advocating that these organizations be "made more accountable . . . [in their] decision-making processes" by opening them up to "feminist participation and scrutiny" (1997, xli). The All India Democratic Women's Association (AIDWA) also called for inspection of the Indian government's primary motives as well as its allying itself "with global and domestic capital" (Oza 2001, 1080; also see N. Shah et al. 1999, 167). Spivak blasts the World Bank, the major supplier of funds and coordinator "of the great narrative of development" and the "phrase 'sustainable development'" [that] has become used universally by all the entities "that manage globality." Like Mahasweta Devi, she vents her outrage with rhetorical questions to which she herself responds. She wants to know "What 'Development'"? and "to sustain what?" in light of the term "global development" being "appropriated" by "racist paternalism (and alas, increasingly, sororalism)" while economically the concern of the so-called global developers is to find "capital-intensive investment" and politically to silence all "resistance," while using "the subaltern as the rhetoric of their protest." Furthermore, "global development's" demands on the state for economic "restructuring" greatly diminishes "redistributive activities" (1999, 373, 418).

4. According to Kumar (1999) in the early 1970s a new kind of protest was begun by women who beat metal plates (*thalis*) with rolling pins (*lathis*) supporting marchers, but they were not part of the demonstrations themselves because they were housebound. Presumably, then, as the demonstrators passed their houses, the women would show their support from their doors. For more details on the expansion and spread of this protest, see N. Shah et al. (1999, 345).

5. Jayapal interviewed a Muslim master weaver who contrasted his community who passed on skills to their children with the workers of Bihar whom he defined as "exploited." He then complained about the banning of Indian carpets as well as the certifying of carpets as "child labor-free" on the grounds that such acts "were part of an international conspiracy." Jayapal adds that a large number of Indians viewed the West's condemnation of child labor as "colonial and patriarchal" (2000, 96). See also Spivak for a broader discussion of this issue, implicating the World Bank and Western feminists and offering better labor laws as the solution (1999, 416).

6. I would argue that this is the case for all women—that they have no caste themselves, but derive their caste from their menfolk. As Natarajan points out, women are excluded from inherently being "brahman" because their "caste can only be 'derived'" (1999, 159).

7. Devi here describes the unfeeling daughters-in-law exactly as Bhikshuk (Chandra Sen) and others had described such women one hundred years earlier, namely as materialistic, ultramodernized, self-centered women who were primarily concerned only with their own appearance and left all household work and duties to their mother-in-law (Chakrabarty 1997, 381). Mukherjee describes the same kinds of complaints by Indian mothers-in-law in the United States during the same period. They see their sons as selfish, their daughters working to stay thin, no grandchildren to pass time with, the daughters-in-law "barren" (1991,

131). Ironically, the mothers-in-law had resented *their* mothers-in-law for a lifetime and, now that they had lived long enough to get their own back, their daughters-in-law were not around for them to boss and/or abuse.

8. In *Duryodhana Vadham* (The Death of Duryodhana and his brother Dushasana), Draupadi is the name of the wife of the Pandavas who lost her to the Kauravas in a game of dice. Dushasana, one of the Kauravas, tried to undress her in front of them all and Draupadi vowed that she would keep her hair undone until she could wash it in Dushasana's blood. One of the Pandavas, Bima, avenges her by slaying Dushasana and bathes her hair in his blood. For numerous variations on this myth and its ending, see Rajeswari Sunder Rajan (1999b).

9. This title, a powerful irony itself, underscores the unspeakable inhumanity of the police. It comes from the popular song heard blaring out and sung by men on all sides from a movie, *Kalnayak* (1993), where the heroine who is a policewoman pretends to be a prostitute. Sunita Mukhi translates the first line of the song somewhat differently, as "Choli ke peeche kya hai? (Guess what is underneath my blouse?)" (1998, 203, 204, fn. 13). It is her heart, which she gives to her beloved, to her friend.

10. Jayawardena (1986, 78), Burton (1994, 58), and Ramusack (1999, 37) write that the Rani died in combat. M. Basu tells us that "she joined the sepoy mutineers and, dressed in male attire, gallantly defended Jhansi till she was killed while fighting on 17 June 1858" (2001, 2). Jayawardena further adds that because the Rani led her troops (on horseback) clad in a military uniform that consisted of a red jacket, red trousers, and a white turban, her sex was concealed. But this does not take into account the necessity of her being veiled. In a myth, the Hadi Rani severs her own head to prevent her husband from being too attached to her and not focusing on the defense of his kingdom during an incursion. He wears her head on his horse on the battlefield, but her head remains modestly covered because the blood effectively keeps her sari clinging to her face (Harlan 1995b, 224, fn. 25).

11. Western definitions differ from Hindu definitions. Hindus define cleanliness as freedom from ritual pollution, not germ-free. For example, the cow is considered sacred and therefore its dung and urine are pure and sometimes used in medicines. Certain castes that work with feces and blood are considered unclean as is meat such as beef and pork (Minturn 1993, 250–251). Furthermore, "purity and pollution" were traditionally ranked according to the relationship "with organic life" such as agriculture, menstruation, and the birth process as "most polluting," but professional "death-dealing" by "the martial castes is exempt from the pollution of death" (Dietrich 1999, 92–93; see also DasGupta Sherma 2000, 27).

12. Curiously, in contrast to Desai's apparent perspective, around this time a "connection . . . between the anticaste dalit movement and feminism" came to be made (R. Kumar 1999, 346).

13. See also M. Naqvi (1998, x), in which she describes "gang-rape" performed after the stripping.

14. Devi cites an 1898 text on the Santhal tribe to explain why some women may not only believe in witchcraft but voluntarily consider themselves witches. Because the religion is mainly focused on the male and since women can only get to heaven through men, they secretly long for "supernatural powers" (1995, 171). But it is the shamans who are the real criminals, for they are the ones who identify the witches, who are then hanged or ostracized and forced out of the community.

Chapter 3: Outsiders Abroad

1. At my health club recently, when the instructor discovered that I had never celebrated Christmas, she shouted, red-faced, in horror: "How can you do this to your children? How

can you deprive them of Christmas and presents?" I responded that as Jews my children and I have been acculturated into entirely different rituals, customs, and celebrations with which we identify. Otherwise, we would not be Jews. Yet she still could not understand how anyone could fail to celebrate Christmas, thereby exposing a failure common to many Americans, especially at Christmas and Easter: to comprehend that Christianity is not a universal religion universally practiced.

2. These are by no means the first riots. For one earlier example, in Calcutta in 1943, five thousand Hindu and Muslim women undertook a hunger march organized by the Calcutta Mahila Atmaraksha Samiti (Women's Self-Defence League—MARS). According to Renu Chakravarty's description:

> The demonstrators in their tattered rags and with babies in arms, famished and emaciated, marched before the eyes of Calcutta's public, telling them what words failed to do, of their pitiful plight. The march was unique, a model of orderly organisation. Neither police nor Communist-baiters, could do anything. The impact of this demonstration was tremendous. It was one of the first militant actions of women which stirred the city of Calcutta. The demonstrators demanded "Open more shops, arrange proper supplies and bring down the price of rice." When they refused to move the Chief Minister distributed 100 bags of rice immediately to the women. (Quoted in Jayawardena 1986, 107)

3. This strategy of workers surrounding a factory and holding their employer hostage became known as *gherao* and was originally initiated by women workers who organized and led the strike for eight months against the British textile mills (Jayawardena 1986, 105).

4. M. N. Srinivas, an Indian sociologist, sees African Americans as Harijans or Untouchables (quoted in Jayapal 2000, 72), which Jayapal points out are below the four varnas or levels that comprise the Hindu caste system. Brahmins are the priestly caste; Kshatriyas are the warriors; Vaishyas are in trade or merchants; Shudras are laborers (2000, 71).

5. Under the British who controlled the interpretation of law, however, "Nayar women in matrilineal arrangements . . . lost their rights to property" (N. Menon 2000, 79) through "new revenue settlements and laws that gave male heads of households sole property rights" (Grewal 1996, 53).

6. According to Spivak, the patriarchy and those complicit with it blame the population explosion on the poor women of the South by situating the depletion of resources globally "between the legs of the poorest women of the South." This, in turn, causes "so-called aid" to be justified, while deflecting "attention from Northern over-consumption [and] . . . pharmaceutical dumping [on the women of the South] of dangerous coercive long-term contraceptives." The North views this practice superficially as "population control," which she distinguishes "rigorously" from "family planning," as the North euphemistically defines it. She contemptuously dismisses Western feminists as "transnationally illiterate benevolent feminists of the North" because they support this practice "wholeheartedly" without examining it, while viewing any criticism as coming from conservatives (1999, 385).

Chapter 4: Outsiders Silenced

1. In the frontispiece to *Cast Me Out If You Will*, her dates given are 1909–1985. In her introduction to the book, Gita Krishnankutty states (on p. xxvi) that Antherjanam died in 1987.

2. In "Lessons from Experience," also in *Cast Me Out if You Will*, Antherjanam records that she was angrily denounced for writing and publishing this story.

3. Because male leaders legislated and regulated women's sexuality, encouraged certain women

to extend their sphere to the public arena, and put into place "modes of surveillance" (Mohanty 1991a, 20) that controlled women's movements outward into various jobs and into politics, some Indian/Third World feminists see a connection between the British male colonial government and the nationalist male leadership.

4. A. Basu states that, nowadays, "the all-India pattern" is in marked contrast in that "elite women of middle-class, upper-caste backgrounds have extensive opportunities to enter the national political arena and are readily accepted when they do so" (1992, 248, fn. 14).

5. After the massacre by General Dyer at Amritsar, Tagore courageously "returned his knighthood to the British" (G. Mehta 1989, 167).

6. DasGupta and Das Dasgupta, writing about post-1965 immigrant Indian women who were teenagers after independence, describe this as a time of nationalism, still with an atmosphere of high morality, restrictions about sexuality, and the separation of public and private spaces that forced women to "hide their sexual selves." Young women were not supposed to possess any awareness of sexuality, and "in most cases, young girls' early sexual experiences were surreptitious touches from male relatives and molestations received in public situations. The shame of these filthy accostings lay absolutely with the victims themselves" (1998, 118).

7. In keeping with her training. A decent woman was supposed to keep her "eyes down" (Markandaya 1954, 14), even when talking to her husband. Only prostitutes looked directly into men's eyes.

8. Eliade seems to have followed Manu's prescription for violating a guru's bed, which he had not done, but he had perhaps done so by violating his guru's hospitality and trust in regard to his daughter. Some of the punishments for doing so are carrying a club like a bedpost, wearing rags, growing a beard, concentrating his mind, and fulfilling the "'painful' vow of the Lord of Creatures for a year in a deserted forest" (Doniger 1995, 164). Jhabvala also describes "sadhus" or "penitents," which gives an approximation of what Eliade looked like during this period. "Some of the sadhus were stark naked, some wore animal skins, all had long, matted hair and beards and were immobile, so that it was easy to believe they had been sitting there for centuries, as rooted and moss-grown as the trees and as impervious as they to snakes and any wild animals there might be prowling around" (1986, 69). A character in Quarratulain Hyder's *River of Fire* makes a comment that resonates with Eliade's state of mind at this time: "Women without men become nuns, sir, men without women turn into sadhus" (1999, 98).

9. In contrast, *shakti* is so much a part of "the mainstream" that the notion of a woman being God or discourse about "women being powerful" is neither "radical or shocking" for Hindus (Erndl 2000, 97).

10. Mukherjee's wonderful character Jasmine is created as a manifestation of both of these aspects at different times. When she takes a razor to her tongue before slaying her rapist, she most clearly represents Kali, whose tongue hanging from her mouth is emphasized in depictions of this goddess. With her tongue, Kali licks up drops of a demon's blood that form human beings. "The black goddess of Time and Destruction," Kali, wears skulls around her neck. She became the consort of Siva, "who destroys the world when its inhabitants can no longer observe their caste duty or *dharma*" and represents the chaotic qualities of life and omnipresent death (Ramusack 1999, 32). Rajan relates Draupadi to Kali, "the avenging goddess worshipped as the fearful feminine principle" (1999, 351). Rajan then goes on to chide the use of avenging feminist heroines based on Hindu mythology such as Mukherjee's Jasmine and Debi. Alexander describes herself as reacting in her poem "Package of Dreams" to the brutality against women in Sarajevo, in Germany, in Omdurman and Ayodhya as: "I

flowed into Kali ivory tongued, skulls nippling my breasts" (1996b, 9). Rajan sees feminists like these who take matters into their own hands as individual examples of revenge against individual oppressors. It diminishes "female power" to portray such heroines as acting within the parameters "set by the oppressor" and by doing so "endorses violence as the (intolerable) solution to social evils." True "feminist praxis" requires "a structural understanding of violence; the possibilities of collective protest; solutions within the framework of law, reform and civil society; and a radical interrogation of the *social* responsibility for individual/collective violence against women" (1999, 352–353, italics the author's).

11. Susie K. Tharu and K. Lalita claim that Das's husband was her uncle, K. Madhava Das (1995, 394).

12. Note that these are all Western authors.

13. He himself is not clear as to this action. It seems to follow the stage he is in, according to the ideal of a Hindu man based on the four life cycles or stages. Gopal, now middle aged, has passed through youth, when he was supposed to study and obey his teachers, and young manhood, when he had to marry and support his family, and is now in the third stage, when he would be expected to retire from worldliness and spend his time in study and spiritual meditation, as he is now doing. In the next stage, he would "renounce the world" (Harlan 1995a, 13) and become a holy man. Harlan adds that even though very few men follow this pattern in their own lives; nevertheless, this renunciatory ideal occasionally causes men to feel ambivalent toward marriage in terms of its being "a lifelong commitment" for themselves. In his meditations and his conduct after leaving his wife and family, Gopal seems to illustrate the passage that P. Chatterjee cites of Ramakrishna in the course of teaching one of his devotees: "When one has true love for God . . . there are no ties of attachment with one's wife or child or kin. There is only compassion. The world becomes a foreign land, a land where one comes to work" (1993, 65). Whereas men honor the "norms" for their four stages "more often in principle than in practice" women, who have only two stages—"daughter and wife"—do "approximate the cultural ideals" in their lives. I would add that women, if not forced to honor these norms, would probably honor them much as men honor theirs. Feminists unite in deploring this "exclusive focus on mothering" (John 2000, 121, fn. 14) and would add more stages to women's lives.

14. This situation is familiar to Divakaruni as one of the founders of *Maitri,* the organization that assists South Asian women, as it is to anyone (like myself) who has worked in a women's shelter.

15. Manjula Padmanaban's short story "Teaser" in *Hot Death, Cold Soup* (1997) is about a seasoned "Eve Baiter" on a public bus who gets his come-uppance.

Chapter 5: Solutions

1. The source of the in-laws' conduct is the dowry which "has come to signify the degradation of the bride, the price her parents must pay to rid themselves of an economic liability. Because she is considered a burden, the bride's in-laws expect gifts from her natal family after marriage, and from her brothers after her father's death" (A. Basu 1992, 112).

2. Antagonism between a wife and her husband's sister frequently occurs because of the wife's resenting the sabbatical the husband's sister gets when she returns to visit "her natal home" (Raheja 1995, 57, fn. 54). "Daughters are considered guests in their parental homes. . . . [M]arried daughters did nothing except take care of their own children when visiting their parental homes. Their presence brought extra mouths to feed for the hardworking *bahus*

who must cook for them and their children" (Minturn 1993, 59). There are also other perqs that the *bahu*'s sister-in-law enjoys when visiting her natal family, and she always outranks the *bahu* in that setting (Minturn 1993, 307–308). Appachana's Americanized *bahu* is incompatible with her husband's family because she is ignorant about these customs that are second nature to them but meaningless to her.

3. Traditionally, a mother-in-law could limit a couple's intercourse in a variety of ways so as to prevent her son from preferring his wife to his natal family, such as keeping the bride up late working when she is required to rise before everyone else, as well as depriving the couple of privacy. Additionally, a husband could see his wife's demands to spend more time with him and to have more privacy as threatening to his relationship with his natal family.

4. In contrast, *Smell* (2001) by Radhika Jha (1960–) offers a far more traditional Cinderella ending. The heroine is forced throughout the text to journey or quest for work and a roof over her head. In the process she is involved in unsuccessful affairs with several men. At the end, instead of starting out on her journey forward into an independent life, Leela is going backward in the sense that she is "going home" [the last words of the novel] to Olivier's home to marry him and to live there with him. A high-born, cultivated, brilliant, low-keyed Englishman, he had befriended Leela in the course of her wanderings and affairs. Very late in the book she discovers that he has loved her all along.

Conclusion

1. Similarly, in the United States, a woman, particularly one living alone or with children and in poverty, or on welfare, is stigmatized by the paternalistic state that acts toward her like a stern father/husband.

Bibliography

Accad, Evelyne. 1991. "Sexuality and Sexual Politics: Conflicts and Contraditions for Contempo-rary Women in the Middle East." In *Third World Women and the Politics of Feminism,* ed. Chandra Talpade Mohanty, Ann Russo, and Lourdes Torres, 237–250. Bloomington, IN: In-diana University Press.

Agnes, Flavia. 1997. "Protecting Women against Violence: Review of a Decade of Legislation, 1980–." In *State and Politics in India,* ed. Partha Chatterjee, 521–565. Delhi: Oxford Univer-sity Press.

———. 2000. "Women, Marriage, and the Subordination of Rights." In *Subaltern Studies XI: Community, Gender and Violence,* ed. Partha Chatterjee and Pradeep Jeganathan, 106–137. New York: Columbia University Press.

Alam, S. M. Shamsul. 1998. "Women in the Era of Modernity and Islamic Fundamentalism: The Case of Taslima Nasrin of Bangladesh." *Signs: Journal of Women in Culture and Society* 23.2: 429–461.

Alcoff, Linda Martín. 2000. "Philosophy Matters: A Review of Recent Work in Feminist Philo-sophy." *Signs: Journal of Women in Culture and Society* 25.3: 841–882.

Alexander, Meena. 1991. *Nampally Road.* San Francisco: Mercury House.

———. 1993. *Fault Lines: A Memoir.* New York: The Feminist Press.

———. 1996a. *The Shock of Arrival: Reflections on Postcolonial Experience.* Boston, MA: South End Press.

———. 1996b. "Package of Dreams." In *Contours of the Heart: South Asians Map North America,* ed. Sunaina Maira and Rajini Srikanth, 9–10. New York: The Asian American Writers' Workshop.

———. 1997. Foreword. *Cast Me Out If You Will: Stories and Memoir.* Trans., ed., intro. Gita Krishnankutty. Foreword Meena Alexander. New York: The Feminist Press.

Antherjanam, Lalithambika. 1997. *Cast Me Out If You Will: Stories and Memoir.* Trans., ed., intro.Gita Krishnankutty. Foreword Meena Alexander. New York: The Feminist Press.

Appachana, Anjana. 1998. *Listening Now.* New York: Random House.

———. (1991) 2000. *Incantations and Other Stories.* New Brunswick, NJ: Rutgers University Press.

Badami, Anita Rau. 2001. *The Hero's Walk*. Chapel Hill, NC: Algonquin Books of Chapel Hill.

Balakrishnan, Radhika. 2001. "Capitalism and Sexuality: Free to Choose?" In *Good Sex: Feminist Perspectives from the World's Religions*, ed. Patricia Beattie Jung, Mary E. Hunt, and Radhika Balakrishnan, 44–57. New Brunswick, NJ: Rutgers University Press.

Banerjee, Sumanta. (1989) 1999. "Marginalization of Women's Popular Culture in Nineteenth Century Bengal." In *Recasting Women: Essays in Indian Colonial History*, ed. Kumkum Sangari and Sudesh Vaid, 127–179. New Brunswick, NJ: Rutgers University Press.

Baruah, Sanjit. 1997. "Politics of Subnationalism: Society versus State in Assam." In *State and Politics in India*, ed. Partha Chatterjee, 496–520. Delhi: Oxford University Press.

Basu, Amrita, and Bharati Ray. 1990. *Women's Struggle: A History of the All India Women's Conference 1927–1990*. New Delhi: Manohar Publications.

Basu, Amrita. 1992. *Two Faces of Protest: Contrasting Modes of Women's Activism in India*. Berkeley and Los Angeles: University of California Press.

———, ed. 1996. *Challenge of Local Feminisms*. Boulder, CO: Westview Press.

Basu, Monmayee. 2001. *Hindu Women and Marriage Law: From Sacrament to Contract*. New Delhi: Oxford University Press.

Basu, Srimati. 1999. "Cutting to Size: Property and Gendered Identity in the Indian Higher Courts." In *Signposts: Gender Issues in Post-Independence India*, ed. Rajeswari Sunder Rajan, 245–292. New Brunswick, NJ: Rutgers University Press.

Bedi, Susham. (1989) 1993. *The Fire Sacrifice (Havan)*. Trans. From the Hindi by David Rubin. Oxford and New York: Heinemann Educational.

Bhabha, Homi. 1997. "Of Mimicry and Man: The Ambivalence of Colonial Discourse." In *Tensions of Empire: Colonial Cultures in a Bourgeois World*, ed. Frederick Cooper and Anna Laura Stoler, 152–160. Berkeley: University of California Press.

Bhattacharjee, Anannya. 1997. "The Public/Private Mirage: Mapping Homes and Undomesticating Violence Work in the South Asian Immigrant Community." In *Feminist Genealogies, Colonial Legacies, Democratic Futures*, ed. M. Jacqui Alexander and Chandra Talpade Mohanty, 308–329. New York and London: Routledge.

———. 1998. "The Habit of Ex-Nomination: Nation, Woman, and the Indian Immigrant Bourgeoisie." In *A Patchwork Shawl: Chronicles of South Asian Women in America*, ed. Shamita Das Dasgupta, 111–128. New Brunswick: Rutgers University Press.

Blaise, Clark, and Bharati Mukherjee. (1977) 1995. *Days and Nights in Calcutta*. Saint Paul, MN: Hungry Mind Press.

Budhos, Marina Tamar. 1995. *House of Waiting*. New York: Global City Press

Burton, Antoinette. 1994. *Burdens of History: British Feminists, Indian Women, and Imperial Culture, 1865–1915*. Chapel Hill: The University of North Carolina Press.

———. 1998. *At the Heart of the Empire: Indians and the Colonial Encounter in Late-Victorian Britain*. Berkeley and Los Angeles: University of California Press.

Chakrabarty, Dipesh. 1997. "The Difference-Deferral of a Colonial Modernity." In *Tensions of Empire: Colonial Cultures in a Bourgeois World*, ed. Frederick Cooper and Anna Laura Stoler, 373–405. Berkeley: University of California Press.

Chakravarti, Uma. (1989) 1999. "Whatever Happened to the Vedic *Dasi*? Orientalism, Nationalism and a Script for the Past." In *Recasting Women: Essays in Indian Colonial History*, ed. Kumkum Sangari and Sudesh Vaid, 27–87. New Brunswick, NJ: Rutgers University Press.

Chatterjee, Milanjana, and Nancy E. Riley. 2001. "Planning in Indian Modernity: The Gendered Politics of Fertility Control." *Signs: Journal of Women in Culture and Society* 26.3: 841–845.

Chatterjee, Partha. 1993. *The Nation and Its Fragments: Colonial and Postcolonial Histories.* Princeton, NJ: Princeton University Press.

——. 1997. "Development Planning and the Indian State." In *State and Politics in India,* ed. Partha Chatterjee, 271–297. Delhi: Oxford University Press.

——, ed. 1997. *State and Politics in India.* Delhi: Oxford University Press.

——, and Pradeep Jeganathan, eds. 2000. *Subaltern Studies XI: Community, Gender and Violence.* New York: Columbia University Press.

Chaudhry, Lubna. 1998. "We Are Graceful Swans Who Can Also Be Crows": Hybrid Identities of Pakistani Muslim Women." In *A Patchwork Shawl: Chronicles of South Asian Women in America,* ed. Shamita Das Dasgupta, 46–61. New Brunswick, NJ: Rutgers University Press.

Collins, Alfred. 2000. "Dancing with Prakriti: The Samkhyan Goddess as *Pativrata* and *Guru.*" In *Is The Goddess a Feminist?: The Politics of South Asian Goddesses,* ed. Alf Hiltebeitel and Kathleen M. Erndl, 69–90. New York: New York University Press.

Cooper, Frederick, and Anna Laura Stoler, eds. 1997. *Tensions of Empire: Colonial Cultures in a Bourgeois World.* Berkeley: University of California Press.

Costa, Claudia de Lima. 2000. "Being Here and Writing There: Gender and the Politics of Translation in a Brazilian Landscape." *Signs: Journal of Women in Culture and Society* 25.3: 727–760.

Courtright, Paul B. 1995. "*Sati,* Sacrifice, and Marriage: The Modernity of Tradition." In *From the Margins of Hindu Marriage: Essays on Gender, Religion, and Culture,* ed. Lindsey Harlan and Paul B. Courtright, 184–203. New York and Oxford: Oxford University Press.

Das, Kamala. (1988) 1996. *My Story.* New Delhi: Sterling Publishers.

Das, Veena. 1999. "Communities as Political Actors: The Question of Cultural Rights." In *Gender and Politics in India,* ed. Nivedita Menon, 441–471. New Delhi: Oxford University Press.

DasGupta, Kasturi. 1995. "The Global Resurgence of Ethnicity: An Inquiry into the Sociology of Ideological Discontent." *Explorations in Ethnic Studies* 18.1: 7–18.

Dasgupta, Shamita Das, and Sayantini DasGupta. 1996a. "Women in Exile: Gender Relations in the Asian Indian Community in the U.S." In *Contours of the Heart: South Asians Map North America,* ed. Sunaina Maira and Rajini Srikanth, 381–400. New York: The Asian American Writers' Workshop.

——. 1996b. "Public Face, Private Space: Asian Indian Women and Sexuality." In *Bad Girls/Good Girls": Women, Sex, and Power in the Nineties,* ed. Nan Bauer Maglin and Donna Perry, 226–243. New Brunswick, NJ: Rutgers University Press.

DasGupta, Sayantini, and Shamita Das Dasgupta. 1998. "Sex, Lies, and Women's Lives: An Intergenerational Dialogue." In *A Patchwork Shawl: Chronicles of South Asian Women in America,* ed. Shamita Das Dasgupta, 111–128. New Brunswick, NJ: Rutgers University Press.

Dasgupta, Shamita Das, ed. 1998. *A Patchwork Shawl: Chronicles of South Asian Women in America.* New Brunswick: Rutgers University Press.

Desai, Anita. 1980. *Clear Light of Day.* New York: Viking Penguin.

——. (1977) 1982a. *Fire on the Mountain.* New York: Penguin.

——. 1982b. *The Village by the Sea: A Family Story.* New York: Viking Penguin.

——. (1978) 1983. *Games at Twilight.* New York: Penguin.

——. 1984. *In Custody.* New York: Harper & Row.

——. (1988) 1990. *Baumgartner's Bombay.* New York: Penguin.

——. 1995. *Journey to Ithaca.* New York: Alfred A. Knopf.

——. 1999. *Fasting, Feasting.* New York: Houghton Mifflin.

Desai, Gaurav. 1993. "The Invention of Invention." *Cultural Critique* 24: 119–142.

Deshpande, Satish. 2000. "Hegemonic Spatial Strategies: The Nation-Space and Hindu Communalism in Twentieth-century India." In *Subaltern Studies XI: Community, Gender and Violence,* ed. Partha Chatterjee and Pradeep Jeganathan, 167–211. New York: Columbia University Press.

Deshpande, Shashi. (1980) 1990. *The Dark Holds No Terrors.* New Delhi: Penguin Books (India) Limited.

———. 1999. *A Matter of Time.* Afterword Ritu Menon. New York: The Feminist Press.

———. 2000. *Small Remedies.* New York: The Feminist Press.

———. (1993) 2001. *The Binding Vine.* New York: The Feminist Press.

Devi, Mahasweta. 1995. *Imaginary Maps,* intro. and trans. Gayatri Chakravorty Spivak. New York: Routledge.

———. 1997. *Breast Stories,* intro. and trans. Gayatri Chakravorty Spivak. Calcutta: Seagull.

———. (1997) 2000. *Dust on the Road: The Activist Writings of Mahasveta Devi,* ed. and trans. Devi Ghabak. Calcutta, India: Seagull Books.

Devi, Maitreyi. (1974) 1995. *It Does Not Die: A Romance.* Chicago: University of Chicago Press.

Dietrich, Gabriele. 1999. "Women, Ecology and Culture." In *Gender and Politics in India,* ed. Nivedita Menon, 72–95. New Delhi: Oxford University Press.

Divakaruni, Chitra Banerjee. 1995. *Arranged Marriage.* New York: Anchor Books Doubleday.

———. 1996. "We the Indian Women in America." In *Contours of the Heart: South Asians Map North America,* ed. Sunaina Maira and Rajini Srikanth, 268–270. New York: The Asian American Writers' Workshop.

———. 1997. *The Mistress of Spices.* New York: Anchor Books Doubleday.

———. 2001. *The Unknown Errors of Our Lives.* New York: Anchor Books Doubleday.

Dobia, Brenda. 2000. "Seeking Ma, Seeking Me." In *Is The Goddess a Feminist?: The Politics of South Asian Goddesses,* ed. Alf Hiltebeitel and Kathleen M. Erndl, 203–238. New York: New York University Press.

Doniger, Wendy. 1995. "Begetting on Margin: Adultery and Surrogate Pseudomarriage in Hinduism." In *From the Margins of Hindu Marriage: Essays on Gender, Religion, and Culture,* ed. Lindsey Harlan and Paul B. Courtright, 160–183. New York, Oxford: Oxford University Press.

Erndl, Kathleen M. 1993. *Victory to the Mother: The Hindu Goddess of Northwest India in Myth, Ritual, and Symbol.* New York: Oxford University Press.

———. 2000. "Is *Shakti* Empowering for Women? Reflections in Feminism and the Hindu Goddess." In *Is The Goddess a Feminist?: The Politics of South Asian Goddesses,* ed. Alf Hiltebeitel and Kathleen M. Erndl, 91–103. New York: New York University Press.

Farooqi, Vimla. 1984. "A Woman Destroyed: An Interview with Rameezabee." In *In Search of Answers: Indian Women's Voices from Manushi,* ed. Madhu Kishwar and Ruth Vanita, 186–188. London: Zed Books.

Feldman, Shelley. 2001. "Exploring Theories of Patriarchy: A Perspective from Contemporary Bangladesh." *Signs: Journal of Women in Culture and Society* 26.4: 1097–1127.

Fernandes, Leela. 1999. "Reading 'India's Bandit Queen': A Trans/national Feminist Perspective on the Discrepancies of Representation." *Signs: Journal of Women in Culture and Society* 25.1: 123–152.

Gandhi, Nandita, and Nandita Shah. 1992. *The Issues at Stake: Theory and Practice in the Contemporary Women's Movement in India.* Delhi: Kali for Women.

———. 1999. "Organizations and Autonomy." In *Gender and Politics in India,* ed. Nivedita Menon, 299–341. New Delhi: Oxford University Press.

Ganesan, Indira. 1990. *The Journey.* New York: Alfred A. Knopf.

———. 1998. *The Inheritance.* New York: Alfred A. Knopf.

Ghabak, Devi, ed. and trans. (1997) 2000. *Dust on the Road: The Activist Writings of Mahasveta Devi*. Calcutta, India: Seagull Books.

Gold, Ann Grodzins. 1995. "The 'Jungli Rani' and Other Troubled Wives in Rajasthani Oral Traditions." In *From the Margins of Hindu Marriage: Essays on Gender, Religion, and Culture,* ed. Lindsey Harlan and Paul B. Courtright, 119–136. New York, Oxford: Oxford University Press.

Goldman, Sally J. Sutherland. 2001. "The Voice of Sita in Valmiki's *Sundarakanda*." In *Questioning Ramayanas: A South Asian Tradition,* ed. Paula Richman, 223–238. Berkeley and Los Angeles: University of California Press.

Gopal, Priyamvada. 1999. "Of Victims and Vigilantes: The 'Bandit Queen' Controversy." In *Signposts: Gender Issues in Post-Independence India,* ed. Rajeswari Sunder Rajan, 293–331. New Brunswick, NJ: Rutgers University Press.

Grewal, Inderpal. 1994. "Autobiographic Subjects and Diasporic Locations: *Meatless Days* and *Borderlands*." In *Scattered Hegemonies: Postmodernity and Transnational Feminist Practices,* ed. Inderpal Grewal and Caren Kaplan, 231–254. Minneapolis: University of Minnesota Press.

———. 1996. *Home and Harem: Nation, Gender, Empire, and the Cultures of Travel*. Durham, NC, and London: Duke University Press.

———, and Caren Kaplan. 1994a. "Introduction: Transnational Feminist Practices and Questions of Postmodernity." In *Scattered Hegemonies: Postmodernity and Transnational Feminist Practices,* ed. Inderpal Grewal and Caren Kaplan, 1–33. Minneapolis: University of Minnesota Press.

———, and Caren Kaplan, eds. 1994b. *Scattered Hegemonies: Postmodernity and Transnational Feminist Practices*. Minneapolis: University of Minnesota Press.

Gupta, Sunetra. 1992. *Memories of Rain*. New York: Grove Weidenfeld.

———. (1993) 1999. *The Glassblower's Breath*. London: Phoenix.

Hancock, Mary E. 1995. "The Dilemmas of Domesticity: Possession and Devotional Experience Among Urgan Smarta Women." In *From the Margins of Hindu Marriage: Essays on Gender, Religion, and Culture,* ed. Lindsey Harlan and Paul B. Courtright, 60–91. New York, Oxford: Oxford University Press.

Harlan, Lindsey. 1995a. "Introduction: On Hindu Marriage and Its Margins." In *From the Margins of Hindu Marriage: Essays on Gender, Religion, and Culture,* ed. Lindsey Harlan and Paul B. Courtright, 3–20. New York, Oxford: Oxford University Press.

———. 1995b. "Abandoning Shame: Mira and the Margins of Marriage." In *From the Margins of Hindu Marriage: Essays on Gender, Religion, and Culture,* ed. Lindsey Harlan and Paul B. Courtright, 204–227. New York, Oxford: Oxford University Press.

———, and Paul B. Courtright, eds. 1995. *From the Margins of Hindu Marriage: Essays on Gender, Religion, and Culture*. New York, Oxford: Oxford University Press.

———. 2000. "Battles, Brides and Sacrifice: Rajput *Kuldevis* in Rajasthan." In *Is The Goddess a Feminist?: The Politics of South Asian Goddesses,* ed. Alf Hiltebeitel and Kathleen M. Erndl, 69–90. New York: New York University Press.

Harriss-White, Barbara. 1999. "Gender-cleansing: The Paradox of Development and Deteriorating Female Life Chances in Tamil Nadu." In *Signposts: Gender Issues in Post-Independence India,* ed. Rajeswari Sunder Rajan, 125–154. New Brunswick, NJ: Rutgers University Press.

Hasnat, Naheed. 1998. "Being 'Amreekan': Fried Chicken versus Chicken Tikka." In *A Patchwork Shawl: Chronicles of South Asian Women in America,* ed. Shamita Das Dasgupta, 33–45. New Brunswick, NJ: Rutgers University Press.

Hiltebeitel, Alf. 1991. *The Cult of Draupadi: On Hindu Ritual and the Goddess*. Chicago: University of Chicago Press.

———. 2000a. "Introduction: Writing Goddesses, Goddesses Writing, and Other Scholarly Concerns." In *Is The Goddess a Feminist?: The Politics of South Asian Goddesses,* ed. Alf Hiltebeitel and Kathleen M. Erndl, 11–23. New York: New York University Press.

———. 2000b. "Draupadi's Question." In *Is The Goddess a Feminist?: The Politics of South Asian Goddesses,* ed. Alf Hiltebeitel and Kathleen M. Erndl, 113–122. New York: New York University Press.

———, and Kathleen M. Erndl. 2000c. "Is the Goddess a Feminist?" In *Is The Goddess a Feminist?: The Politics of South Asian Goddesses,* ed. Alf Hiltebeitel and Kathleen M. Erndl, 24–51. New York: New York University Press.

———, and Kathleen M. Erndl, eds. 2000d. *Is The Goddess a Feminist?: The Politics of South Asian Goddesses.* New York: New York University Press.

Hossain, Rokeya Sakhawat. (1908) (1929) 1988. *Sultana's Dream and Selections from The Secluded Ones.* ed. and trans. Roushan Jahan. New York: The Feminist Press.

Humes, Cynthia Ann. 2000. "Is the Devi Mahatmya a Feminist Scripture?" In *Is The Goddess a Feminist?: The Politics of South Asian Goddesses,* ed. Alf Hiltebeitel and Kathleen M. Erndl, 123–151. New York: New York University Press.

Hyder, Qurratulain. (1959) 1999. *River of Fire.* New York: New Directions.

Islam, Naheed. 1996. "Signs of Belonging." In *Contours of the Heart: South Asians Map North America,* ed. Sunaina Maira and Rajini Srikanth, 85–93. New York: The Asian American Writers' Workshop.

———. 1998. "Naming Desire, Shaping Identity: Tracing the Experiences of Indian Lesbians in the United States." In *A Patchwork Shawl: Chronicles of South Asian Women in America,* ed. Shamita Das Dasgupta, 46–61. New Brunswick, NJ: Rutgers University Press

Ismail, Qadri. 2000. "Constituting Nation, Contesting Nationalism: The Southern Tamil (Woman) and Separatist Tamil Nationalism in Sri Lanka." In *Subaltern Studies XI: Community, Gender and Violence,* ed. Partha Chatterjee and Pradeep Jeganathan, 212–282. New York: Columbia University Press.

Jahan, Roushan, ed. and trans. 1988. *Sultana's Dream and Selections from The Secluded Ones.* New York: The Feminist Press.

Jayapal, Pramila. 2000. *Pilgrimage: One Woman's Return to a Changing India.* Seattle, WA: Seal Press.

Jayawardena, Kumari. 1986. *Feminism and Nationalism in the Third World.* London: Zed Books

———. 1995. *The White Woman's Other Burden: Western Women and South Asia During British Rule.* New York: Routledge.

Jha, Radhika. 2001. *Smell.* New York: Soho Press.

Jhabvala, Ruth Prawer. 1986. *Out of India: Selected Stories.* New York: William Morrow.

John, Mary E. and Janaki Nair, eds. 1998. *A Question of Silence?: The Sexual Economics of Modern India.* New Delhi: Kali for Women.

———. 1999. "Gender, Development and the Women's Movement: Problems for a History of the Present." In *Signposts: Gender Issues in Post-Independence India,* ed. Rajeswari Sunder Rajan, 100–124. New Brunswick, NJ: Rutgers University Press.

Jung, Patricia Beattie, Mary E. Hunt, and Radhika Balakrishnan, eds. 2001. *Good Sex: Feminist Perspectives from the World's Religions.* New Brunswick, NJ: Rutgers University Press.

Kamani Ginu. 1995. *Junglee Girl.* San Francisco: Aunt Lute Books.

———. 1996. "Just After 'Just Between Indians.'" In *Contours of the Heart: South Asians Map North America,* ed. Sunaina Maira and Rajini Srikanth, 353—380. New York: The Asian American Writers' Workshop.

Kamdar, Mira. 1998. *Cultural Portraits of India.* Photographs by Lindsay Hebberd, Essays by Mira Kamdar. New Delhi: Cultural Portraits Poductions.

Kannabiran, Vasantha, and Kalpana Kannabiran. 1997. "Looking at Ourselves: The Women's Movement in Hyderabad." In *Feminist Genealogies, Colonial Legacies, Democratic Futures,* ed. M. Jacqui Alexander and Chandra Talpade Mohanty, 259-279. New York and London: Routledge.

———, and K. Lalitha. (1989) 1999. "That Magic Time: Women in the Telangana People's Struggle." In *Recasting Women: Essays in Colonial History,* ed. Kumkum Sangari and Sudesh Vaid, 180-203. New Brunswick, NJ: Rutgers University Press.

Kaplan, Caren. 1994. "The Politics of Location as Transnational Feminist Critical Practice." In *Scattered Hegemonies: Postmodernity and Transnational Feminist Practices,* ed. Grewal Inderpal and Caren Kaplan, 137-152. Minneapolis: University of Minnesota Press. Press.

———. 1996. *Questions of Travel: Postmodern Discourses of Displacement.* Durham, NC: Duke University.

Kapur, Manju. 1998. *Difficult Daughters.* New Delhi: Penguin Books India.

Kapur, Ratna, and Brenda Cossman. 1999. "On Women, Equality and the Constitution: Through the Looking Glass of Feminism." In *Gender and Politics in India,* ed. Nivedita Menon, 197-261. New Delhi: Oxford University Press.

Khan, Shahmaz. 1998. "Muslim Women: Negotiations in the Third Space." *Signs: Journal of Women in Culture and Society* 23.2: 463-494.

Khan, Surina. 1998. "Sexual Exiles." In *A Patchwork Shawl: Chronicles of South Asian Women in America,* ed. Shamita Das Dasgupta, 62-71. New Brunswick, NJ: Rutgers University Press.

Khanna, Vandana. 1999. "Spell." *Callaloo* 22.1: 25.

Kishwar, Madhu, and Ruth Vanita, eds. 1984. *In Search of Answers: Indian Women's Voices from Manushi.* London: Zed Books.

Kishwar, Madhu. 1999. *Off the Beaten Track: Rethinking Gender Justice for Indian Women.* New Delhi: Oxford University Press.

———. 2001. "Yes to Sita, No to Ram: The Continuing Hold of Sita on Popular Imagination in India." In *Questioning Ramayanas: A South Asian Tradition,* ed. Paula Richman, 285-308. Berkeley and Los Angeles: University of California Press.

Krishnan, Satya P., Malahat Baig-Amin, Louisa Gilbert, Nabila El-Bassel, and Anne Waters. 1998. "Lifting the Veil of Secrecy: Domestic Violence Against South Asian Women in the United States." In *A Patchwork Shawl: Chronicles of South Asian Women in America,* ed. Shamita Das Dasgupta, 145-162. New Brunswick, NJ: Rutgers University Press.

Kumar, Radha. 1994. *The History of Doing: An Illustrated Account of Movements for Women's Rights and Feminism in India, 1800-1990.* London: Verso.

———. 1999. "From Chipko to *Sati:* The Contemporary Indian Women's Movement." In *Gender and Politics in India,* ed. Nivedita Menon, 342-369. New Delhi: Oxford University Press.

Lahiri, Jhumpa. 1999. *Interpreter of Maladies.* Boston and New York: Houghton Mifflin.

Leach, Laurie. 1997. "Conflict over Privacy in Indo-American Short Fiction." In *Ethnicity and the American Short Story,* ed. Julie Brown, 197-212. New York: Garland Press.

Lee, Rachel C. 2001. "Book Review." *Signs: Journal of Women in Culture and Society* 26.3: 561-565.

Lokugé, Chandani, ed. 1998. *Saguna: The First Autobiographical Novel in English by an Indian Woman.* Delhi: Oxford University Press.

MacKinnon, Catherine A. 1987. *Feminism Unmodified: Discourses on Life and Law.* Cambridge: Harvard University Press.

MacLeod, Arlene. 1991. *Accommodating Protest.* New York: Columbia University Press.

———. 1992. "Hegemonic Relations and Gender Resistance: The New Veiling as Accommodating Protest in Cairo." *Signs: Journal of Women in Culture and Society* 17.3: 533-557.

Maira, Sunaina, and Rajini Srikanth, eds. 1996. *Contours of the Heart: South Asians Map North America*. New York: The Asian American Writers' Workshop.

Mani, Bakirathi. 1996. "Moments of Identity in Film." In *Contours of the Heart: South Asians Map North America,* ed. Sunaina Maira and Rajini Srikanth, 174–187. New York: The Asian American Writers' Workshop.

Mani, Lata. (1989) 1998. "Contentious Traditions: The Debate on *Sati* in Colonial India." In *Recasting Women: Essays in Colonial History,* ed. Kumkum Sangari and Sudesh Vaid, 88–126. New Brunswick, NJ: Rutgers University Press.

———. 1999. *Contentious Traditions: The Debate on Sati in Colonial India.* Berkeley and Los Angeles: University of California Press.

Markandaya, Kamala. 1954. *Nectar in a Sieve.* New York: Signet.

Mazumdar, Rinita. 1998. "Marital Rape: Some Ethical and Cultural Considerations." In *A Patchwork Shawl: Chronicles of South Asian Women in America,* ed. Shamita Das Dasgupta, 129–144. New Brunswick, NJ: Rutgers University Press.

Mazumdar, Sucheta. 1996. "Afterword: Identity Politics and the Politics of Identity." In *Contours of the Heart: South Asians Map North America,* ed. Sunaina Maira and Rajini Srikanth, 461–469. New York: The Asian American Writers' Workshop.

Meer, Ameena. 1996. "I Want to Give you Devotion." In *Contours of the Heart: South Asians Map North America,* ed. Sunaina Maira and Rajini Srikanth, 92–106. New York: The Asian American Writers' Workshop.

Mehta, Diane. 1996. "A Better Life." In *Contours of the Heart: South Asians Map North America,* ed. Sunaina Maira and Rajini Srikanth, 276–277. New York: The Asian American Writers' Workshop.

Mehta, Gita. 1989. *Raj.* New York: Ballantine Books.

———. (1979) 1991. *Karma Cola: Marketing the Mystic East.* New York: Fawcett Columbine.

———. 1997. *Snakes and Ladders: Glimpses of Modern India.* New York: Bantam Doubleday Dell Publishing Group.

Menon, Nivedita. 1999a. "Rights, Bodies and the Law: Rethinking Feminist Politics of Justice." In *Gender and Politics in India,* ed. Nivedita Menon, 262–296. New Delhi: Oxford University Press.

———, ed. 1999b. *Gender and Politics in India.* New Delhi: Oxford University Press.

———. 2000. "Embodying the Self: Feminism, Sexual Violence and the Law." In *Subaltern Studies XI: Community, Gender and Violence,* ed. Partha Chatterjee and Pradeep Jeganathan, 66–105. New York: Columbia University Press.

Menon, Ritu. 1999. Afterword. *A Matter of Time.* New York: The Feminist Press.

———, and Kamla Bhasin. 1998. *Borders and Boundaries: Women in India's Partition.* New Brunswick, NJ: Rutgers University Press.

Menon, Usha, and Richard A. Shweder. 2000. "Power in its Place: Is the Great Goddess of Hinduism a Feminist?" In *Is The Goddess a Feminist?: The Politics of South Asian Goddesses,* ed. Alf Hiltebeitel and Kathleen M. Erndl, 151–165. New York: New York University Press.

Mercer, Kobena. 1990. "Welcome to the Jungle: Identity and Diversity in Post-modern Politics." In *Identity, Culture, Difference,* ed. Jonathan Rutherford, 43–72. London: Lawrence & Wishart.

Mernissi, Fatima. 1987. *Beyond the Veil: Male-Female Dynamics in Modern Muslim Society.* Bloomington: Indiana University Press.

Mills, Sara. 1991. *Discourses of Difference: An Analysis of Women's Travel Writing and Colonialism.* New York: Routledge.

Minh-ha, Trinh T. 1989. *Woman, Native, Other: Writing Postcoloniality and Feminism.* Bloomington and Indianapolis: Indiana University Press.

Minturn, Leigh. 1993. *Sita's Daughters: Coming Out of Purdah: The Rajput Women of Khalapur Revisited.* New York and Oxford: Oxford University Press.

Mitra, Anuradha M. 1996a. "The Spelling Bee." In *Contours of the Heart: South Asians Map North America,* ed. Sunaima Maira and Rajini Srikanth, 3–5. New York: Asian American Writers' Workshop.

——. 1996b. "Romantic Stereotypes: The Myth of the Asian American Khichri-Pot." In *Contours of the Heart: South Asians Map North America,* ed. Sunaima Maira and Rajini Srikanth, 425–429. New York: Asian American Writers' Workshop.

Moglen, Helene. 1993. "Redeeming History: Toni Morrison's *Beloved.*" *Cultural Critique* 24: 17–40.

Mohanty, Chandra Talpade. 1991a. "Cartographies of Struggle: Third World Women and the Politics of Feminism." In *Third World Women and the Politics of Feminism,* ed. Chandra Talpade Mohanty, Ann Russo, and Lourdes Torres, 1–47. Bloomington: Indiana University Press.

——. 1991b. " 'Under Western Eyes': Feminist Scholarship and Colonial Discourses." In *Third World Women and the Politics of Feminism,* ed. Chandra Talpade Mohanty, Ann Russo, and Lourdes Torres, 51–80. Bloomington: Indiana University Press.

——, Ann Russo, and Lourdes Torres. 1991. *Third World Women and the Politics of Feminism.* Bloomington: Indiana University Press.

——. 1997. "Women Workers and Capitalist Scripts: Ideologies of Domination, Common Interests, and the Politics of Solidarity." In *Feminist Genealogies, Colonial Legacies, Democratic Futures,* ed. M. Jacqui Alexander and Chandra Talpade Mohanty, 3–29. Routledge: New York and London.

Mufti, Aamir R. 2000. "A Greater Story-writer than God: Genre, Gender and Minority in Late Colonial India." In *Subaltern Studies XI: Community, Gender and Violence,* ed. Partha Chatterjee and Pradeep Jeganathan, 1–36. New York: Columbia University Press.

Mukherjee, Bharati. 1971. *The Tiger's Daughter.* New York: Fawcett Crest.

——. 1975. *Wife.* Boston: Houghton Mifflin.

——. 1985. *Darkness.* New York: Fawcett Crest.

——. 1988. *The Middleman and Other Stories.* New York: Fawcett Crest.

——. 1991. *Jasmine.* New York: Fawcett Crest.

——. and Clark Blaise. (1977) 1995. *Days and Nights in Calcutta.* Saint Paul, MN: Hungry Mind Press.

——. 1997. *Leave It to Me.* New York: Random House.

Mukhi, Sunita Sunder. 1998. "'Underneath My Blouse Beats My Indian Heart'": Sexuality, Nationalism, and Indian Womanhood in the United States." In *A Patchwork Shawl: Chronicles of South Asian Women in America,* ed. Shamita Das Dasgupta, 186–205. New Brunswick, NJ: Rutgers University Press.

Nair, Anita. 2001. *The Better Man.* New York: Picador USA.

Nair, Hema. 1996. "Burning Turtles." In *Contours of the Heart: South Asians Map North America,* ed. Sunaina Maira and Rajini Srikanth, 332–347. New York: The Asian American Writers' Workshop.

Namjoshi, Suniti. 1989. *The Mothers of Maya Diip.* London: The Women's Press Limited.

——. 1996. *Building Babel.* Melbourne, Australia: Spinifex Press.

——. 2000. *Goja.* Melbourne, Australia: Spinifex Press.

Naqvi, Maniza. 1998. *Mass Transit.* New York: Oxford University Press.

Naqvi, Tahira. 1997. *Attar of Roses and Other Stories from Pakistan.* Boulder, CO: Lynne Rienner.

Narayan, Uma. 1997. *Dislocating Cultures: Identities, Traditions, and Third World Feminism.* New York: Routledge.

——. 2000. "Undoing the 'Package Picture' of Cultures." *Signs: Journal of Women in Culture and Society* 25.4: 1083–1086.

Natarajan, Nalini. 1994. "Woman, Nation, and Narration in *Midnight's Children*." In *Scattered Hegemonies: Postmodernity and Transnational Feminist Practices,* ed. Grewal Inderpal and Caren Kaplan, 76–89. Minneapolis: University of Minnesota Press.

——. 1999. "Gender, Caste and Modernity: A Reading of U.R. Anantha Murthy's *Sanskara* in its Intellectual Context." In *Signposts: Gender Issues in Post-Independence India,* ed. Rajeswari Sunder Rajan, 155–187. New Brunswick, NJ: Rutgers University Press.

Nicholas, Ralph W. 1995. "The Effectiveness of the Hindu Sacrament (*Samskara*): Caste, Marriage, and Divorce in Bengali Culture." In *From the Margins of Hindu Marriage: Essays on Gender, Religion, and Culture,* ed. Lindsey Harlan and Paul B. Courtright, 137–160. New York, Oxford: Oxford University Press.

Nilsson, Usha. 2001. "Grinding Millet But Singing of Sita: Power and Domination in Awadhi and Bhojpuri Women's Songs." In *Signposts: Gender Issues in Post-Independence India,* ed. Rajeswari Sunder Rajan, 137–158. New Brunswick, NJ: Rutgers University Press.

Niranjana, Tejaswini. 2000. "Nationalism Refigured: Contemporary South Indian Cinema and the Subject of Feminism." In *Subaltern Studies XI: Community, Gender and Violence,* ed. Partha Chatterjee and Pradeep Jeganathan, 138–166. New York: Columbia University Press.

Oza, Rupal. 2001. "Showcasing India: Gender, Geography, and Globalization." *Signs: Journal of Women in Gender and Society* 26.1: 1067–1096.

Padmanabhan, Manjula. 1997. *Hot Death, Cold Soup*. Reading, UK: Garnet Publishing Ltd.

Pandian, M.S.S. 1997. "Culture and Subaltern Consciousness: An Aspect of the MGR Phenomenon." In *State and Politics in India,* ed. Partha Chatterjee, 367–390. Delhi: Oxford University Press.

Panjabi, Kavita. 1997. "Probing 'Morality' and State Violence: Feminist Values and Communicative Interaction in Prison Testimonios in India and Argentina." In *Feminist Genealogies, Colonial Legacies, Democratic Futures,* ed. M. Jacqui Alexander and Chandra Talpade Mohanty, 151–169. New York and London: Routledge.

Peres da Costa, Suneeta. 1999. *Homework*. New York: Bloomsbury Publishing.

Péres-Torres, Rafael. 1993. "Nomads and Migrants: Negotiating Multicultural Postmodernism." *Cultural Critique* 26: 161–190.

Persaud, Lakshmi. 1990. *Butterfly in the Wind*. Leeds: Peepal Tree Press.

Pfeil, Fred. 1994. "No Basta Teorizar: In-Difference to Solidarity in Contemporary Fiction, Theory, and Practice." In *Scattered Hegemonies: Postmodernity and Transnational Feminist Practices,* ed. Grewal Inderpal and Caren Kaplan, 197–230. Minneapolis, MN: University of Minnesota Press.

Pintchman, Tracy. 2000. "Is the Hindu Goddess Tradition a Good Resource for Western Feminism?" In *Is The Goddess a Feminist?: The Politics of South Asian Goddesses,* ed. Alf Hiltebeitel and Kathleen M. Erndl, 187–202. New York: New York University Press.

Pratt, Mary Louise. 1992. *Imperial Eyes: Travel Writing and Transculturation*. London: Routledge.

Raheja, Gloria Goodwin. 1995. "'Crying When She's Born, and Crying When She Goes Away': Marriage and the Gift in Pahansu Song Performance." In *From the Margins of Hindu Marriage: Essays on Gender, Religion, and Culture,* ed. Lindsey Harlan and Paul B. Courtright, 19–59. New York, Oxford: Oxford University Press.

Rajan, Rajeswari Sunder, ed. 1999a. *Signposts: Gender Issues in Post-Independence India*. New Brunswick, NJ: Rutgers University Press.

——. 1999b. "The Story of Draupadi's Disrobing: Meanings for Our Times." In *Signposts: Gender Issues in Post-Independence India,* ed. Rajeswari Sunder Rajan, 332–359. New Brunswick, NJ: Rutgers University Press.

———. 2000. "Real and Imagined Goddesses: A Debate." In *Is The Goddess a Feminist?: The Politics of South Asian Goddesses,* ed. Alf Hiltebeitel and Kathleen M. Erndl, 269–284. New York: New York University Press.

Ramusack, Barbara N. 1999. "Women in South Asia." In *Women in Asia: Restoring Women to History,* ed. Barbara N. Ramusack and Sharon Sievers, 15–76. Bloomington and Indianapolis: Indiana University Press.

———, and Sharon Sievers, eds. 1999. *Women in Asia: Restoring Women to History.* Bloomington and Indianapolis: Indiana University Press

Rao, Anupama. 1999. "Understanding Sirasgaon: Notes Towards Conceptualizing the Rule of Law, Caste and Gender in a Case of 'Atrocity.'" In *Signposts: Gender Issues in Post-Independence India,* ed. Rajeswari Sunder Rajan, 205–248. New Brunswick, NJ: Rutgers University Press.

Rao, Velcheru Narayana. 2001. "The Politics of Telugu *Ramayanas:* Colonialism, Print Culture, and Literary Movements." In *Questioning Ramayanas: A South Asian Tradition,* ed. Paula Richman, 159–185. Berkeley and Los Angeles: University of California Press.

Ray, Bharati, ed. 1995. *From the Seams of History: Essays on Indian Women.* Delhi: Oxford University Press.

Ray, Sangeeta. 2000. *En-Gendering India: Woman and National in Colonial and Postcolonial Narratives.* Durham, NC: Duke University Press.

Richman, Paula. 2001a. "The Ramilla Migrates to Southall." In *Questioning Ramayanas: A South Asian Tradition,* ed. Paula Richman, 309–328. Berkeley and Los Angeles: University of California Press.

———, ed. 2001b. *Questioning Ramayanas: A South Asian Tradition.* Berkeley: UCLA Press.

Roy, Arundhati. 1998. *The God of Small Things.* New York: Harper Perennial.

Roy, Manisha. 1998. "Mothers and Daughters in Indian-American Families: A Failed Communication?" In *A Patchwork Shawl: Chronicles of South Asian Women in America,* ed. Shamita Das Dasgupta, 97–110. New Brunswick, NJ: Rutgers University Press.

Sahgal, Nayantara. 1988a. *Mistaken Identity.* New York: New Directions Publishing.

———. (1986) 1988b. *Rich Like Us.* New York: New Directions Publishing.

———. (1977) 1988c. *A Situation in New Delhi.* New Delhi: Penguin.

Sangari, Kumkum, and Sudesh Vaid. 1999a. "Institutions, Beliefs, Ideologies: Widow Immolation in Contemporary Rajasthan." In *Gender and Politics in India,* ed. Nivedita Menon, 383–440. New Delhi: Oxford University Press.

———. (1989) 1999b. "Recasting Women: An Introduction." In *Recasting Women: Essays in Colonial History,* ed. Kumkum Sangari and Sudesh Vaid, 1–26. New Brunswick, NJ: Rutgers University Press.

———. (1989) 1999c. *Recasting Women: Essays in Colonial History.* New Brunswick, NJ: Rutgers University Press.

Saraswati, Pandita Ramabai. (1886) 1888. *The High Caste Hindu Woman.* Philadelphia: no publisher.

Sassen, Saskia. 1998. *Globalization and Its Discontents: Essays on the New Mobility of People and Money.* New York: New Press.

Satthianadhan, Krupabai. (1887–1888) 1998. *Saguna: The First Autobiographical Novel in English by an Indian Woman,* ed. Chandani Lokugé. Delhi: Oxford University Press.

Sen, Ilina. 1999. "Feminists, Women's Movement, and the Working Class." In *Gender and Politics in India,* ed. Nivedita Menon, 370–380. New Delhi: Oxford University Press.

Shah, Nandita, Sujata Gothoskar, Nandita Gandhi, and Amrita Chhachhi. 1999. "Structural Adjustment, Feminization of Labour Force and Organizational Strategies." In *Gender and Politics in India,* ed. Nivedita Menon, 145–177. New Delhi: Oxford University Press.

Shah, Sonia. 1998. "Three Hot Meals and a Full Day at Work: South Asian Women's Labor in the United States." In *A Patchwork Shawl: Chronicles of South Asian Women in America,* ed. Shamita Das Dasgupta, 206–222. New Brunswick, NJ: Rutgers University Press.

Shamsie, Kamila. 2000. *Salt and Saffron.* New York: Bloomsbury.

Sherma, Rita DasGupta. 2000. " '*Sa Ham:* I Am She': Woman as Goddess." In *Is The Goddess a Feminist?: The Politics of South Asian Goddesses,* ed. Alf Hiltebeitel and Kathleen M. Erndl, 24–51. New York: New York University Press.

Shiva, Vandana. 1999. "Colonialism and the Evolution of Masculinist Forestry." In *Gender and Politics in India,* ed. Nivedita Menon, 39–71. New Delhi: Oxford University Press.

———. 2001. *Tomorrow's Diversity.* New York: Thames and Hudson

Sidhwa, Bapsi. 1991. *Cracking India.* Minneapolis: Milkweed Editions.

———. 1993. *An American Brat.* Minneapolis: Milkweed Editions.

Spivak, Gayatri Chakravorty, ed. and trans. 1997. *Breast Stories.* Calcutta, India: Seagull Books.

———. 1999. *A Critique of Postcolonial Reason: Toward a History of the Vanishing Present.* Cambridge, MA: Harvard University Press.

Sprague, Joey. 2001. "Comment on Walby's 'Against Epistemological Chasms: The Science Question in Feminism Revisited: Structured Knowledge and Strategic Methodology.'" *Signs: Journal of Women in Culture and Society* 26.3: 527–536.

Srikanth, Rajini. 1996. "For James and Buffalo—Who Launched Me Off." In *Contours of the Heart: South Asians Map North America,* ed. Sunaina Maira and Rajini Srikanth, 174–187. New York: The Asian American Writers' Workshop.

Sundaresan, Indu. 2002. *The Twentieth Wife.* New York: Pocket Books.

Talwar, Vir Barhat. (1989) 1999. "Feminist Consciousness in Women's Journals in Hindi: 1910–1920." In *Recasting Women: Essays in Colonial History,* ed. Kumkum Sangari and Sudesh Vaid, 204–232. New Brunswick, NJ: Rutgers University Press.

Tharu, Susie K. (1989) 1999. "Tracing Savitri's Pedigree: Victorian Racism and the Image of Women in Indo-Anglian Literature." In *Recasting Women: Essays in Colonial History,* ed. Kumkum Sangari and Sudesh Vaid, 254–268. New Brunswick, NJ: Rutgers University Press.

———, and Tejaswini Niranjana. 1999. "Problems for a Contemporary Theory of Gender." In *Gender and Politics in India,* ed. Nivedita Menon, 494–525. New Delhi: Oxford University Press.

———, and K. Lalita, eds. 1991. *Women Writing in India 600 B.C. to the Present.* Vol. I: *600 B.C. to the Early Twentieth Century.* New York: The Feminist Press.

———, and K. Lalita, eds. 1995. *Women Writing in India 600 B.C. to the Present.* Vol II: *The Twentieth Century.* New York: The Feminist Press.

Tilak, Lakshmibai. (1934–1937) 1950. *I Follow After: An Autobiography,* trans. E. Josephine Inkster. London: Oxford University Press.

Tripp, Aili Mari. 2000. "Rethinking Difference: Comparative Perspectives from Africa." *Signs: Journal of Women in Culture and Society* 25.3: 649–676.

Umrigar, Thrity. 2002. *Bombay Time.* New York: Picador USA.

Vanita, Ruth. 1999. "Thinking Beyond Gender in India." In *Gender and Politics in India,* ed. Nivedita Menon, 529–539. New Delhi: Oxford University Press.

———, and Saleem Kidwai, eds. 2000. *Same-Sex Love in India: Readings from Literature and History.* New York: Palgrave.

Virthal, B. P. R. 1997. "Evolving Trends in the Bureaucracy." In *State and Politics in India,* ed. Partha Chatterjee, 208–231. Delhi: Oxford University Press.

Visweswaran, Kamala. 1994. *Fiction of Feminist Ethnography.* Minneapolis: University of Minnesota Press.

Wadley, Susan S. 1995. "No Longer a Wife: Widows in Rural North India." In *From the Margins of Hindu Marriage: Essays on Gender, Religion, and Culture,* ed. Lindsey Harlan and Paul B. Courtright, 92–118. New York, Oxford: Oxford University Press.

Walby, Sylvia. 2001. "Against Epistemological Chasms: The Science Question in Feminism Revisited." *Signs: Journal of Women in Culture and Society* 26.2: 485–510.

Index